HR Manager's Guide to Human Resources Management Systems: A Practical Approach

Third Edition

Glen M. Rampton | Ian J. Turnbull | J. Allen Doran

© 2007 Thomson Canada Limited

NOTICE AND DISCLAIMER: All rights reserved. No part of this publication may be reproduced, stored in a retrieval system, or transmitted, in any form or by any means, electronic, mechanical, photocopying, recording, or otherwise, without the prior written permission of the publisher (Carswell).

Carswell and all persons involved in the preparation and sale of this publication disclaim any warranty as to accuracy or currency of the publication. This publication is provided on the understanding and basis that none of Carswell, the author's or other persons involved in the creation of this publication shall be responsible for the accuracy or currency of the contents, or for the results of any action taken on the basis of the information contained in this publication, or for any errors or omissions contained herein. No one involved in this publication is attempting herein to render legal, accounting, or other professional advice.

Library and Archives Canada Cataloguing in Publication

Rampton, Glenn M.
    HR manager's guide to human resources management systems: a practical approach / Glenn M. Rampton, Ian J. Turnbull, Allen Doran. – 3rd ed.

First eds. had title: Human resources management systems.
Includes index.

ISBN 978-0-7798-0007-0

1. Information storage and retrieval systems – Personnel management. 2. Personnel management – Data processing.
I. Turnbull, Ian J. II. Doraqn, J. Allen. III. Title.

HF5549.5.D37R34 2007   658.300285   C2007-900358-3

Composition: Computer Composition of Canada Inc.

One Corporate Plaza, 2075 Kennedy Road, Toronto, Ontario M1T 3V4
Customer Relations:
Toronto 1-416-609-3800
Elsewhere in Canada/U.S. 1-800-387-5164
Fax 1-416-298-5094
E-mail carswell.reference@thomson.com

Brief Contents

About the Authors		xi
Preface		xv
Acknowledgements		xix
Chapter 1	Introduction	1
Chapter 2	The Need for an Effective HRMS	25
Chapter 3	Return on Investment	35
Chapter 4	Planning a New HRMS	53
Chapter 5	Designing and Developing a New HRMS	73
Chapter 6	Implementation	107
Chapter 7	Maintaining the HRMS	127
Chapter 8	Human Resources Strategic and Tactical Planning	139
Chapter 9	Staffing	161
Chapter 10	Training and Development	181
Chapter 11	Total Compensation — Salary, Benefits, Pension, Payroll and Time and Attendance	195
Chapter 12	Occupational Health and Safety	229
Chapter 13	Trends in HRMS	245
Index		273

CONTENTS

About the Authors xi
Preface xv
Acknowledgments xix

Chapter 1: Introduction 1
1.1   Introduction 1
1.2   Historical Background 4
    (a)   The 1800s 4
    (b)   Pre-World War II 5
    (c)   The Postwar Period 5
    (d)   The Mid-1950s and Early 1960s 6
    (e)   The Mid-1960s 7
    (f)   The 1970s 9
    (g)   The Internet 10
    (h)   The 1980s 11
    (i)   The Late 1980s and Early 1990s 12
1.3   Evolving Human Resources Management Information
    Requirements for the New Millennium 16
1.4   Business/Technological Trends 16
1.5   Models of the Human Resources Function 17
1.6   Summary 22
1.7   References 22

Chapter 2: The Need for an Effective HRMS 25
2.1   Introduction 25
2.2   Employee Lists 25
2.3   Attrition Reporting/Monitoring 26
2.4   Employment Equity Tracking/Monitoring 27
2.5   Salary Benefits 28
2.6   Seniority Lists 28
2.7   Applicant Tracking 29
2.8   Grievance Tracking and Analysis 29
2.9   Workers' Compensation (WC) and Long-Term Disability (LTD)
    Tracking 29
2.10 HRMS "Reports" 30
2.11 Human Resources/Strategic Planning 30
    (a)   Strategic Planning 31
    (b)   Succession Planning 31
    (c)   Internal Population Analysis 31
2.12 Summary 32
2.13 References 32

Chapter 3: Return on Investment 35
3.1 Introduction 35
3.2 Example: Employee Lists 40
3.3 Legislative Requirements 41
3.4 Salary/Benefits Reporting and Modeling 42
3.5 Examples 43
3.6 Human Resources Planning, Development, Research, and
    Related Issues 45
    (a) Quality Control of Canadian Forces Recruiting
        and Selection 48
3.7 Summary 49
3.8 References 49

Chapter 4: Planning a New HRMS 53
4.1 Introduction 53
4.2 Planning 53
4.3 The Planning Process 54
4.4 Project Management 55
4.5 The Communications Process 59
4.6 Critical Success Factors 60
4.7 Dealing with Change 63
4.8 Planning and Implementation 66
4.9 Training and Documentation 66
    (a) Purpose of Documentation and Training 67
    (b) Training Phases 67
    (c) In-House or Off-the-Shelf Systems 68
    (d) Timeliness of Documentation 69
    (e) Timeliness of Training 70
4.10 Summary 70
4.11 References 71

Chapter 5: Designing and Developing a New HRMS 73
5.1 Introduction 73
5.2 General Design Considerations 74
5.3 Applications: Breadth and Depth 74
5.4 Language and Currency Requirements 77
5.5 Security and Privacy 78
    (a) Privacy 78
    (b) Privacy in Canada 79
    (c) Privacy in the U.S.A. 80
    (d) Date Effectivity 80
    (e) Reports 81
    (f) Technical Issues 82
    (g) The Internet 83
5.6 Analysis of Business Processes 83
    (a) Analysis Phase 84

Contents

	(b)	Problem-Solving Phase	84
5.7		Tools to Assist in HRMS Design and Development	86
	(a)	Flow Charts	86
	(b)	Benchmarking and Best Practices	87
5.8		HR Metrics	88
5.9		Build or Buy	91
5.10		Typical HRMS Components	94
5.11		Screening and Selecting Software	96
	(a)	Definition of Requirements	97
	(b)	Development of an RFI/RFP	98
	(c)	Assessment of Vendor Responses	98
	(d)	Demonstrations	100
	(e)	Supplier and Product Reliability	101
5.12		Building an HRMS or Contracting Out	101
	(a)	Contracting Out Example: Payroll Services	101
5.13		Summary	103
5.14		References	104

Chapter 6: Implementation — 107

6.1		Introduction	107
6.2		Change	107
6.3		Pitfalls in HRMS Implementation	108
6.4		Implementation Phases	109
6.5		Implementation Planning	109
	(a)	Priorities	110
	(b)	Implementation Schedules	111
6.6		The HRMS Project Implementation Team	111
6.7		The HRMS Manager	113
6.8		Policy and Procedure Issues	113
6.9		The Role of the Steering Committee	114
6.10		Corporate/Executive Sponsor	114
6.11		Project Team Training	115
	(a)	The Training Plan	115
	(b)	Technical Team Training	116
	(c)	Extended Team Training	117
	(d)	Training of Other Users	117
6.12		Installation	117
6.13		Fit Analysis	118
	(a)	Reliance on Vendor	119
6.14		Modifying the System	120
6.15		Unit Testing	120
6.16		Conversion	121
6.17		Parallel Testing	122
6.18		Summary	123
6.19		References	123

Chapter 7: Maintaining the HRMS ... 127
7.1 Introduction ... 127
7.2 Shared Services ... 128
7.3 Vendor Relations ... 129
    (a) User Groups ... 130
7.4 Coordination with Other Clients/Users ... 131
    (a) Internal ... 131
7.5 Hardware and Communications Maintenance ... 132
7.6 Software Maintenance ... 132
7.7 Business Process Maintenance ... 133
7.8 Roles ... 134
7.9 Responsibilities ... 135
    (a) Functional Maintenance ... 135
    (b) Technical Maintenance ... 136
    (c) Functional/Technical Maintenance ... 136
7.10 New Functional Requirements ... 137
7.11 User Support ... 137
7.12 Summary ... 137
7.13 References ... 137

Chapter 8: Human Resources Strategic & Tactical Planning ... 139
8.1 Introduction ... 139
8.2 Internal and External Trends ... 141
8.3 The Importance of Effective Human Resources Planning ... 142
8.4 Demand and Supply Forecasting ... 142
8.5 The Use of an HRMS in Human Resources/Succession Planning ... 145
8.6 Case Study — Application of an HRMS in Human Resources Planning ... 150
8.7 Measuring HRM Practices and Value ... 151
8.8 Outsourcing ... 153
8.9 Case Study — Safety Statistics ... 154
8.10 Summary ... 158
8.11 References ... 159

Chapter 9: Staffing ... 161
9.1 Introduction ... 161
9.2 Staffing Model ... 161
9.3 Staffing Programs: An Overview ... 163
9.4 Applications ... 163
    (a) Shortages of Qualified Workers ... 165
    (b) Internet Job Sites ... 166
    (c) Management Staffing ... 171
        (i) Recruitment On-line ... 171
        (ii) Referral Programs ... 172
        (iii) Exit Interviews ... 173
        (iv) Accommodation ... 173

Contents

	(v) No Staffing Software?	174
9.5	Program Monitoring for Staffing	175
9.6	Summary	176
9.7	References	177

Chapter 10: Training and Development 179
- 10.1 Introduction 179
- 10.2 Strategic Context 179
- 10.3 Training and Development Options 180
- 10.4 Training and Development: An HR Model 182
- 10.5 Training Management Information 185
- 10.6 Training Delivery 190
- 10.7 Application 191
- 10.8 Attitude Surveys 192
- 10.9 Summary 192
- 10.10 References 193

Chapter 11: Total Compensation — Salary, Benefits, Pension, Payroll and Time and Attendance 195
- 11.1 Introduction 195
  - (a) Payroll 198
  - (b) HR Model 199
  - (c) Benefits 201
- 11.2 Modeling/Analyses 204
- 11.3 Trends 204
  - (a) Coordination of Benefits 205
  - (b) Flexible Benefits 205
  - (c) Pensions 207
- 11.4 HRMS Requirements for Total Compensation 207
- 11.5 Program Evaluation/Metrics 223
- 11.6 Summary 225
- 11.7 References 225

Chapter 12: Occupational Health and Safety 229
- 12.1 Introduction 229
- 12.2 Occupational Health and Safety Model 229
- 12.3 Legislation 231
- 12.4 Application 232
- 12.5 Relationships Between OH&S and HRM Data 233
- 12.6 Occupational Health and Safety Inspections 234
- 12.7 Accident Reporting 235
- 12.8 Increased Awareness of OH&S Issues 237
- 12.9 Security and Privacy 239
- 12.10 Health and Employability 240
- 12.11 Summary 241
- 12.12 References 242

Chapter 13: Trends in HRMS 245
13.1 Introduction 245
13.2 The New Economy 245
13.3 Globalization 246
13.4 Outsourcing/Contracting Out 246
13.5 Restructuring Work 247
13.6 Technological Advances 247
13.7 Flexibility 248
13.8 Other Technical Issues 248
13.9 Impact of the Internet and Related Innovations 249
13.10 Internet/Intranet 251
13.11 E-Commerce 255
13.12 Networking 258
13.13 Information Management 263
13.14 Non-Traditional HRM Approaches 265
    (a) Competencies 265
    (b) Workflow 266
    (c) Teams 266
    (d) Downsizing 267
13.15 Human Resources Information Management 267
13.16 Summary 270
13.17 References 270

Index 273

ABOUT THE AUTHORS

GLENN M. RAMPTON

Glenn Rampton is currently chief executive officer of Kerry's Place Autism Services. Previously, Dr. Rampton held senior executive and human resources positions in a variety of settings. He retired as senior psychologist of the Canadian Forces in 1983, after a distinguished career as a military behavioural scientist. During his tenure with the Forces, Dr. Rampton was responsible for a number of innovations that led to the more effective and efficient staffing and utilization of human resources within the Department of National Defence.

Prior to his appointment as senior psychologist, Dr. Rampton served as commanding officer of the Canadian Forces Personnel Applied Research Unit and as an associate professor of leadership and management at the Royal Military College. Dr. Rampton represented Canada on a number of international committees and working groups, including the Steering Committee of a prestigious panel of senior scientists from the United States, Great Britain, Australia and New Zealand. He also served as president of the Military Testing Association (MTA), representing more than 1,000 scientists engaged in applied research in 15 research institutes from eight countries in Europe, Australia and North America. In this capacity he acted as chair of the MTA's 22nd Annual Conference in Toronto.

Dr. Rampton has also held appointments as the director of Human Resources Planning and Development for Canada Post Corporation and as assistant vice-president (human resources) for York University. In both of these positions, he was responsible for overseeing the development and implementation of corporate human resources programs in the context of great organizational change. He is the author or co-author of three books along with numerous publications and invited addressess.

IAN J. TURNBULL

Ian Turnbull is Managing Director of Laird & Greer Management Consultants, focusing on Human Resource Management Systems (HRMS). Laird & Greer offers a wide variety of services, including change management; strategic planning; perspectives on e-HR and Human Capital Asset Management; HR metrics and best practices; software requirements definition; system assessment and selection; project organization/management/implementation; and re-engineering of business processes.

He is also a Director of the Canadian Privacy Institute and Editor and chief author of a recent book published by CCH, *Privacy in the Workplace – the Employment Perspective*, 2004. The Institute is a private organization that offers information, consulting services, software and education alternatives to help organizations understand and meet the practical challenges of Canada's privacy laws in a global context.

He is a Certified Human Resource Professional (CHRP), the Human Resource Professionals Association of Ontario (1991) and in October 2002, was given the President's Award from the International Public Management Association of Canada (IPMA) for making an outstanding contribution to the practice of human resources management in Canada.

Ian received a Master of Business Administration (1975) from the Richard Ivey School of Business at the University of Western Ontario in London Ontario and a Bachelor of Arts (1973), also from UWO.

His service to the HR and wider business community includes:

- Director, the Human Resource Management Systems Professionals (HRMSP)
- Past-Chair, the International Association of Human Resource Information Management (IHRIM)
- Past-Chair the Canadian Council of Human Resource Associations (CCHRA)
- Past-Chair, National Standards Steering Committee, CCHRA
- Director, the Workforce Privacy Network
- Director, Human Resource Professionals of York Region (HRPYR)
- Member of the Board, Community Legal Clinic of York Region
- Member, Human Resource Professionals Association of Ontario (HRPAO)
- Member, the Society for Human Resources Management (SHRM)

Mr. Turnbull has written numerous articles and spoken at professional conferences and workshops throughout North America and in Europe on general management, human resources, payroll, time management, privacy and security issues. He has taught the practical aspects of HRMS at the University of Toronto's Centre for Industrial Relations, contributed two modules of the Canadian Payroll Association Certification Program and has edited and authored numerous modules for the Canadian HR Study Guide series.

Turnbull assists organizations through a wide variety of services, including change management; strategic planning; requirements definition; system assessment and selection; project organization/management/implementation; and engineering of business processes. Specializing in human resources, payroll and time and attendance, he has also dealt with general management and operational issues. Mr. Turnbull has consulted throughout Canada and the United States in such industries as consulting engineering, distribution, education, energy, health care, government, manufacturing, mining, forestry and retail.

J. ALLEN DORAN

Al Doran is president and chief executive officer of Phenix Management International, a consulting firm head- quartered in Toronto and specializing in assisting

About the Authors

organizations of all sizes to develop and maintain effective human resources management systems.

Previously, Mr. Doran was director, Human Resources Management Information and Payroll at York University, Toronto, Ontario. He has more than 25 years of experience in the design, development and application of computer-based information systems, with particular emphasis in personnel, payroll and human resources planning functions.

While at York, Mr. Doran was responsible for the development and implementation of a "state of the art" human resources information system for the university. He was also responsible for an annual payroll in excess of $200 million. Using the latest methodologies, Mr. Doran worked on the re-engineering of current human resources practices to streamline operating procedures, reduce paper and distribute management information to line managers.

In his previous assignment, Mr. Doran was responsible for directing the development of all personnel and labour relations systems for one of Canada's largest Crown corporations, Canada Post. He was responsible for coordinating a major project to develop a comprehensive and coherent structure that will be used as the blueprint for all future HR systems development.

As manager of the Research Information Systems at the Canadian Forces Personnel Applied Research Unit in Toronto, he developed one of the most comprehensive people databases in Canada.

Mr. Doran is a Certified Human Resource Professional (CHRP), the Human Resource Professionals Association of Ontario (1991), In 1996 Mr. Doran was the first Canadian recipient of the Summit Award, IHRIM's highest honour, for "his significant, long-standing contributions to the Association's mission and goals."

Mr. Doran is Secretary of the Human Resource Management Systems Professionals (HRMSP) and a past president of the Board of the International Association for Human Resources Information Management (IHRIM).

His volunteer roles in human resources and other areas have included:

- Board Member and Founding Member HRMS Professionals Association
- Board Member, International Association for Human Resources Information Management, 2000-2003
- Board Member, Canadian Council of Human Resource Associations, 2000-2003
- Board Member, Ontario Chapter, IHRIM, 1999-2005
- Director, National Board, Canadian Association of Human Resource Systems Professionals, 1989-1995
- President, Ontario Chapter, IHRIM, 1999-2005
- Chair, Higher Education Special Interest Group, IHRIM, 1996-1997

Human Resources Management Systems

- Chair, HR Technology Committee, HRPAO, 1998-2000
- Committee member, IHRIM Internet Advisory Board, 1995-2000
- Member, IHRIM Journal Advisory Board, 1997-1999
- Member, Human Resources Development Canada, Internet Advisory Board, 1998-2000
- Director, Integral Canadian Chapter Users Group, Conference Director 1990, 1991, 1992, 1993
- Member, Human Resource Systems Professionals of Ontario (HRPAO), 1988
- Web Site Director – International Softball Congress – 1999-

Mr. Doran is a regular speaker at IHRIM and personnel/payroll conferences in Canada, the U.S.A., China and Australia. He often contributes articles on the effective use of technology in managing human resources information to a variety of publications.

PREFACE

Writing the second — or in this case, the third — edition of a book is a careful balancing act. The trick is to keep all that is good while adding in the new and removing the old.

In the case of this book we were extremely pleased by the strength of the earlier editions when we reviewed them. Much of the first and second editions have been kept because the conceptual framework contained therein was and is sound.

The primary additions to this edition were with regard to the use of the web. Electronic HR, or "eHR" as it has become known, is all the rage. The evolution of technology has made the internet the primary delivery method for most new software application. The focus has been technology as the enabler, allowing organizations to leverage HR-based functionality to the larger managerial, supervisory and employee communities.[1]

In addition to this being a primary focus of the new content, over the course of writing editions one through three of this book, the Internet has become increasingly important as our primary source of research. While we mourn the passing of musty library carols, we do appreciate the ease of the new process.

Many of the events predicted by the second (1999) edition have come to pass, with countless uses of the Internet being key. Not all of these uses have been a resounding success and we note those in the respective chapters. What has not changed are the continuing challenges faced by users to populate the software with accurate data and then to fully use the software to manage that same data.

A human resources management system (HRMS) is more than a human resources information system (HRIS). It is what the name implies; an information management system accessible to staff at all levels, designed to ensure that the organization's most important resources — its people — are recruited, selected, developed, employed, deployed and supported most effectively.

Texts on human resources information systems commonly focus on developing and implementing systems that gather, store and report human resources data in a timely fashion, in forms that are useful to human resources personnel, line management and other users. In writing this book, we have attempted to go further than this, by focusing as well on the uses of an HRMS as a critical management tool.

This book is designed to reach a diverse audience, including:

1. human resources and/or payroll managers and functional specialists who want to know more about what an HRMS can do, or who are involved with, or contemplating the development of a new HRMS;

---

[1] Gueutal, Hal G. and Stone, Dianna L., eds. The Brave New World of eHR. Jossey-Bass, 2005.

2. executives and general managers who understand that their human resources are their most important resource and are looking to the strategic and pragmatic value of an HRMS in terms of helping them manage their human resources;

3. information systems professionals who will be working on an HRMS project and want to learn more about the business and user perspective on such systems; and

4. post-secondary school students taking a general HRMS course.

The content of *HRM Systems* is based on advancements in the professional literature, together with the authors' combined first-hand experience in developing, implementing and using numerous human resources management systems in private and public sector organizations. The perspectives of human resources, payroll, operations, human resources information specialists and management systems specialists are all addressed, as are the different issues facing small, medium and large organizations.

This and previous editions of this book were written to provide basic reference materials for Human Resources Management programs in colleges and universities. The prior editions have been used as the primary text in a variety of human resources management programs in academic institutions throughout the world. They have distinguished themselves from the other texts on a similar topic by appealing to an international audience and business people, both HR and others.

Exercises that were previously included at the end of each chapter of the book have been placed on the website: <http://www.pmihrm.com/>, along with MSPowerpoint lecture slides for each chapter of the book and other supporting materials for using the book as a text in college and university settings. As time goes on this website will be updated on the basis of feedback from and for the convenience of, professors, lecturers and students.

The text begins with the history of HRMS. Chapter 2 "The Need for an Effective HRMS," discusses the typical reasons why organizations begin a search for an HRMS. Using examples, Chapter 3, "Return on Investment," explores the value that an HRMS can add to an organization's efficiency and effectiveness. These two chapters together provide a framework by which practitioners can develop their own business cases for an HRMS.

Chapter 4, "Planning a New HRMS," outlines the planning processes to be considered in researching the requirements of a new HRMS, with emphasis on the importance of a complete, realistic and documented plan. An experienced human resources practitioner should be able to use the processes outlined to arrive at an HRMS plan. At the beginning of an HRMS development project, those responsible are generally faced with the decision of whether to upgrade the existing system, to build a new one from scratch, or to buy one.

Preface

Chapter 5, "Designing and Developing a New HRMS," describes the steps involved in building (designing/developing) a system in-house, or in adapting existing commercial software packages to meet the needs of the organization. The strengths and weaknesses of each approach are discussed. There are currently many sophisticated, reasonably priced HRMSs on the market. Consequently, most organizations find it more cost-effective to buy a new HRMS "off the shelf." This chapter therefore also outlines the steps involved in identifying the best software packages, including preparing requests for proposals, short-listing proposals, how to approach systems demonstrations, hidden issues surrounding the decision and the final choice. Chapter 5 also discusses what is required to prepare a feasibility report and a business case to present the options, arguments and recommendations so that an informed decision may be made. Many organizations have existing manual, semi-automated, or automated processes and systems in place. This chapter examines how to determine whether opportunities exist to better use or improve on those systems and processes and, thus, avoid the expense of buying or building a new HRMS.

The many issues involved with implementing an HRMS are discussed in Chapter 6. We believe that most texts do not give adequate attention to this important subject.

Once implemented, an HRMS must be maintained, or it and the information the system contains, will soon become out-of-date. Chapter 7, "Maintaining the HRMS," discusses the ongoing requirements of an information system's maintenance, as well as who should be involved. The "users," whoever they may be, must be schooled in both the concept and operation of an HRMS to fully and successfully integrate it into their everyday work.

Continuous systems testing is required in the development, implementation and operation of an HRMS. It is better to test and retest rather than to allow errors to go unidentified and uncorrected, resulting in a lack of confidence that would take much longer to correct than any testing process.

Without giving users the ability to generate information, an HRMS is simply a bucket for data—*and data are not necessarily information.* This chapter points out that on-line and hard-copy reports, graphics and analysis, are the keys for successful system use. Adapting the HRMS to new legal requirements, changing business needs, turnover in personnel and new technology is a challenge requiring continuous improvement. A successful HRMS will never be "finished". It must be flexible enough to grow and change with the needs of the organization. Included is a discussion of who should do what, when an HRMS is "live."

Using actual examples drawn from the authors' experience, Chapters 8 through 12 describe how an effective HRMS can be used to further the work of the core human resources functions. Chapter 13, "Trends in HRMS," discusses the impact that the ever increasing technological and organizational change is having on HRMSs, as well as how this technology may be used to support the human resources function and in turn, the larger organization which the human resources function supports.

The three authors are Canadian and have worked primarily in Canada, so many of the examples are Canadian. However every effort has been made to provide examples that are generic to the function of HRMS and the business of HR throughout the world. The authors would welcome comments from readers everywhere regarding this book and examples and ideas for inclusion in our next book on this subject.

ACKNOWLEDGEMENTS

We dedicate this book to a good friend and colleague whose untimely death late in 2005 shocked and saddened us. Robert Stambaugh (Bob) was a pioneer in the field of HRMS and worked tirelessly to make the field a better one. Always opinionated, often argumentative, and never sedate, Bob contributed heavily to our understanding and vision of HRMS, and therefore, to this book and our prior editions. He is sorely missed.

We offer a tribute to our many friends in the global HRMS community who are never reluctant to share their visions of human resources, payroll or human resources management systems, and who make this business such a fun industry in which to work. Thanks as well to the anonymous reviewers who provided extremely useful feedback on early chapters of the book.

Glenn Rampton would like to thank Barbara and Sherene for all the sacrifices that they made while he was preoccupied with this project.

Ian Turnbull thanks Susan, Katherine and Elizabeth for their continued loving support, Bob Grose for mentoring Ian's early years in HR, and a special note of thanks to Bob Delaney, President of Canadian HR Press, who continues to challenge Ian's vision of human resource management in order to create better products for the HR community.

Al Doran would like to dedicate this work to his children, Wendy and Michael, who make it all worthwhile. He would also like to thank his co-authors for their patience, and Glenn for being his mentor in HRM and in life.

Chapter 1: Introduction

1.1 — Introduction

The "Information Age" is a name given to a period lasting from approximately 1971 to 1991, after the industrial age and before the Knowledge Economy. It is a term applied to the period lasting from approximately 1971 to 1991, where movement of information became faster than physical movement. It could be argued though, that it actually began during the later half of the nineteenth century with the invention of the telephone and telegraphy.[1]

The Information Age also heralded the era where information was a scarce resource and its capture and distribution generated competitive advantage, and so it is not only a description of technology, but of communication and economic theory. It is often used in conjunction with the term post-industrial society.

Microsoft became one of the largest companies in the world based on its influence in creating the underlying mechanics to facilitate information distribution.

Around 1991 information ceased being scarce, beginning the Knowledge Economy that continued to approximately 2002 giving way to a new economic era, the Intangible Economy. In the Intangible Economy, four factors of production are the four key resources from which economic activity and competitive advantage are primarily derived and delivered today:

- Knowledge assets (what people know and put into use),
- Collaboration assets (who people interact with to create value),
- Engagement assets (the level of energy and commitment of people), and
- Time quality (how quickly value is created).

Google is now a serious competitor to Microsoft as it relies on Intangible Economy principles to run its operations.[2]

---

1 Gathered 06-10-20 from <http://en.wikipedia.org/wiki/Information_age>.
2 *Ibid.*

1.1 Human Resources Management Systems

Figure 1.1 Ages Spiral Ever Faster

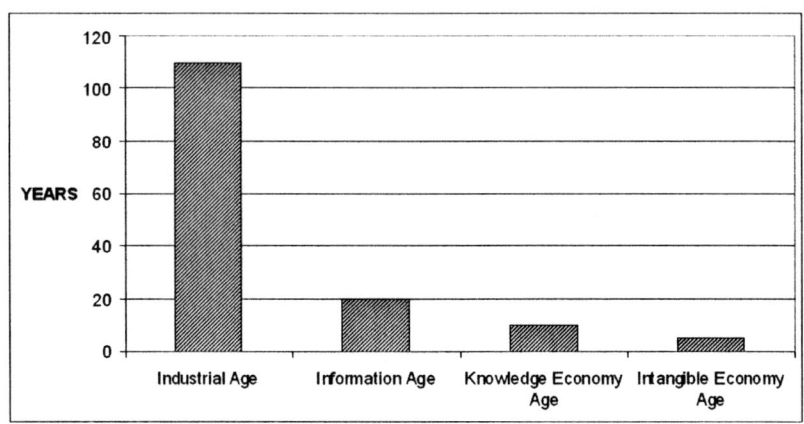

Automation and information technology are revolutionizing the way we do business and, as the following example illustrates, Human Resources Management is no exception.

Suppose you are an operational manager in a large organization. The planning committee has determined that a need exists for an industrial systems engineer in your area; you have advertised the vacancy in the newspaper, trade journals, in relevant on-line publications, and on your company's World Wide Web home page. Several candidates have responded via e-mail. By accessing the on-line HRMS on your office computer, you compare each candidate's qualifications against the job requirements and determine what testing procedure will be used to demonstrate each qualified individual's abilities. The test is administered via computer, and the results, along with all other recruitment and selection information, are automatically collected, edited, stored, and made available to those who have authorized access to it by the on-line HRMS. Using these results, you determine which candidate is best suited for the job, and make a formal offer of employment to Ms. Mary Smith.

Once the successful candidate, Mary Smith, has been hired, a file is opened in the HRMS computer and all key information (address, education, etc.) is automatically transferred into it from the applicant file. On her first day at work, Ms. Smith is assigned a log-in name and selects a password; from now on, she will be able to log in to her HRMS file directly from any terminal. This will allow her to access the HR data files in order to find and retrieve information on her company benefits and pension account and update her biographical information. On-line access also allows Ms. Smith to use title or name keywords to find out who is responsible for various functions within the multinational organization, where they are located, and how they may be reached by telephone or e-mail.

As Ms. Smith's role and responsibilities change to adapt to the growing needs of your organization, her HRMS file is continually updated. Throughout her tenure, these responsibilities are translated into goals and priorities that are updated monthly on the HRMS. Ms. Smith reports on these goals, and on the status of various projects within her portfolio, by submitting a monthly report to you which she simply uploads into your office terminal on the first Monday of every month.

One morning, you are scheduled to meet with Ms. Smith to discuss a new department initiative, but as you drive in to work your Blackberry advises you that due to an accident Ms. Smith will be unable to attend the meeting. She reported her absence by phone to the Interactive Voice Response attachment of the HRMS, which recorded her absence, deducted the day from her sick leave balance, checked the employee scheduling and calendar system and automatically sent you an e-mail message notifying you that the meeting will have to be rescheduled.

The HRMS also automatically prompts you to schedule regular work planning and career development sessions, including quarterly reviews, with each of your employees. The work planning process involves the translation of company goals into individual achievement objectives, which form the basis for quarterly job performance reviews; all of this is documented on the HRMS for easy reference by yourself and the employees, and is linked by the HRMS with the organization's individual and department-based merit (or bonus) pay programs. Career development information stored on the HRMS might include vocational interests entered by the employee, career development objectives entered by both the employee and the manager, and the results of training or qualifications gained during the employee's tenure, all of which will assist you in making decisions concerning employee promotions, transfers, and pay raises.

The HRMS also provides a forum for employee feedback. Just as the performance of each employee is evaluated each quarter, so too does each employee have the opportunity to provide his or her views on organization culture, leadership, and initiatives through specially formatted HRMS screens. This data is then grouped together by the HRMS to provide a comprehensive and detailed portrait of the company to management. Using this information, management is able to track changes in employee attitudes, assess reactions toward current organizational programs, identify strengths and areas for improvement, and design programs leading to greater employee satisfaction and increased productivity.

The technology described above exists, not as one seamless software/hardware package, each of which is available to be acquired and implemented. This book discusses the issues that must be taken into account by the human resources practitioner or HRMS specialist when developing, implementing, and maintaining a leading edge HRMS such as the one described here.

The electronic management of human resources information is referred to as "human resources management systems," or "HRMS." The term used to describe the HRMS of any particular company may vary: HRMS is often used interchangeably with a number of other terms, including Human Resources Information Systems (HRIS), Employee Data Base (EDB), Personnel Data Base (PDB), and

Personnel Management Information System (PMIS). Whatever they are called, however, HRMSs have evolved to the point where they have become essential business support tools for today's progressive organizations.

This chapter provides a brief outline of the historical context of human resources management systems and related issues. It then introduces current HRMS issues and trends, and presents a model showing the relationships between an HRMS and other human resources programs. (This model will appear in subsequent chapters in modified forms, adapted to specific functions.)

1.2 — Historical Background

(a) — The 1800s

The information technologies of the nineteenth century allowed faster and wider dissemination of information than previously possible. However, ultimately such information had to be reduced to the same form which had been the final form for centuries: paper, whose analogs go back to stone and clay tablets.

In 1837, Samuel Morse created a device which converted physical movement into electrical impulses that could travel over large distances. In 1844, telegraphy was used to transmit data along an experimental telegraph line from Washington, D.C. to Baltimore, Maryland. Slightly more than 20 years later, the first telegraph cables were stretched across the Atlantic Ocean, in 1858, but failed to stay in operation; however, uninterrupted service began in 1866.

This invention set off a stream of devices used for the processing of information, the typewriter, the mechanical calculator, and finally, the telephone in 1876. "Informationalization" of previous devices occurred, such as the player piano.

The ability to distribute large runs of printed material had created the means for information transmission to change economic and social behavior. Telephones and ticker tape machines would be part of the infrastructure for the growth of stock markets, as well as the ability to trade precious metals, such as gold. It was the telegraph that allowed the news of Krakatau's explosive eruption to spread around the world rapidly.

Recording added a new means of distribution: namely that of sound. However, the distribution was either person to person, as in the telegraph, or through the distribution of a physical object. Since physical objects cannot be transported as quickly as electrical signals, the next stage of information technology was to be able to transmit pure information, as the telegraph did, but with mass reception.[3]

With the development of what was called wireless transmission, when combined with the ability to transmit voice and sound from the telephone, and recording technology, a new medium began to be born, which placed a different final result

---

3 *Ibid.*

in the hands of the individual. These technologies would eventually become radio.[4]

(b) — Pre-World War II

In the first half of the twentieth century, human resources, or personnel, as it was then known, was undervalued. Prior to the mid-1940s, the *personnel* function was often regarded as a reactive, caretaker activity that provided very little to the bottom-line of the corporation. Seen as "paper pushers," those in the personnel department were generally regarded as caretakers of employee records and such. At the time, these functions ranked below those of operations, marketing and finance.

During this period, there was no significant automation of any personnel or payroll function: the technology available was limited, and that which did exist was not generally applied. However, the fact that the personnel (or human resources, as it is now generally known) came late to applying automation technology is a little ironic, given that the first large-scale application in information automation was, effectively, a human resources application.

In the 1880s the United States Census Bureau discovered that it could not publish the 1880 census on time using manual techniques. Consequently, the United States government commissioned Herman Hollerith to adapt technology invented in the 1820s by the Englishman, Charles Babbage. This technology made use of punched cards and a variety of equipment — card punchers, sorters, tabulators, printers — to process the cards and the data they contained. Application of this technology was very successful and, with refinements, it was used for more than 50 years.

The "Hollerith" punched card continued to be widely used (until the 1970s) to input data into the electronic computers that eventually replaced mechanical equipment in data automation, thus forming the main link between the eras of mechanical and electronic automation. In fact, the standard "IBM card," so familiar only a few decades ago, was the same size as the United States currency of the 1880s because the equipment that Hollerith used to produce the "blanks" for his punch cards was the same as that used to produce American bank notes of the day.

(c) — The Postwar Period

The first computerized personnel systems were the payroll systems that evolved in the 1940s and 1950s. These were very basic recordkeeping files maintained on tabulating and electrical accounting machinery (EAM). These early payroll systems met the requirements of the time, which, from a human resources point of

---

4 *Ibid.*

view, were really limited to what we now think of as staffing or employment data. The "data dictionary" of the 1950s would have included only such basic information as the name, address, sex, work location, and department code (for budget purposes) of employees.

Payroll systems did not evolve until the demand for information could not be met with simple paper ledgers. As the demand for industrial products and services grew, so did the numbers of workers. Employees worked in shifts, in different locations, at different jobs, and for varying rates of pay. In addition to the sheer volume of information that had to be kept, there was the additional complexity of collecting enough information to comply with labour laws. In the United States, for example, the Fair Standards Act of 1934 and subsequent amendments provided the stimulus for time clocks and payroll. In Canada, the equivalents to the Fair Standards Act are the Employment Standard Acts of the provinces and the Canada Labour Code for the federal government. These acts do not generally require either time clocks or payroll systems, but do typically require specific records retentions and accurate pay.

With recording technologies, transmission, and with early computers, it didn't take very long for scientific advances to merge together into the new field of Information Technology. Information technology is the use of technology to enhance the speed and the efficiency of the transfer of information.[5]

(d) — The Mid-1950s and Early 1960s

Television followed radio, allowing video to be displayed with sound. While radio brought the world's events to our homes, it was television that brought the first pictures of the world to many people. Televisions were first used as a way to get information and news from other places, but quickly became a very important entertainment device, as well as a useful tool for learning. Unlike radio, television brought with it a whole new industry of content delivery, mainly cable television providers. Not only were stations producing and broadcasting their own shows, but the broadcasting industry allowed homes to receive more and more channels. With the later advances in technology, direct services such as cable and satellite television provided increasingly diverse amounts of content.[6]

Computer technology began to accelerate by the early 1960s. Unfortunately, the availability of these tools was not generally taken advantage of by those working in Personnel, but there were notable exceptions in the aerospace and defence industries, where the first known nonpayroll personnel systems were developed. These industries were leaders in the use of technology. They identified the need for information on employees and potential employees with specific skill sets,

---

5 *Ibid.*
6 *Ibid.*

and then developed automated systems to gather, store, and access it. The first known human resources inventory applications were developed in the late 1950s.

These particular industries had to be ready to respond to a rapidly growing demand for special skills for projects. Behavioural scientists developed instruments to survey existing employees who were already working on projects. These instruments determined levels of education, experience, etc., for each special skill. The information gathered was recorded on computer cards. Once analyzed, it told the Personnel department which of their employees had specific skills; they could then be identified for new projects, as required. As well, surveys and tests were developed for applicants that would help indicate whether an individual had a specific skill.

The computers available, although offering capabilities only previously dreamed of, were cumbersome to program. Many of the programmers and analysts of the time were engineers and scientists, and the applications they developed tended to serve the areas they knew, or which were pressing for assistance. During this period, only the larger companies could afford programmers. But some of these companies began to recognize the value of having information available on their employees. They learned over time that collecting and analyzing such information was expensive but sometimes necessary. Gradually, new applications were developed; however, these occurred in a piece-meal fashion rather than as a total solution.

Much of the data was collected on Hollerith cards. These 80-column paper cards were punched with code to record basic information. Often, several cards were required to record all of the information on one employee. When it was determined that additional information was required, new cards were often needed. Even with the use of magnetic tape, only a "card image" was available to store information. Since the storage media was so inflexible, most new applications were developed to handle specific needs. One file might hold basic personnel biographical data, while another contained skill information, and still others time information, training information, etc. Very few applications were developed where the full picture of an employee was available. This was the era of the second generation computer.

(e) — The Mid-1960s

As organizations realized the power of the computer, more and more applications were developed, and inefficiencies corrected. Computer storage was relatively expensive, yet there was much duplication of information. Dozens of personnel records could exist for each individual, each having an employee identifier recorded as well as name and department. Eventually it was realized that this duplication could be prevented if the records could be longer. As well, it was realized that information, if properly captured once, near the source, could potentially be accessed for a variety of uses. Time worked, for example, was generally captured to determine the amount to pay the employee. In many cases, other

1.2 Human Resources Management Systems

applications were developed separately to capture labour distribution and product costs. It would clearly be beneficial to tie these records together, and when possible, link them to one employee record.

The adoption of this "longitudinal file" concept coincided with the development and introduction of the IBM/360 and related mainframe computers. Management Information Systems (MIS) departments became involved in massive projects to track information flow and create new applications that managed whole business events. Some of these projects included payroll and personnel applications, but generally speaking, payroll received more attention. This was a trend that would continue for some time, as it was seen to be more important to pay people accurately and on time than to use automation for other human resources management purposes.

During the 1960s, a number of very large projects were initiated to develop systems to manage all of an organization's business information needs in one application, including personnel and payroll. While conceptually feasible, the technology did not exist to support the complexity of these systems, so that these initiatives were generally not successful.

The American Equal Pay Act of 1963 is said to have provided the most significant business case of all for developing an automated personnel system. This legislation was designed to ensure equality in pay between men and women for work that was substantially equal. To comply, companies needed data and statistics. Employers needed to collect large amounts of data about their employees, including job content, pay levels, and so on. Existing personnel systems were generally unprepared to meet these needs. The Equal Pay Act of 1963 was followed by Title VII of the Civil Rights Act in 1964. This act forbade discrimination in employment (as well as housing, education, and other areas) and subsequent amendments were enacted to remedy these deficiencies. An Equal Opportunities Commission (EOC) was established, and it brought a new discipline to personnel processes. It also set forth recordkeeping rules for employers with 25 or more employees.

There were some success stories in the 1960s. White collar and clerical labour costs for processing paper-handling tasks in the larger banks and insurance companies were high. These resources were not unionized, and management consequently saw opportunities to save by paring administrative and turnover costs. They saw benefits in automating the processing of personnel documents, and in reducing turnover and training costs. This was accomplished with automated systems that tracked skills and assisted in the selection of the "right person for the right job".

It was in the 1960s that the first commercial HRMS packages were developed. In May 1965, several individuals who worked at IBM got together and formed a new company called Information Science Incorporated (known as INSci); this company was to develop the first packaged personnel system. Their first product,

PICS (Personnel Information Communication System), used the concepts of skills systems. INSci developed a system to match jobs with people: résumés were coded and matched against existing job criteria to assist employers in filling jobs.

Although the first INSci system was not a tremendous success, it generated some interest with employers who were experiencing problems with their personnel records functions. INSci responded by developing a number of customized personnel systems to meet the specific needs of individual companies. In 1970, for instance, it developed HRS II, a mainframe-based HRMS system designed for banks.

Western military forces quickly became leaders in applying the development and implementation of computer technology to human resources. In an early example, the United States Air Force Human Resources Laboratory (AFHRL) distributed thousands of task inventories to airmen in all enlisted jobs in the Air Force. Through the use of computers and statistical software, called the Comprehensive Occupational Data Analysis Programs (CODAP), these data were analyzed to identify different jobs, job families, and the requirements for each. Such efforts not only established the most effective and comprehensive approach to job analysis yet attempted, but clearly identified the potential power and impact of the use of computers in personnel.

Many of the programs put into place by military forces to select the right people for the right job were copied by their civilian counterparts, expanded to include attitudinal surveys and other human resources tools. For instance, Ontario Hydro, a Canadian company, successfully used CODAP in the 1970s and 1980s.

These developments resulted in a heightened awareness of the fact that human resources was an increasingly significant part of a company's budget. By controlling these costs, a company could be more competitive. Further, the importance of employee morale was recognized as crucial to retaining the best people. Motivational and opinion surveys consequently evolved.

New human resources programs were developed to ensure that a supply of properly skilled and motivated employees was available. Job evaluation systems were created to rate jobs according to established criteria. Salary ranges were established; so too were performance criteria, and performance evaluations were developed to track progress. Pay was thus linked to performance.

(f) — The 1970s

In the United States in the early 1970s, government legislation related to Equal Employment Opportunity (EEO) and other employee programs forced most companies of a few thousand employees or more to develop automated personnel systems. During this time, the cost of storing and processing information started to fall, and pre-programmed commercial HRMSs made personnel systems less expensive.

1.2 Human Resources Management Systems

Amendments to American EEO legislation in the 1970s established the concept of "affirmative action." This new legislation created requirements for calculating "availability," setting goals and targets, producing utilization reports, and generating workforce analysis. This level of legislation was the strongest to date and American business began to seriously monitor their workforce in order to comply with the recordkeeping requirements. Computerization was the most efficient way for many larger companies to comply with the legislation. Many organizations added new data elements to their existing payroll systems, as this area had already been automated.

In the late 1970s, the scope of systems was expanded greatly for many organizations. Many HRMS projects were completed, but many others were abandoned along the way. Some were halted when they ran out of funding while others simply ran out of time, and a new project was started. This was a frustrating period for those involved with HRMS projects. The human resources function turned out to be much more difficult to automate than many people anticipated.

(g) — The Internet

The Internet was originally conceived as a distributed, fail-proof network that could connect computers together and be resistant to any point of failure. In the fifties and early sixties, prior to the widespread inter-networking that led to the Internet, most communication networks were limited by their nature to only allow communications between the stations on the network. Some networks had gateways or bridges between them, but these bridges were often limited or built specifically for a single use. One prevalent computer networking method was based on the central mainframe method, simply allowing its terminals to be connected via long leased lines. This method was used in the 1950s by Project RAND to support researchers such as Herbert Simon, in Pittsburgh, Pennsylvania, when collaborating across the continent with researchers in Santa Monica, California, on automated theorem proving and artificial intelligence.

In January 1960, J.C.R. Licklider had articulated a pioneering idea calling for "a network of such [computers], connected to one another by wide-band communication lines" which provided "the functions of present-day libraries together with anticipated advances in information storage and retrieval and [other] symbiotic functions." In October 1962, Licklider was appointed head of the United States Department of Defense's DARPA information processing office, and formed an informal group within DARPA to further computer research.

As part of the information processing office's role, three network terminals had been installed, each with three different sets of user commands. At the tip of the inter-networking problem lay the issue of connecting separate physical networks to form one logical network. At the same time others were working on a notion of a network — the Internet — that could survive a nuclear attack through decentralization to avoid combat damage compromising the entire network.

Introduction **1.2**

The first links of what was to become the internet was established between the University of California, Los Angeles and the Stanford Research Institute on 21 November 1969. By 5 December 1969, a four-node network was connected by adding the University of Utah and the University of California, Santa Barbara. The ARPANET started in 1972 and was growing rapidly by 1981 with 213 hosts and with a new host being added approximately every twenty days.

ARPANET became the technical core of what would become the Internet, and a primary tool in developing the technologies used. Meanwhile the British Post Office, Western Union International and Tymnet collaborated to create the first international packet switched network, referred to as the International Packet Switched Service (IPSS), in 1978. This network grew from Europe and the U.S. to cover Canada, Hong Kong and Australia by 1981. By the 1990s it provided a worldwide networking infrastructure.

In 1979, CompuServe became the first service to offer electronic mail capabilities and technical support to personal computer users. The company broke new ground again in 1980 as the first to offer real-time chat with its CB Simulator. There were also the America Online (AOL) and Prodigy dial in networks and many bulletin board system (BBS) networks such as The WELL and FidoNet. FidoNet in particular was popular amongst hobbyist computer users, many of them hackers and amateur radio operators.

(h) — The 1980s

In the late 1970s and early 1980s, personnel functions went through a transformation. The number of functions and services offered grew: job analysis became more rigorous; compensation became quite complex; employment equity programs were put in place; large investments were made in staff development; employee testing became quite common; and organization development arrived. Each area required specialized expertise. Even mid-size companies (those with 1000 to 4000 employees) found that they could justify their own HRMS. Many did not need the power of a mainframe, and chose instead to utilize a mid-size computer. Packaged HRMS products were utilized that did not take a lot of time to customize, install, and maintain.

The early HRMS packages had many limitations, and by the early 1980s many organizations were experiencing problems. The number of processes to be automated was growing in number and complexity and the available packages could not readily accommodate them. Seemingly straightforward applications such as recruitment and selection left vast gaps in what could easily be automated. This reflected the recordkeeping basis of the HRMS systems in place at the time.

Existing HRMSs were generally not as effective as they might have been because they were not designed to meet the specific requirements of the host organization. For example, the process of transferring an existing employee from one job to another in the same organization may sound simple. But this is generally not the case, as company policies and labour agreements can come into play. Each process must be fully reviewed and agreed upon before it can be decided that a process is correct and work can commence in automating it. Another example is defining an "applicant." The definitions may differ by union affiliation or by plant site.

In the 1980s however, small computers started to become available. A personal computer, or PC, is generally a microcomputer intended to be used by one person at a time, and suitable for general purpose tasks such as word processing, programming, editing or playing a personal computer game, and is usually used to run purchased or other software not written by the user. Unlike minicomputers, a personal computer is often owned by the person using it, indicating a low cost of purchase and simplicity of operation. The user of a modern personal computer may have significant knowledge of the operating environment and application programs, but is not necessarily interested in programming nor even able to write programs for the computer.

The term PC was popularized by Apple Computer and soon after many other companies began offering personal computers. International Business Machines Corporation (IBM) developed the first open standard Personal Computer (IBM PC launched in U.S. markets in 1981, the first deliveries to European markets were in 1982 and 1983), which standardized the software development. For the first time in the world history we had PC's that used the similar operating systems that allowed the computers' users to communicate by using the same platform.

Soon after, we saw the birth of what we know as current information technology: personal computers in our own homes, using communication devices known as modems, to access information on remote servers. The first incarnation of those were BBS servers, setup by education facilities or even individual people, to store both information and allow discussion with chat and messages.[7]

With the invention of the World Wide Web in 1989 the Internet took off as a global network.

(i) — The Late 1980s and Early 1990s

The introduction of the microcomputer or personal computer (PC) had a dramatic impact on human resources, for it offered some relief for the problems created by rapidly changing requirements. This relief came in several ways:

- Microcomputers were a lot less expensive than mainframes and mid-ranges.
- Micro-based systems could be installed in a few short months whereas larger systems could take years.
- Micro-based systems could be maintained by the HR user.

---

7 *Ibid*.

Introduction 1.2

- They were easy to modify.
- They were easy to use.
- They could be used in conjunction with office productivity tools such as spread sheets, document processing, other databases, and electronic mail.

When microcomputers first became available to the business community, HR applications had to be built by the user. Few, if any packages were available, and local MIS resources were not yet trained to program the microcomputers. The use of microcomputers in many organizations was originally banned or severely restricted: MIS departments put such strong impediments in the way that most users could not acquire a micro without going through impossible roadblocks. A number of reasons for restricting access to computers were provided, but many micro-users today believe that the primary explanation lies in the insecurity of the then mainframe-oriented MIS department, which feared loss of control and of jobs.

However, many of the concerns voiced have actually turned out to be valid. Some of these include:

- Inadequate or no routine back-up of important files.
- Data not secure.
- Lack of standards when developing supplementary databases in-house, incompatible files.
- Lack of adequate documentation for user-built systems and subsystems.
- Databases not integrated, resulting in redundancy of data, inconsistent or outdated data, or data in multiple systems that do not match.

This revolution continues, however, and MIS resistance has given way to reluctant acquiescence or to enthusiastic support.

During the late 1980s, the major issue facing HRMS was the marriage of microcomputers to mainframes. Connectivity was an issue. In large companies, some of the business applications remained on mainframes and the microcomputer was used like a "dumb terminal," merely to access the HRMS on-line to the mainframe. There were many problems related to complex access protocols and data standards. Moving data back and forth between mainframe databases and micro-based productivity tools was very difficult. Downloading a subset of HRMS data to a spreadsheet such as LOTUS for analysis, for example, was very difficult. Users found it difficult to enjoy the full benefit of the information resource available only on the mainframe HRMS. Also, microcomputer users found it difficult or impossible to share information that was only resident on their micro-units.

During the late 1980s great improvements were made in linking computers together into networks. Wide Area Networks (WANs) and Local Area Networks (LANs) became possible after improvements in the technology. LANs, both independent from or connected to the mainframe, provided access to common data for users who had common interests, such as HR. Human Resources, however, was seldom the first, or even the second function in a company to take advantage of this new technology.

The Digital Revolution is a recent term describing the effects of the rapid drop in cost and rapid expansion of power of digital devices such as computers and telecommunications (e.g. mobile phones). It includes changes in technology and society, and is often specifically used to refer to the controversies that occur as these technologies are widely adopted. Technological advances such as mobile phones, high speed connections, Voice Over IP (VOIP) have changed lifestyles around the world and spawned new industries around controlling and providing information.[8]

Some of the reasons for Human Resources being slower in utilizing networks were related to the following considerations:

1. In large companies, the HRMS was already established on the mainframe and provided some level of satisfactory service.
2. Moving the HRMS off the mainframe and onto a LAN, or at least integrating the two, had to be "cost-justified" before closing down the mainframe-based HRMS.
3. There was a distinct lack of micro- or LAN-based HRMS applications available.
4. The first applications were generally "stand alone applications," for use on one microcomputer, which would deny access to others in Human Resources and to line management.
5. Customizing a stand-alone micro-HRMS application to work on a network was expensive and time-consuming.
6. Most human resources practitioners were not as computer literate as their colleagues in Finance and Operations. As a result, they often failed to convince management to invest in the new technology.
7. There were many technical problems associated with HRMS installation. End users were simply not prepared to contend with the numerous problems with downtime, hardware problems, lost data, and new releases of software. These were not sophisticated technology users; they were HR users with little technical training and a low tolerance for paving new ground.

Basically, there was a reluctance to try new solutions even when they did become available, especially when it was widely believed that LANs were unreliable and

---

8 *Ibid.*

that a mainframe offered more stability. This issue was not really resolved in many organizations until employees who were more comfortable with computers entered the HR workforce.

In the past, human resources practitioners were generally not knowledgeable or skilled in data automation or computer-related areas, and so were dependent on systems analysts and other "experts" to design and implement systems for them. However, these systems/computer experts frequently did not understand the content areas for which they were designing the systems, leading to communications problems. This in turn led to the design and implementation of systems that were not as effective or as efficient as they otherwise might have been. Because the human resources generalists did not understand the potential inherent in automation, and the systems specialists generally did not understand human resources requirements at anything but a superficial level, many such systems wound up being little more than an automation of existing paper files and practices.

To bypass these communications problems, the systems people developed and adopted an extensive, complicated set of needs analysis and project management protocols designed to obtain user-input and feedback at various stages. The problem with this process was that it was "owned and operated" by the management information specialists. Too often it was not applied under the direction of someone knowledgeable in both human resources and computer applications and ended up automating current or even past practices rather than allowing for future innovations. Adding to this the fact that the process was long and inefficient, it is no wonder that many of the systems developed were verging on obsolescence before being implemented.

Because human resources practitioners have not traditionally been computer experts, and especially in small organizations purchasing a human resources management information system for the first time, the following problems may be encountered:

1. Practitioners may go with what they are comfortable, in terms of implementing a system that merely automates existing paper and labour-intensive practices.
2. Management information specialists may be given the job of conducting needs analysis, choosing software, and implementing the system, without adequate awareness of human resources requirements.
3. Human resources practitioners and others in the organization may be persuaded to purchase and implement a system that is more or less sophisticated than the organization requires at its current level of technical evolution.

Thus, the marriage of Human Resources (HR) and Information Systems (IS) has not always been as smooth as it might have been. Human resources and information systems professionals tended to have very different approaches and philosophical outlooks and, as a consequence, neither understood each other nor communicated well.

In an attempt to bridge that gap the International Association for Human Resource Information Management (IHRIM) was formed in 1996 out of the Canadian Association of Human Resource Systems Professionals (CHRSP) and the Association of Human Resource Systems Professionals (HRSP) creating a new international association. IHRIM began strongly and expanded to chapters in the U.K. and Australia and holding conferences in North America, but gradually it moved away from its international founding vision retaining less than half of its founding membership numbers.

In Canada the void has been filled by the HRMS Professionals Association (HRMSP)/Association des professionnels en SGRH (PSGRH). HRMSP has grown slowly but steadily since its formation in 2005 offering information and networking to those with an interest in HRMS in Canada.

1.3 — Evolving Human Resources Management Information Requirements for the New Millennium

Flexibility and effectiveness in the strategic structuring and managing of human resources is becoming increasingly important. While we are in a period of great change, and there is uncertainty as to how best to achieve these goals, it is clear that doing so requires data gathering, storage, retrieval, and analysis from an appropriate HRMS.

1.4 — Business/Technological Trends

Valaskakis, Coull and Clermont (1991) have pointed out that, for most organizations, corporate success will increasingly depend on the coordinated, strategic management of the organization's human resources and information technology.

In the future, those responsible for developing, implementing, operating, and maintaining an HRMS must have a broad knowledge of: the organization's human resources programs; the relationship between human resources programs and other organizational functions, particularly strategic planning and operations; the potential inherent in computer and data automation; and how to capitalize on this potential, and explain and "sell it" to others in the organization.

An HRMS must therefore be geared to the strategic and business requirements of the organization, and harmonized with its other systems. It must also be sufficiently flexible to adapt and grow with evolving requirements and technology. Those responsible for designing and implementing new systems must understand the evolving strategic, business, and technological trends of the organization, and its external environment.

For many organizations, these evolving trends may be summarized as follows:

1. Office and process automation technologies are profoundly modifying the organization of work with the following outcomes:

    - the information-based organization is flatter, requiring significantly fewer levels of management; and,

    - the nature of management is changing, emphasizing technical knowledge and facilitation rather than supervision.

2. Managerial, professional, and administrative occupations are increasingly relying on distributed computing as an essential part of their business.

3. Computers are increasingly used to gather, analyze, and communicate or report crucial information, facilitated by electronic mail and local area networks.

4. Information technology can increase the speed and quality of managerial decision making.

5. There has been a shift in office automation from support staff to business professionals.

6. Office automation has become a continuing, dynamic process of combining all the interactive elements of the office: people, information, functions, and procedures.

1.5 — Models of the Human Resources Function

Many human resources practitioners begin as employment counsellors, compensation and benefits clerks, or labour relations officers, whether directly from university or college, or on transfer from other functions. They may spend their careers administering or managing human resources programs such as those outlined below.

- Recruiting and Selection
- Training and Development
- Time and Attendance
- Payroll
- Compensation and Benefits
- Employee/Labour Relations
- Employee/Performance Problems
- Employee Assistance
- Equity Programs
- Retirement/Pensions

1.5 Human Resources Management Systems

As organizations mature, they generally find that they require more effective means for assessing, keeping track of, and managing their human resources. Recently, the impetus for this has come from the need to develop tools to satisfy legislative requirements, as well as the need to respond more effectively and efficiently to evolving strategic/business pressures. These tools include job analysis, work planning and review, performance/personnel assessment, and an HRMS.

Figure 1.2 A Human Resources Model

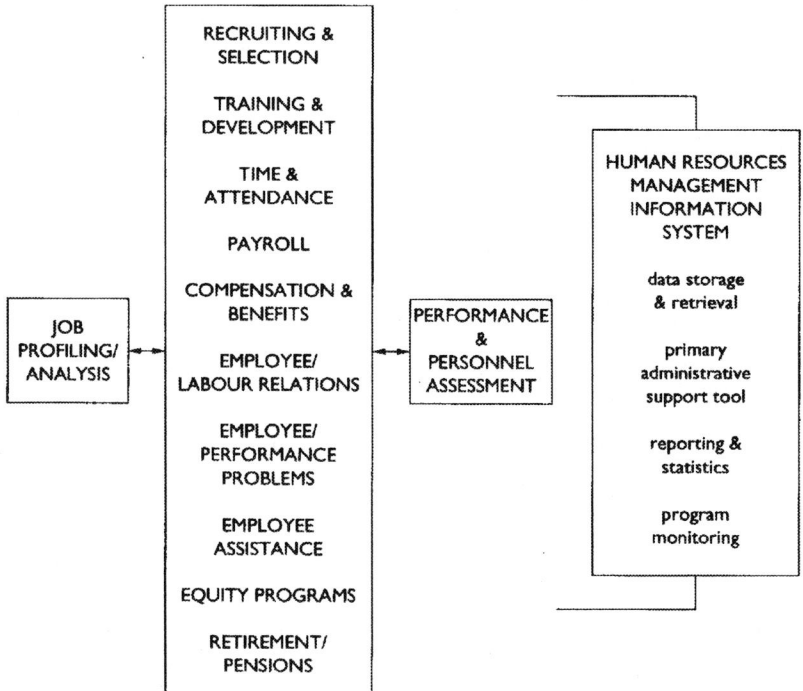

With respect to HRMSs, Lederer (1991) argues that a broader range of organizations is finding that they require automation to handle their human resources information management needs. Furthermore, as discussed in succeeding chapters, there are many new developments in HRMS software and hardware. This means that many systems that have been in place for five or ten years are now obsolete, particularly if they were not originally based on sound needs analysis or on state-of-the-art technology existing at the time of implementation. A combination of circumstances, therefore, has conspired to make this a time when many organizations are looking to obtain a new HRMS. Included among these are:

  1. relatively small but growing organizations looking for their first system;

2. organizations that are restructuring because of the need to be competitive in the increasingly international marketplace, and require new systems as strategic tools in support of this goal; and

3. an increasing number of organizations with established human resources information systems that are looking to upgrade their existing systems to keep up with evolving technology.

An HRMS provides an organization with data storage and retrieval, primary administrative support, reporting and statistics, and program monitoring capabilities. These four capabilities in turn may allow the human resources function to move beyond administering and managing programs of the sort listed in Figure 1.2, to human resources planning and related functions (see Figure 1.3).

Figure 1.3 Addition of Human Resources/Succession Planning to the Human Resources Model

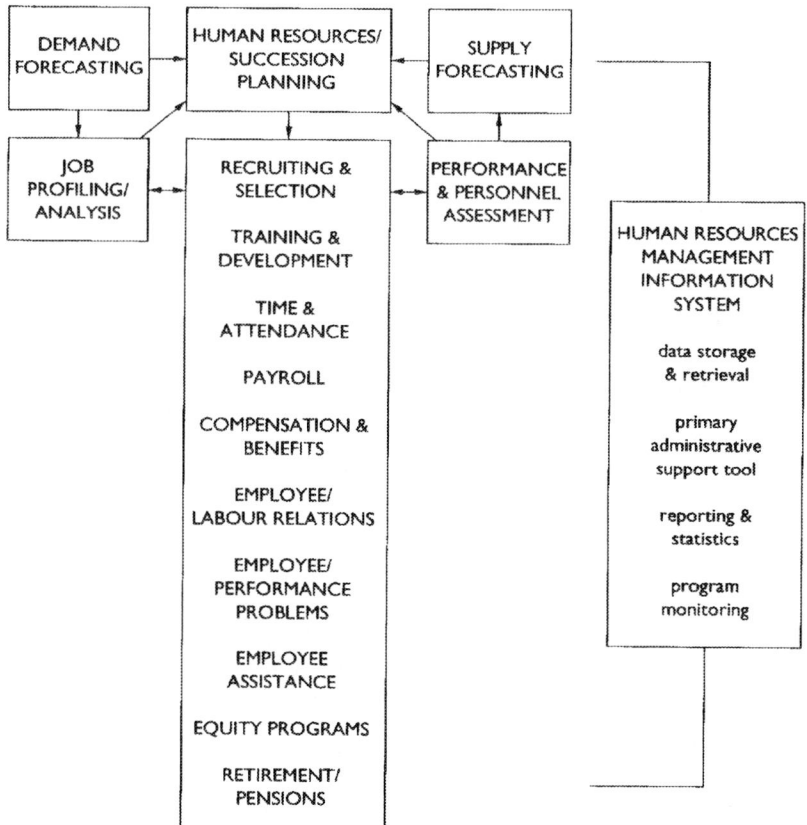

1.5 Human Resources Management Systems

As noted by Cascio and Thacker (1994), progressive Human Resources departments have been able to place all of these programs in the context of external environmental influences and the organization's strategic/business focus (see Figure 1.4).

Figure 1.4 provides a model showing the components comprising the human resources functions of most organizations, along with their interrelationships. The reader will note that this model is organized into rows and columns.

Row 1 contains contextual, strategic components of the model. Thus, component C1 deals with the external issues, including the socioeconomic and legislative context impinging on the organization. Knowledge of these influences affects issues in component A1, which involves the organization's strategic, business planning processes.

Row 2 contains forecasting and planning processes required to identify the need/potential inherent in Row 1, and translate these into effective human resources programs.

Row 3 contains the programs that most practitioners recognize as the traditional human resources functions, including job/position evaluation, recruiting and selection, training and development, labour relations, compensation and benefits, performance management and evaluation, etc.

Row 4 involves the program evaluation or auditing function required to ensure that the previous components are working as they should. Thus, the model is not just driven from the top down. This and other components should feed back to and influence functions higher in the model, so that problems are self-correcting.

Column A consists of components that assess or reflect the "demand" or requirements for human resources. That is, the global requirements of the organization should be reflected in its strategic and business plans; these, in turn, are further analyzed and planned for in the organization's demand forecasting. The organization's strategic/business plans should also drive the structure of the organization, which are then reflected in the job description/job evaluation process.

Column B consists of what one commonly thinks of as the "traditional human resources functions." These are the functions and processes that serve as the link, interface, or means of satisfying gaps between the requirement for human resources at various levels and its supply.

Column C consists of components that assess or reflect the "supply" of human resources. That is, external conditions determine the skills and availability of individuals that might be recruited, as well as socioeconomic and legislative influences on other components in the model. These, in turn, can be further analyzed and planned for the organization's supply forecasting. Performance management and evaluation processes not only represent the means of planning for and getting the work of the organization done through the efforts of its employees, but also reflect and provide an inventory of the skills, expertise, and qualification of the internal workforce.

Column D represents the various modules and tools that, together, comprise the HRMS.

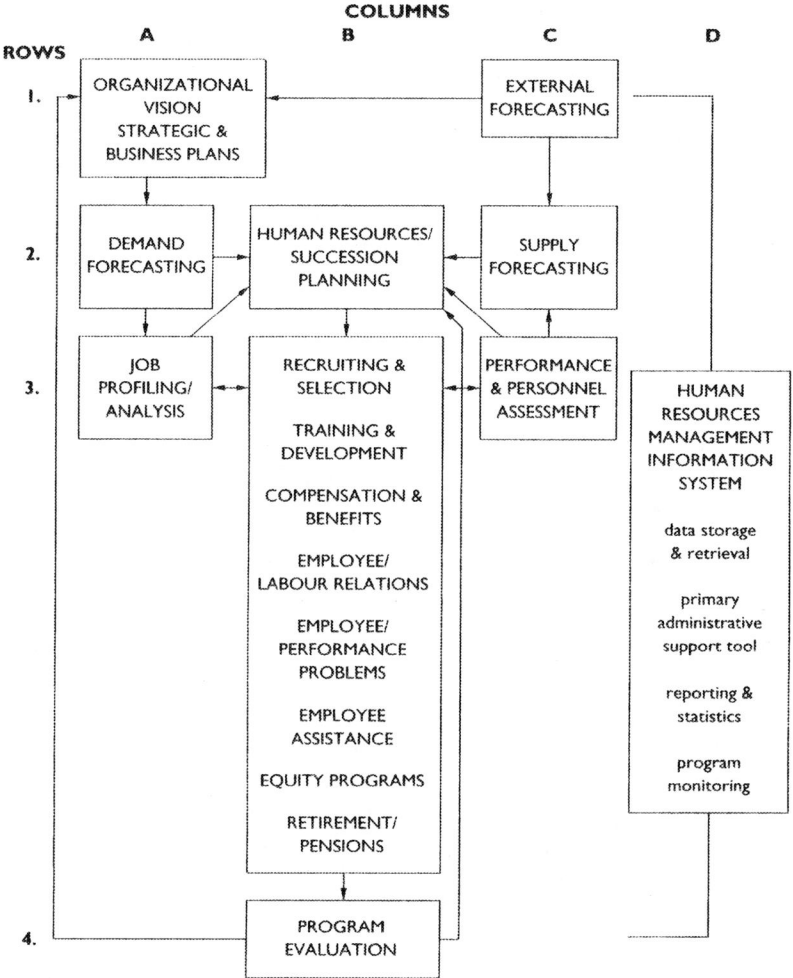

Figure 1.4 General Human Resources Model

Not all of the components of this model may be included in every human resources department. All of them exist, however, whether explicitly or implicitly, in every organization.

The challenge of the human resources professional is to understand the relationships among the various components of the model and to become proficient in using them effectively. As mentioned above, many human resources practitioners do not understand that their role could extend beyond programs outlined in row 3, column B of the model. Others understand the need for demand and supply forecasting cum human resources/succession planning (row 2, columns A, B, and C), but are unable to use this knowledge to provide input into and influence the organization's strategic plan (row 1, columns A, B, and C). Furthermore, they are unlikely to gain this influence and the status that comes with it without a sound working knowledge of how to use an HRMS effectively (column D) in support of the remaining programs.

1.6 — Summary

This chapter began by providing an historical overview of HRMSs, from their earliest beginnings, as a means of compiling the first United States Census, through the evolution of Hollerith computer cards, "batch" payroll application, mainframe driven, tape-resident longitudinal files, to today's direct-access, PC-networked systems.

The chapter went on to describe how, in today's dynamic business environment, those responsible for planning for and developing a new HRMS are faced with many challenges. A new or updated HRMS must be fully capable of adapting to new requirements. These trends have been reviewed to set the stage for more detailed discussion on how process re-engineering and other methods discussed later in the book may be used to define requirements, and then to plan, develop, implement, and maintain an HRMS.

1.7 — References

Berry, W.E. 1993. "New Role for HR Requires a New Vision for Management Systems." *HR Focus* 70, no. 3 (March): 22.

Bloom, N.L. 1991. "Corporate Needs for HR Information." In A.L. Lederer, ed., *Handbook of Human Resources Information Systems*. New York: Warren, Gorham and Lamont.

Broderick, R., and J.W. Boudreau. 1992. "Human Resource Management, Information Technology, and the Competitive Edge." *The Executive* 5, no. 2 (May): 7–17.

Cascio, W.F., and J.W. Thacker. 1994. *Managing Human Resources*. Toronto: McGraw-Hill Ryerson.

Ceriello, V.R. 1991. *Human Resource Management Systems: Strategy, Tactics, and Techniques*. Toronto: Maxwell Macmillan.

Christal, R.E. 1974. *The United States Air Force Occupational Research Project, AFHRL-TR-73-75*. Lackland Airforce Base, Texas: Airforce, Occupational Research Division.

CHRSP Resource Magazine 5, no. 3, 1995.

Doran, J.A., and G.M. Rampton. 1994. "Making a Business Case for a New Human Resources Management Information System." *Canadian Human Resources Systems Professionals Resource Magazine* (June): 4–8.

Encyclopedia Britannica (Micropaedia, vol. V). 1975. Toronto: Helen Hemingway Benton, p. 92.

French, W. 1974. *The Personnel Management Process: Human Resources Administration*, 3rd ed. Boston, Mass.: Houghton Mifflin.

Haltrecht, E. 1980. "CODAP: Introduction and Uses in a Large Public Facility." In G.M. Rampton, ed., *Proceedings of the 22nd Annual Conference of the Military Testing Association*. Toronto: Canadian Forces Personnel Applied Research Unit, ha10 - ha115.

Hennecke, M. 1984. "The People Side of Strategic Planning." *Training* (November): 25–34.

Horsfield, D. 1991. "Human Resources Planning Applications." In A.L. Lederer, ed., *Handbook of Human Resources Information Systems*. New York: Warren, Gorham and Lamont.

Kavanagh, M.J., H.G. Gueutal, and S.I. Tannenbaum. 1990. *Human Resource Information Systems: Development and Application*. Boston, Mass.: PWS-Kent.

Kazanas, H.C. 1988. *Strategic Human Resources Planning and Management*. Englewoods Cliffs, N.J.: Prentice-Hall.

Lederer, A.L. 1991. *Handbook of Human Resources Information Systems*. New York: Warren, Gorham and Lamont.

Mackey, C.B. 1991. "Conducting a Preliminary Study for an HRIS Project." In A.L. Lederer, ed., *Handbook of Human Resources Information Systems*. New York: Warren, Gorham and Lamont.

Miracle, M. 1993. "The Trend to Client/Server is Maturing into Acceptance." *National Underwriter Life/Health/Financial Services* 97, no. 45 (November): 2–8.

Mueller, B. 1994. "Changing Attitudes Help Shape HR Systems." *Systems Management* 22, no. 3 (March): 82–89.

Niehaus, R.J. 1987. *Strategic Human Resources Planning Applications*. New York: Plenum Press.

Pasqualetto, J. 1993. "New Competencies Define the HRIS Manager's Future Role." *Personnel Journal* 72, no. 1 (January): 91–99.

Rampton, G.M., and J.A. Doran. 1994. "A Practitioner's Guide for a New HRIS." Paper presented at the 9th Annual CHRSP Conference (October 4-7).

Richards-Carpenter, C. 1994. "Personnel takes Pragmatic Approach to Technology." *Personnel Management* 26, no. 7 (July): 55–56.

Rummler, G.A., and A.P. Brache. 1991. "Managing the White Space." *Training* (January): 55–70.

Schuler, R.S. 1984. *Personnel and Human Resources Management*, 2nd ed. New York: West Publishing.

Stambaugh, R. 1991. "Determining HRIS Requirements." In A.L. Lederer, ed., *Handbook of Human Resources Information Systems*. New York: Warren, Gorham and Lamont.

Stright, J.F. 1993. "Strategic Goals Guide HRMS Development." *Personnel Journal* (September): 68-78.

United States Department of Labor. 1967. "Equal Pay for Equal Work under the Fair Labor Standards Act." *Interpractices Bulletin*. Title 27, Part 800.

Valaskakis, K., R. Coull, and R. Clermont, R. 1991. *Information Technology and Human Resources: Prospects for the Decade*. Report prepared for the Canadian Human Resources Scanning Association. Toronto (April).

Walker, A.J. 1982. *A Project Team Guide to Building an Effective Personnel Information System*. New York: Van Nostrand Reinhold.

Walker, J.W. 1980. *Human Resource Planning*. New York: McGraw Hill.

Wetherbe, J.C., N.P. Vitalari, and A. Milner. 1994. "Key Trends in Systems Development in Europe and North America." *Journal of Global Informations Management* 2, no. 2 (Spring): 5–20.

Chapter 2: The Need for an Effective HRMS

2.1 — Introduction

To be competitive in today's demanding and rapidly changing business environment, management needs accurate and timely information on the organization's most important resources, its employees. Many organizations are finding that the traditional ways of managing human resources information are not up to the challenge, and must be updated or completely revamped. This chapter begins by discussing some of the reasons why organizations are coming to this conclusion. Included is a discussion of the organizational information needs that a modern HRMS can satisfy. This discussion is then expanded by functional area in each of the functional Chapters, 8 – 12.

Human resources information requirements are becoming more complex and demanding for most organizations. This is due, in part, to the need to comply with greatly increased requirements for information to satisfy government legislation in such areas as employment equity (affirmative action in the U.S.), pay equity, pensions, payroll, and taxation. It is also due to the fact that more effective access to workforce information is becoming more and more necessary if organizations are to be competitive in today's rapidly changing business environment.

Information technology has evolved to the point where organizations with as few as 50 to 100 employees are finding it cost effective to implement and maintain an HRMS. Companies that have never had an HRMS are exploring the feasibility of implementing their first system. In larger organizations, line managers and human resources practitioners are discovering that technological advancements have rendered existing systems obsolete, leading them to believe that their organizations would benefit from either modernizing an existing HRMS or purchasing a new one.

Organizations will often decide to implement a new HRMS either to develop the capability to do the applications described below, or to do them better than is possible using the technology currently available to the organization.

2.2 — Employee Lists

As simple as this sounds, basic lists are at the top of many organization's requirements. Most have many lists of all kinds such as addresses, employees by organization unit, phone numbers, etc. They reside in paper files, in spreadsheets, word processing files or small databases, and often in all those forms. In many organizations every HR person and every Supervisor and Manager keeps their own versions of these lists, rarely with two alike.

2.3   Human Resources Management Systems

Such information may also be partially available in automated form in payroll files, but it may not be readily accessible to identify different groups of employees or to communicate with them for a variety of purposes, such as:

1. distributing surveys to assess employee attitudes to proposed changes in administrative policies or benefits programs;
2. communicating widely regarding employee recognition programs;
3. advising employees about changes regarding administrative or operational programs; or
4. saving money on postage by sending payroll tax returns to each individual's work address rather than to their homes.

There are many occasions during the course of a year where managers at all levels are required to identify employees with specific characteristics, and to produce tables of the numbers of individuals having these characteristics. These lists should be simple to produce, but many organizations do not have the means of doing so quickly and accurately. Such lists should allow employees to be grouped by plant, department, sex, age, years of service, grade, salary, employee affiliation, employment status (part-time/full-time), etc., for such purposes as:

1. providing a record of all the employees reporting to a new manager;
2. documenting all employees in Department A, age 60 and older, listing name, job title, grade, age, length of service, as background information for a human resources planning exercise;
3. producing a list of casual employees by time in position to monitor violations of a collective agreement; and
4. producing a list of full and vacant positions by department.

2.3 — Attrition Reporting/Monitoring

If Canadian organizations are to compete successfully in the increasingly international marketplace, employees must be regarded as a renewable resource to a much greater extent than they are now. This means attracting well-qualified applicants, making the most of their talents through progressive training and effective employment practices, and retaining the individuals that you want to keep. There is a considerable body of research evidence that suggests that North American organizations lag behind others in the industrialized world in making the most of their human assets.

As automation and information technology become more pervasive, investment in associated skills in a broader range of employees increases. The generic skills of typing or shorthand for secretaries or administrative assistants, for example, have largely been replaced by word processing, spreadsheets, electronic mail, and electronic information and storage devices, all resident on local area networks. Further, these applications are often tailored to the specific organization, so that individuals with experience in one organization may require retraining before they can be fully productive in a new organization.

Thus, in today's competitive environment, an organization requires effective recruiting, selection, training, compensation, and employment programs, along with effective information systems to support them. It also requires the means of monitoring who is leaving the organization, and for what reasons. Depending on an analysis of the reasons for attrition, its consequences, and the options available to the organization, the company could:

1. accept the situation and
    a. do nothing; or
    b. respond to the high turnover by increasing recruiting and training costs; or
2. try to decrease attrition by
    a. increasing compensation and benefits in an effort to make it more attractive for individuals to stay; or
    b. addressing motivation problems by examining leadership practices, increasing employee empowerment, quality of working life, etc.

2.4 — Employment Equity Tracking/Monitoring

For many years employment equity legislation of one sort or another has applied to all employers and employees in Canada and the United States. Corporations are finding that minority group recruiting is good business, as it broadens the population from which to select individuals with hard-to-find skills. As documented in Chapter 1, legislation has made it absolutely essential for organizations to develop accurate information gathering, retrieval, and analysis systems capable of:

1. reporting on the numbers and status in the organization of individuals from four designated groups (women, visible minorities, individuals with disabilities, and aboriginal people);
2. supporting the development of action plans for ensuring that individuals from the designated groups are approximately represented in all functions and levels in the organization in the same proportion that they are represented in the population from whence employees are recruited; and
3. monitoring the effectiveness of these action plans and modifying them as required.

A complication for those organizations covered by both federal and provincial legislation is that the reporting requirements for each, while similar in principle, differ significantly in format and detail.

Over the past few years, legislative changes have led to increasing pressures and constraints for most employers. Pay and employment legislation, for example, have had a significant impact on the field of human resources generally, and HRMS specifically, as systems must be adapted to provide for data and reporting requirements.

2.5 — Salary/Benefits

The compensation (salary and benefits) structure of most organizations having more than one or two hundred people can become quite complex. Yet situations arise (e.g., contract negotiations, pay equity planning, corporate restructuring, social contract planning) in which it is essential to be able to quickly estimate the costs of various changes in salary and benefits plans. In a typical application, the organization might have a total amount of money that can be divided between salary and benefits in different ways. A series of quick but realistic "what-if" analyses might have to be done to demonstrate that whatever is negotiated does not exceed budget limitations. Horror stories exist in many organizations about the lasting effects of agreements that were not accurately costed.

Salary and benefits budgets are a common requirement since it is important to be able to accurately and efficiently track salary and benefits costs to date, and to make projections against authorized budgets, given staffing levels and authorized staff complement. This capacity is crucial to budget management and budget planning. This often requires integration of the HRMS with the organization's financial systems.

2.6 — Seniority Lists

Seniority is an important consideration governing employment conditions in many union contracts and several organizations have multiple levels of seniority, sometimes inter-relational. Included are rights to:

- Overtime
- Vacation scheduling
- Bids for new positions where more than one employee meets the qualifications
- Bumping when positions are declared redundant

Employers are typically responsible for producing accurate seniority lists to be sent to the union and posted to be seen by the union membership. Errors or omissions in such lists are then open to grievance/arbitration processes.

In situations where seniority can be affected by different kinds of leave or working relationships, calculating seniority can be complicated. However, being able to produce accurate lists is very important to the organization, the union, the individuals concerned, and the relationships among all three.

2.7 — Applicant Tracking

This area of functionality has exploded in direct response to the economic climate and the increasing shortage of knowledge workers.

Because of the increasing shortage there is a need to act quickly on every qualified applicant even if they aren't right for a current vacancy. It is important to be able to cross-reference applicants from one competition to another, and to be able to track each applicant through the selection process because applicants passed over from one competition may be a good match for another. If this matching can be done effectively and efficiently, it is possible to save significantly on recruiting costs, such as advertising and administration.

It should also be possible for the information that is collected to be passed on to other human resources systems modules. For example, biographical information should not have to be collected more than once, and information on applicant characteristics should be available for employment equity reporting.

2.8 — Grievance Tracking and Analysis

In unionized settings there is an obligation on both management and unions to process grievances according to steps and timing stipulated in union contracts. An effective automated grievance management information system can save money, avoid unnecessary ill-will, and avoid the prospect of losing grievances or arbitrations for technical reasons.

The information gathered to manage grievance processes is also very important in providing a picture of the "who, why, what, and where" of the incidence of grievances and arbitrations. By analyzing trends one can often identify problem areas that can be worked on to reduce grievances and effect better employee relations. An important aspect of this process is to feed back to managers the types of grievances that have arisen over particular time periods, as well as their disposition and cost to the organization.

2.9 — Workers' Compensation (WC) and Long-Term Disability (LTD) Tracking

Organizations that have established effective means of managing workers' compensation and long-term disability costs can save hundreds of thousands of dollars annually. To be able to manage these costs effectively, the organization must be able to track the incidences and reasons (who, what, where) for accidents or illnesses. Effective management of WC and LTD means: determining what kinds of accidents or illnesses are happening, and where and when they are happening, to provide the basis for identifying and addressing problem areas; identifying potential fraudulent claims and taking corrective action; and getting individuals back on the job as quickly as possible, even if this means appropriate workplace accommodation.

WC provides financial inducements to employers that are successful in reducing workplace accidents and minimizing costs. The situation for LTD is similar except that, instead of being funded through an agency like a Workers' Compensation Board, LTD is self-funded (in the case of large organizations for whom this is economical), or funded indirectly through the payment of premiums to an insurance carrier.

While WC has traditionally focused on workplace accidents, stress-related illnesses have recently begun to be funded. If the analyses shows that these or similar ailments funded by LTD are prevalent, wellness programs or employee assistance programs may be useful in reducing costs by either preventing them from developing, or stopping them from getting worse.

2.10 — HRMS "Reports"

"Reports" can be traditional paper-based or on-screen. HRMS reports can include population snapshots or overviews, including such important variables as present employee make-up, population flows, population forecasts, and the implications that these have for staffing, human resources planning and development, and other personnel programs. These reports can serve as important benchmarks for the monitoring of population shifts and the identification of trends, potential problems, and areas meriting more detailed analysis.

2.11 — Human Resources/Strategic Planning

Business is carried out through and by people. The role of human resources planning, supported by an effective HRMS, is to provide managers with human resources data to influence and aid them in decision making, so that the right quantity and quality of people are available in the future to carry on sound and effective business.

Business decisions made today affect present human resources availability and the balance between future human resources demand and supply. An effective HRMS is required to support the following important human resources functions: strategic planning, succession planning, and internal population analysis. Each of these is discussed in more detail below.

(a) — Strategic Planning

Planning the future activities of the organization generates specific human resources needs and requirements to carry out the planned operations. A sound understanding of external and internal human resources trends is required to anticipate their potential impact on the supply/demand balance. This is particularly true in today's rapidly changing environment.

One objective of human resources planning is to monitor business plans closely and to integrate upcoming human resources requirements with strategic business and operating plans to avoid unanticipated imbalances between labour force supply and demand. The quality of an organization's adaptation to human resources needs generated by business plans is dependent on the quality of the information received. The role of human resources planning must have a proactive effect on strategic business planning, in terms of providing an appreciation of the organization of the labour force and its capacity to accommodate changes in business requirements.

(b) — Succession Planning

Human resources planning is oriented towards achieving a balanced state between human resources demand and supply, where shortages and surpluses are anticipated and dealt with to harmonize the flow of human resources throughout the organization.

All organizations must cope with the fact that employees, regardless of their positions, move internally and eventually leave the organization. To ensure stability and continuity in its operations, an organization must examine mobility, turnover, and separation statistics, and be prepared to allocate human resources to best satisfy the requirements of vacant positions.

Succession planning is a special case of human resources planning in which real or probable vacancies in specific key or vulnerable positions are identified, often with the assistance of specially designed HRMS modules. The next step is to identify potential in-house candidates, and to provide them with opportunities to prepare for and acquire skills to suit them for the key and/or vulnerable positions when vacancies occur.

(c) — Internal Population Analysis

Factors to be monitored through internal population analyses may include mobility of the labour force within the organization, aging of the employee population, hiring and promotion practices, and surplus of resources.

The development of a systematic capability for modelling (forecasting) attrition/retention can provide management with an effective tool for planning staffing needs. Techniques such as Markov analyses can be incorporated into the HRMS to do "what if" scenarios to evaluate such issues as promotion rates, transfer rates, hiring rates, reorganization, and downsizing, on the distribution of employees.

Effectively anticipating supply and demand problems, developing people to fill key or vulnerable positions, and recognizing the potential that different types of people bring to the organization are becoming increasingly important to ensuring long-term organizational success.

2.12 — Summary

Recent technological changes, together with greatly increased demands for human resources information, have converged to make it cost-effective for organizations with as few as 50 employees to develop and implement a new HRMS. Parallel trends have contributed to HRMSs in larger organizations becoming obsolete, so that many of these organizations are in the process of replacing or upgrading their current systems. This chapter has discussed some of the human resources management needs that may lead an organization to develop a new HRMS or to upgrade their old one. The next chapter discusses issues relative to cost-justifying human resources management systems in modern organizations.

2.13 — References

Beaman, K., ed. 2002. *Boundaryless HR: Human Capital in the Global Economy*. Austin: IHRIM Press.

Belcher, D.W., and T.J. Atchison. 1987. *Compensation Administration*. Englewood Cliffs, N.J.: Prentice-Hall.

Berry, W.E. 1993. "New Role for HR Requires a New Vision for Management Systems." *HR Focus* 70, no. 3 (March): 22.

Bozman, J.S. 1993. "Minority Hiring Getting More Attention, Help." *Computerworld* 27, no. 44 (November): 101.

Broderick, R., and J.W. Boudreau. 1992. "Human Resource Management, Information Technology, and the Competitive Edge." *The Executive* 5, no. 2 (May): 7–17.

Burak, E.H. 1980. *Creative Human Resource Planning and Applications: A Strategic Approach*. Englewood Cliffs, N.J.: Prentice-Hall.

Burgess, L.R. 1984. *Wage and Salary Administration: Pay and Benefits*. Columbus, Ohio: Merill.

Cascio, W. 1978. *Applied Psychology in Personnel Management*. Reston, VA.: Reston Publishing.

_____. and J.W. Thacker. 1994. *Managing Human Resources.* Toronto: McGraw-Hill Ryerson.

Ceriello, V.R. 1991. *Human Resource Management Systems: Strategy, Tactics, and Techniques.* Toronto: Maxwell Macmillan.

Director, S. 1985. *Strategic Planning for Human Resources.* New York: Pergamon.

Doran, J.A., and G.M. Rampton. 1994. "Making a Business Case for a New Human Resource Management Information System." *Canadian Human Resources Systems Professionals Resource Magazine* (June): 4–8.

Downey, J., and McCamus, D. 1990. *To Be Our Best: Learning For the Future.* Montreal, P.Q.: Corporate Higher Education Forum.

Fitz-enz, Jac 1997. The 8 Practices of Exceptional Companies, New York: Amacom.

Fitz-enz, Jac 2000. The ROI of Human Capital. New York: Amacom.

Fogel, W. 1984. *The Equal Pay Equity Act: Implications for Comparable Worth.* New York: Praeger.

Hennecke, M. 1984. "The people side of strategic planning." *Training* (November): 25–34.

Kavanagh, M.J., H.G. Gueutal, and S.I. Tannenbaum. 1990. *Human Resource Information Systems: Development and Application.* Boston, Mass.: PWS-Kent.

Kazanas, H.C. 1988. *Strategic Human Resources Planning and Management.* Englewoods Cliffs, N.J.: Prentice-Hall.

Larson, P.E., and Blue, M.W. 1991. *Training and Development 1990: Expenditures and Policies* (Report 67-91). Ottawa: The Conference Board of Canada.

Lederer, A.L. 1991. *Handbook of Human Resource Information Systems.* New York: Warren, Gorham and Lamont.

McCaffrey, R.M. 1988. *Employee Benefits Programs: A Total Compensation Perspective.* Boston, Mass.: PWS-Kent.

Meade, J.G. 2003. The Human Resources Software Handbook, San Francisco: Jossey-Bass/Pfeiffer.

Miracle, M. 1993. "The Trend to Client/Server is Maturing into Acceptance." *National Underwriter Life/Health/Financial Services* 97, no. 45 (November): 2–8.

Mueller, B. 1994. "Changing Attitudes Help Shape HR Systems." *Systems Management* 22, no. 3 (March): 82-89.

2.13 Human Resources Management Systems

Murray, L.A., and G.M. Rampton. 1986. *Human Resource Planning*. Ottawa: Directorate of Human Resources Planning and Development Report, Canada Post Corporation.

National Committee on Pay Equity. 1987. *Pay Equity: An Issue of Race, Ethnicity, and Sex.* Washington, D.C.

Niehaus, R.J. 1987. *Strategic Human Resources Planning Applications.* New York: Plenum Press.

Rampton, G.M. 1989. "Entrenching Equity in Employment Practices." *The Equal Times: The Newsletter for Human Resource Professionals* 2, no. 3: 19–21.

———. and J.A. Doran. 1994. *A Practitioners Model for a New Human Resources Management Information System.* Paper presented at the annual Canadian Human Resources Systems Professionals Conference. Toronto (October).

Stambaugh, R.H., ed. 2000. 21 Tomorrows: HR Systems in the Emerging Workplace of the 21st Century, Austin: IHRIM Press.

Tannenbaum, S.I. and Alliger, G.M. 2000. Knowledge Management: Clarifying the Key Issues. Austin: IHRIM Press.

Valaskakis, K., R. Coull, and R. Clermont. 1991. *Information Technology and Human Resources: Prospects for the Decade*. A Report Prepared for the Canadian Human Resources Scanning Association. Toronto (April).

Walker, J.W. 1980. *Human Resource Planning*. New York: McGraw Hill.

CHAPTER 3: RETURN ON INVESTMENT

3.1 — Introduction

One of the most significant challenges facing human resources managers today is justifying the cost of upgrading or purchasing a new HRMS. Yet, in today's tight economy, it is imperative that this cost justification be done if the HRMS is to receive due weight in the context of other organizational priorities.

The cost justification of an HRMS has always presented a challenge. Only recently, have executives and human resources practitioners turned their attention to quantifying costs and benefits of personnel systems. Compared to financial and operating information systems, HRMS cost/benefit analysis is a recent development, and still relatively rare. While hard costs are a significant piece of the puzzle in most cases the numbers alone are insufficient to fully describe either the costs or the benefits expected of a HRMS. Therefore, this chapter addresses concepts relevant to justifying an HRMS.[1]

Human resources comprise the largest part of many organizations' operating costs. These costs can range upwards of 80 to 90% of total operating budgets for organizations whose primary function is to provide public services, such as universities, schools, government departments, social service agencies, or consulting firms. Proportional human resources costs are also high in the emerging high-tech/information-based industries, especially in the software development area. Even in heavy industry and the natural resources sector, human resources typically account for 50% or more of total operational costs.

In many respects, human resources are also an organization's most complicated and difficult resource to manage. Human resources management information and the automated systems that support them are consequently becoming important strategic tools. However, one of the most significant challenges facing human resources managers today is the justification of costs associated with the purchase and implementation of an HRMS. As Stright (1993) points out:

> HR has to earn its keep. If you can't specify exactly how you contribute to the bottom line, you'll have increasingly few resources available. Not only does the HRMS have to generate a significant return, but also, customers need to understand exactly how it's accomplishing that return. (p. 70)

Many organizations already have a policy of cost-justifying new technology, but this approach has been adopted more frequently in functional areas other than Human Resources. ROI models are as varied as the organizations that use them and range from a single page of text to 50 or more pages of text and spreadsheet analysis. The right model will be completely reflective of the executive group

---

[1] The Human Resources Software Handbook, James Meade, 2003.

3.1 Human Resources Management Systems

that is being addressed, and therefore never one consistent approach or look and feel.

Typical measures can include (Meade 2003):

- Managing salary
- Managing turnover
- Lowering the cost of hiring
- Saving HR time (p. 193)

Human resources departments have begun to cost justify the implementation of new innovations and are finding that, in some cases, very significant advances can be made without a great deal of cost.

A good example of this was demonstrated in Canadian Tire, a large, national retailer of hardware, garden supplies, household, and vehicle parts.

Canadian Tire's first corporate web page was designed for posting jobs. In 1999 Canadian Tire found that they received 15% of their applications from the Internet, and of those, 50% were new graduates. As well, it appeared that over 50% of their candidates overall visited their web site to obtain information about the company. Since that time the proportion of web-based applications grew, satisfying Canadian Tire that the return, while not fully quantifiable, was many times the total investment for the web structure investment.

Another example of an organization that is using the Internet for recruiting purposes is Silicon Graphics, a large California based software company. Silicon Graphics reported that they have achieved savings in recruiting costs of $70,000 a day in paper costs related to recruiting; and $73,000 annual savings in new employee forms. Less tangible benefits reported included:

- lower turnover, better qualified candidates
- reports generated faster, and elimination of unnecessary reports
- better, quicker decision making
- faster turnaround in filling vacancies
- improved company image
- improved image of Human Resources

The contributions of the human resources function are often undervalued and not well understood by others in the organization. Part of the explanation for this may be that human resources practitioners have failed to justify their role in a way that other managers readily understand. Human resources practitioners are not used to cost-justifying what they do. Many may not even believe that this can, or should, be done. It is no wonder that other functions look on Human Resources as a "necessary liability" that does not contribute to the "bottom line" in the same way as the more "relevant, hard functions," such as operations, marketing, customer service, and finance.

Techniques for assessing the dollar value of human resources programs have existed for some time, but human resources practitioners have either been unaware of them or disinclined to use them. This is changing, however, and as human resources functions are able to demonstrate that their input is relevant to organizational success, they are slowly but surely gaining more credibility, influence, and input into strategic decision making.

As the HRMS market has matured over the past 25 years — that is, as more organizations have implemented an HRMS — another side of the ROI equation has emerged. Organizations have begun to question the long-term return on investment of their "new" HRMS. The cost-benefit analysis produced to justify the original acquisition and implementation are often not reflected in the usage of the system since that time. The effectiveness of the entire human resource management (HRM) process, of which the HRMS is but a part, is being held up for examination, and HR departments (and often, external consultants) are being asked to create opportunities for HRM and HRMS to add more value.

The underlying principles in producing pragmatic, defensible cost-benefits analysis are similar for an HRMS of any size, although the scale of analyses may be quite different. The various methods that can be used to perform human resources cost-benefits analyses are largely based on HR Metrics. A detailed discussion of all of the possible metrics and their application is beyond the scope of this book: the interested reader is instead referred to Cascio (1991), Fitz-Enz (1995 and 2000), or Watson (1993) for an extensive treatment of these issues. We have included examples of some common HR metrics in the succeeding functionally-oriented chapters.

Let us consider a typical (but simplistic) acquisition financial costing model analysis where the software will be acquired by Organization XXX.

Many organizations make the mistake of focusing only on the license fee. If the imaginary organization used here — Organization XXX — had approval for a total expenditure of $150,000 they would have somewhat embarrassed to discover they had overspent by 2/3 because in this sample purchase model (Figure 3.1) the core software acquisition cost of $150,000 (Primary Software, Year 0) is just 30.4% of the year "0" costs, and just 15% of the cumulative costs over years "0", "1", and "2".

3.1 Human Resources Management Systems

Figure 3.1 Total Compensation Model[2]

Item \ Year	0	1	2	3,4,5,...	
Acquisition:					
• Primary Software	$150,000	$0	$0	etc	One time cost
• Additional Software	$ 45,000	$0	$0	etc	Various bits to add on
• Hardware	$ 95,000	$0	$0	etc	One time, may require upgrades
• Training	$ 50,000	$ 50,000	$20,000	etc	Recurring cost
• Implementation	$ 30,000	$0	$0	etc	One-time
Sub-total	$370,000	$ 50,000	$20,000	....	
• Depreciation	$	$ 65,000	$ 65,000	etc.	Over X years
• Cost of funds	$	$ 1,200	$ 1,200	etc.	Will vary based for each organization
• Hosting (if any)	$	$	$	etc.	
Sub-total	$0	$ 66,200	$66,200	....	
Primary Maintenance	$ 40,000	$42,000	$44,100	....	@ 20%; Can range from 15% to 26%
Secondary Maintenance	$ 9,000	$ 9,450	$ 9,923	....	@20% also
Internal Support	$ 75,000	$78,750	$82,688	....	In I/T, a special HRMS unit, ...
Sub-total	$124,000	$130,200	$136,711	....	
TOTAL	$494,000	$246,400	$222,911	....	
Cumulative Total	$494,000	$740,400	$963,311		

Note: The list of expense items is not exhaustive and all of the values are illustrative

Conversely, if $150,000 was the ceiling for the project then Organization XXX should have limited its search to software that would have a license cost of $50,000-$75,000. That should help them avoid exceeding the $150,000 limit.

That ratio, that the license price is approximately 33% of total year one costs, is a good guideline, but readers should be aware that the ratio can be as high as 50% (50% license and 50% everything else in the first year), to as low as 10% or 15% (15% license and 85% implementation).

Organizations also need to understand that the acquisition of a new software application is not a one-year expense, but rather one that continues year-after-year. In the example below we have extended Organization XXX's costs over seven years, a not unreasonable length of time for the life a software application.

You can see that the annual costs peak in the first year (Year 0) but continue at a predictable rate thereafter. This chart reflects a 5% annual cost-of-living increase. Some organizations would rather use constant dollar valuation but the net effect is the same.

---

[2] Laird & Greer Management Consultants, 2005.

Return on Investment 3.1

Figure 3.2 Total Compensation Model[3]

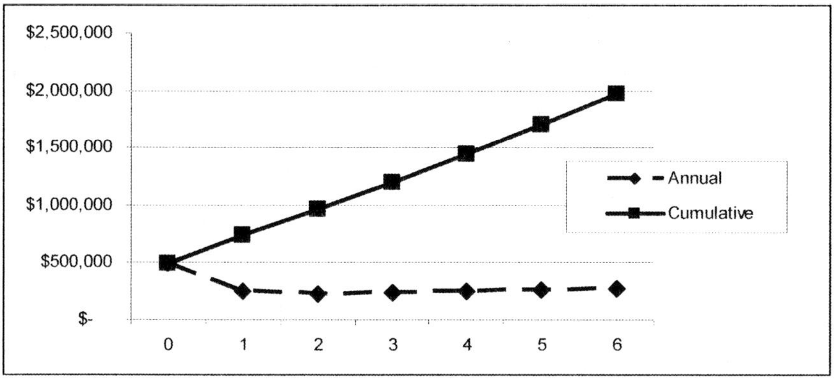

Year 0 Acquisition license price $150,000

The number of variables that go into these amounts are considerable and vary by organization. It is up to the CFO of the organization to determine such issues as:

- What costs will be included, or not.
- Whether depreciation or cost of money is an issue.
- What costs are operational (can be 100%) and what are capital (can also be 100%).
- If internal staff time (HR, Payroll, I/T, etc) will be "loaned" to the project without being an attributable cost, or, if internal staff time will be charged to the project.
- If time spent in training is attributable to the project (if a self-service model is selected then all managers, supervisors and employees will need some level of training — is that also chargeable to the project?

There are no absolute right answers since organizational policy may dictate one choice over another. The important part of this discussion is to recognize that the costs are greater than the license fee, normally by a minimum of 100% and often by far more.

The remainder of this chapter discusses cost benefits concepts for the reader interested in justifying the cost of the first-time implementation of an HRMS, or in the replacement of one that has become obsolete, whether due to changes in the needs of the organization or to changes in technology.

---

[3] *Ibid.*

3.2 — Example: Employee Lists

The use of an HRMS to produce employee lists is a simple application, and one that is familiar to most practitioners. Let us consider how cost justification of such a simple example might be done.

In some medium to large-sized organizations (5,000 to 10,000 employees), human resources information specialists may typically receive 10 or more requests a day to prepare address labels for a variety of purposes, such as sending pension information to recent retirees, informing selected employees about the way in which restructuring of their organizational unit could affect them, advising members and their spouses about changes in benefits programs, etc.

In one real-life example, the organization had the capacity for providing address labels for its members and retirees through its HRMS. Once managers learned that Human Resources could produce address labels in much less time and at a fraction of the cost than they could be produced through other means, the demand to produce such labels grew to the extent that it began to consume about one-fifth of the time of a human resources information officer.

Rather than discourage the use of the information officer's time in producing address labels, the manager responsible decided to do a rough cost-benefits analysis of this activity. He first determined that if his employee did not produce the labels, the various people who wanted them would simply find other means of obtaining them. The information officer was paid about $35,000 per annum; he calculated that it was costing about $7,000 (in salary-related costs alone); that is, one-fifth of $35,000, to produce the address labels.

The manager also estimated that the information officer was able to produce the address labels in about one-eighth of the total time that it would have taken others to produce them. Thus, approximately 1.6 person-years of clerical time would otherwise have been required to produce the labels (since the task occupied one-fifth of the information officer's time, and, on average, she was able to produce the labels eight times faster than those requiring them — 8/5 = 1.6). Even assuming that the individuals who would otherwise have produced the address labels earned somewhat less (say $5,000 less per annum) than the information officer, the total cost of producing the labels would have been in the order of $48,000 ($30,000 × 1.6). The total saving that the organization effected by having the information officer produce the labels was, therefore, $41,000 ($48,000 − $7,000). This is undoubtedly an underestimate, because it assumes that other costs to produce the labels were equal no matter how the labels were produced, when, in fact, there was strong evidence that costs of supplies and wastage were less when the labels were produced by the information officer. Further, many of the individuals who might otherwise have produced the labels made as much or more, per year, as the information officer.

We note that sending mail is a "push" approach that could also be offered by e-mail or internal mail, or by the "pull" approach of having employees go to a website and draw out the information. Each solution has its own sets of pros and cons, but if you accept as given that traditional mail using address labels is the preferred and accepted method, this cost benefit analysis clearly shows that the solution offers an acceptable ROI.

3.3 — Legislative Requirements

As mentioned above and in Chapter 2, organizations must be able to produce lists of their employees broken down in many different ways, accurately, quickly, and efficiently. This is necessary not only to develop and manage their human resources, but to meet legislative requirements for information in the area of taxation, pay equity, employment equity, and so on. Legislative requirements often demand a general organizational response. With respect to pay equity legislation in the province of Ontario, for example, before it can be determined whether individuals in female-dominated job classes are paid less than individuals in male-dominated jobs of equal value, this information must be available in an accessible form. Similarly, with respect to employment equity legislation, in most jurisdictions, to determine how individuals in any of the designated groups compare to others with respect to salary or position in the organization, this information must be available in the system in suitable form, and the system must have the capability to report it.

The penalty for not being able to meet legislative requirements can be significant, as much as $50,000 or more in the province of Ontario, in the case of pay equity. Faced with such penalties, most organizations find a way of meeting these requirements, even if it means processing the requisite information by hand. Doing so, however, is much less effective and more costly than anticipating the need for such information, having it resident in the HRMS, and being able to produce the information quickly and accurately. The principle of cost justification in such cases is exactly the same as in the previous example.

In one large Canadian university, the position control module of the existing HRMS had never been activated since the system was purchased, as doing so would have required alterations costing about $35,000. A pay equity program for administrative staff was negotiated in July 1992, two and one-half years after the implementation of pay equity legislation in Ontario. This meant that considerable amounts of retroactive salary were owed to many individuals.

Further, every individual who had ever been in a female-dominated job since the pay equity implementation date on January 1, 1990, had to be tracked and, if applicable, paid for the time that they were in such positions, including those individuals who resigned, retired, or left temporarily for such reasons as maternity leave. Without the automatic tracking capability of the position control module, much of the tracking had to be done by hand, on a post-hoc basis. With more than

1,200 employees, in a largely female-dominated group, this required an enormous amount of time, effort, and resources. More than five person-years of extra administrative help were necessary for the clerical aspects of the tracking process alone. This expense by itself resulted in additional personnel costs of more than $165,000. It is therefore readily apparent that not spending the $35,000 to implement the position control module in a timely fashion was a false economy. In fact, the more than $130,000 savings evident from the figures presented is an underestimate of the total savings since it ignores additional materials and other costs incurred. It also does not take into account the time and effort that had to be devoted by supervisory and management staff that could have been spent more profitably elsewhere.

3.4 — Salary/Benefits Reporting and Modelling

In one way or another, most organizations have automated their payroll information, even if they contract their payroll to an external agency. It is also likely that payroll information will be among the most accurate of the organization's automated information. However, despite the fact that salary and benefits costs comprise a substantial portion of the operating costs in many organizations, few organizations have invested in more sophisticated means of tracking trends in salary and benefits costs, or of performing "what if" analyses to help find ways of keeping costs in check.

As noted in MacPherson and Wallace (1992), until the decades of the 1950s and into the 1960s, benefits such as medical, dental, sick leave, long-term disability, and life insurance, accounted for a relatively small percentage of each individual's overall compensation package and were often referred to as "fringe benefits." In the 1960s, 1970s, and 1980s benefits coverage was expanded, with employers picking up more and more of the overall cost. And from the late 1980s and early 1990s, costs for such benefits as long-term disability and health, dental, and drug programs have tended to escalate much faster than the cost of inflation. In addition, governments have begun to alter social programs in directions that effectively shift more of the costs of health care and drugs on to employers. This may take the form of implementing payroll taxes to pay for health insurance costs; it may also involve reducing the range of health and drug coverage, thus forcing company-sponsored plans to pick them up.

Many organizations today are finding it necessary to provide closer control over salary and benefits costs. The only feasible way of doing this is by means of an effective HRMS, which contains accurate salary and benefits information and has the flexible analysis and reporting capability required to produce "what if" models on demand.

For payroll purposes, for example, this means being able to examine the results of various salary increase options, whether in the form of across-the-board percentage increases, flat dollar increases, or some combination of the two. The ability to produce such analyses during labour negotiations can lead to settlements that are not only more economical in and of themselves, but that can also be instrumental in avoiding costly work stoppages.

It is also important that an HRMS be able to provide analyses of various benefits options. In the past, organizations tended to negotiate salary and benefits as separate issues. Increasingly, however, organizations are negotiating the total cost of salary and benefits, so that tradeoffs are possible within the various options as long as overall costs remains within a total dollar "envelope." Accurate and relevant automated salary and benefits data, along with an effective analysis and reporting capability, are mandatory. Huge cost savings then become possible, in that even a small percentage saving in a salary and benefits settlement can lead to large dollar amounts, given that, as we have seen, human resources costs form such a large part of the operating budgets of many organizations.

3.5 — Examples

In one set of difficult labour negotiations having ready access to such a reporting capability by management negotiations led to a significant savings. The negotiations were with a bargaining unit consisting of about 1,200 predominately white-collar administrative, technical, and laboratory staff, with a total salary and benefits package of about $50,000,000. The labour climate in the organization had been strained for several years and there was little trust between the two parties. Strikes had been involved in previous contract settlements, and it seemed that these negotiations were headed in that direction.

Some degree of trust was established by using the HRMS to produce a clear and accurate picture of the organization's financial situation. This allowed management to demonstrate that the $250,000 required for the additional .5 percent in benefits costs that were requested by the union would result in the loss of at least 10 jobs. This demonstration would not have been as timely or convincing without access to the HRMS, and it led to acceptance of the lower management offer by the union. In terms of HRMS cost justification, it is important to note that the $250,000 was an annualized cost saving. Total costs would grow in a compounded manner each year. Harder to quantify perhaps, but very important, was the fact that a potentially costly strike was avoided.

After these negotiations, a great deal of work was done to improve the labour relations climate within the organization. Part of this campaign involved using the HRMS to provide the union with more accurate and timely information. This included information that was required in the collective agreement (e.g., seniority lists), as well as information that had never previously been provided (e.g., statistics on the use of casual and relief help). The campaign was successful in reducing the number of grievances and leading to a more healthy labour relations climate overall. The savings that resulted due to fewer grievances and the increased productivity arising from the improvement in labour relations would be

3.5   Human Resources Management Systems

difficult to quantify, but it is certainly safe to say that the HRMS played a significant role in achieving them. The example described above demonstrates how HRMS information can be used to limit benefits costs through labour negotiations. Benefits costs can also be controlled by:

1. negotiating better deals with insurance carriers; or
2. managing the costs of benefits programs by more efficient administration, so that benefits can be maintained or even improved at the same or lower cost (or, at least, with minimum cost increases).

In organizations with more than 200 employees, these tasks again, require access to accurate automated benefits data, as well as an effective analysis capability.

The pension and benefits staff in one organization, with about 10,000 employees, used the HRMS to track benefits costs over a five-year period, and then used this information to project future cost trends. The analyses indicated increasing cost trends in the order of 38% per annum. Because of these unacceptably high increases, it was decided to implement a program of cost containment while maintaining the overall quality and level of the benefits provided. Needless to say, the HRMS was critical in supporting the development, implementation, and monitoring of the cost-control measurers.

Some of the highlights of this cost-control program were as follows:

1. *Coordination of benefits.* The coordination of benefits coverage with spousal coverage was implemented, resulting in savings in unnecessary payments in health and dental claims with an overall savings in excess of $40,000.
2. *Long-term disability.* Tighter monitoring and control of who was on long-term disability, for how long, and for what reasons, together with a worker accommodation program, led to annual savings of more than $50,000.
3. *Workers' compensation.* Implementation of a more effective occupational health and safety program, a workers' accommodation program, and other measures led to a lower WC category and avoidance of penalties, resulting in annual savings in excess of $100,000.
4. *Self-administration.* Using the HRMS to do analyses and produce reports previously done by consultants resulted in an annual saving in excess of $35,000.
5. *Pension administration system.* Internal demographic studies conducted using the HRMS indicated that retirements would accelerate over the next decade to the point where staff would not be able to cope using current technology. Handling the workload would take at least three additional staff members, although it was doubtful that the existing data system could handle the extra volume even with the additional staff. Therefore, it was decided to implement a new pension administration system for an overall

cost of about $250,000. Even discounting the payoff from the greatly increased efficiency, accuracy, and service of the new system, the $250,000 cost involved in acquiring it would soon be more than amortized by the $120,000 annual salary savings.

It is easy to see from the above examples how the cost of an HRMS may be justified by its use in identifying and implementing salary and benefits cost control measures.

3.6 — Human Resources Planning, Development, Research, and Related Issues

In the early 1970s, researchers and information systems staff at the Canadian Forces Personnel Applied Research Unit (CFPARU) began work on an HRMS that was designed to contain recruiting, selection, aptitude tests, training, performance appraisal, and status information on everyone who applied for and joined the Canadian Forces from July 1968 onwards. This is undoubtedly one of the earliest examples of an effective, large-scale HRMS in Canada, and its history and contribution to its parent organization merits some discussion. While some of the requirements of an HRMS in an organization like the Canadian Forces may differ from those facing many of the readers of this book, others will be recognized as highly similar.

The system described eventually contained millions of records on hundreds of thousands of individuals. This system served partially as a data storage and reporting facility for authorities requiring information for human resources management purposes. A more important function, however, and in fact, the reason for its conceptualization and development was its use as an applied research tool. Therefore, in addition to the longitudinal information mentioned above, that was collected regularly on each individual, a great deal of additional information was collected, usually in survey form, and maintained in cross-sectional files.

The Canadian Forces is a large and costly federal government organization and regularly comes under the close scrutiny of such financial watchdogs as the Auditor General, to ensure responsibility to the public purse. As a consequence, great care is taken to ensure that all important personnel decisions are thoroughly costed and based on sound research and analysis. Over the years the CFPARU HRMS was an important tool in many of these research programs. Included were studies:

1. to develop and implement aptitude tests and associated procedures to select the several thousand individuals entering the Forces as officers and in trades training;

2. to develop and implement assessment centers for officer training plans, including aircrew, combat arms, and naval officers;

3. to develop and validate leadership assessment instruments used in officer training plans;

4. to support human resources scanning and demographic analyses, including applicant demand and supply forecasts;

5. to examine the relationship of individual and organizational variables on attrition;

6. to develop new performance appraisal systems for all Canadian Forces personnel;

7. to implement quality of working life and organizational development procedures;

8. to examine the factors that facilitate or hinder the movement of military personnel into the civilian labour force; and

9. to provide an action research base for trials to integrate women into all environments and roles in the Canadian Forces.

This information system evolved from rather humble beginnings over a period of more than 25 years. The initial version prototype of the HRMS was developed in-house, and brought on-line for a capital investment of $5,800. Since then, many times this amount was invested on upgrades to allow the system to become a state-of-the-art data management and research tool.

The total amount invested over the years, however, was much less than the return from the system. For example, on average, it costs more than one million dollars to train each pilot to operational standard. If research supported by this HRMS led to even a 5% savings in training costs, spread over the thousands of pilots who have been selected and trained by the Canadian Forces over the years, the savings would amount to several millions of dollars.

Although the per training cost of most other trades and officer classifications is less than that for pilots, the total number selected and trained over the past 25 or so years amounts to hundreds of thousands of individuals. The total savings realized through more effective selection and trade/occupational classification and training, made possible by research supported by this HRMS, has been much greater.

We have looked at only one of the many applied research areas that have been supported by the CFPARU HRMS; the Canadian Forces benefited from many others that have contributed to the more effective planning for, accession, development, and utilization of its personnel. It is true that the same sorts of research studies would have been required whether or not this particular system had ever been developed. However, it is also true that because of the volume of data and the complexity of the analyses involved, some system would undoubtedly have been required, or only a fraction of the research would have been accomplished, and that research would have been supported by less accurate data.

Although this example begins over 30 years ago in the 1970s, and therefore the dollar values seem amazingly small in today's inflated terms, the value of the lessons learned remain unchanged. It also illustrates that the period considered for ROI need not be limited to a five or seven year financial model since operational benefits of a well-designed and used system can extend years and decades beyond traditional financial modeling time periods.

An HRMS can only be as good as its data. The needs analysis stage of HRMS development is therefore particularly critical. The CFPARU HRMS benefited from some fortunate early decisions about the information that it was to contain. As the software and hardware of this system evolved, the nature of the core data contained in the system remained intact. This has allowed personnel applied research in the Canadian Forces to reflect a longitudinal or long-term perspective in which individuals were tracked over their entire careers, if necessary, to assess the long-term effects of implementing new personnel programs. This allowed for a more thorough validation of new research initiatives than has previously been available to most organizations.

With technology evolving so quickly, and information requirements apparently doing the same, it is easy to fall into the trap of designing a system for its "here and now," short-term payoff, with the assumption that in a few years it will probably be obsolete. While technology may become obsolete quickly, the same is not necessarily true for relevant and accurate personnel data. In fact, such information should be recognized and fostered by all organizations as a valuable part of their asset base.

It is important then, that the needs analysis of such systems be done so that the data may be maintained, with updates and refinements, as the software and hardware evolves around it. The longitudinal perspective which this allows means that the cost benefit perspectives of such systems are generally much greater than those of more temporary ones, which must go through several costly needs analysis, systems development, data gathering/transformation, and systems implementation cycles as the organization decides that old systems have to be replaced.

When a system like an HRMS has been in existence for some time, uses are generally found for it that were not intended when the system was being developed. Being able to capitalize on these new applications enhances the cost benefit of the system. Although it may not be possible to anticipate these in the initial systems planning and development stages, they can and should be used to justify the cost of systems upgrades and enhancements. Often these "opportunity applications" take the form of solutions to problems that line management, or those responsible for other functions in the organization, cannot resolve, or cannot resolve as effectively or efficiently as a human resources practitioner with the aid of the HRMS could. Being able and willing to help out in this way is often highly visible, and can do much to enhance the status of human resources practitioners and of the human resources function.

The following example, again involving the CFPARU, demonstrates the way in which new applications can arise.

(a) — Quality Control of Canadian Forces Recruiting and Selection

The Canadian Forces operates a very effective aptitude-testing program. In the 1970s, item analyses and validation studies to upgrade aptitude tests for both officer and trades training plans were undertaken. All Canadian Forces Recruiting and Selection Centres were asked to send all of their completed test answer sheets to CFPARU, where the item responses on them could be automated by being physically key-punched. In addition to being used in the item analyses, automation of the items on each sheet allowed a computer program to be written to score each aptitude test and compare the result with that contained on the individual's file. Even though such reports and returns were cross-checked at least once, a significant number of the aptitude test scores contained one or more errors, whether in the recording of the scores, or in the purely clerical job of documenting them or any other information that was required on each candidate's selection documentation. Any errors in test scores, however caused, were very important to control because they could eliminate individuals from being considered for programs for which they might otherwise be eligible.

A quality control exercise was implemented with the cooperation of the 16 Recruiting and Selection Centres across Canada. As part of this exercise, CFPARU began sending reports back to all Centres providing a statistical summary of the errors that each had made the previous month. All reports with errors were sent back to the Centre concerned so that it could review the errors, and determine how they occurred and how they might be corrected. After a few months of this process, "error rate" averages in all 16 Centres dropped from a range of 5 to 10%, to the point where one or more errors on fewer than 1% of the forms were being made. Many individual Centres would go months without making even a single error on thousands of documents generated.

Although it started as a rather simple attempt to help the Recruiting and Selection Centres improve their documentation, this service was considered important enough to help CFPARU justify the purchase of optical scanning equipment to facilitate automation of the answer sheet marking. The optical scanning equipment, in turn, allowed CFPARU to develop a much more effective survey capability, since it allowed thousands of survey forms to be gathered and marked automatically.

When combined with the data analysis capability and data already contained on the CFPARU HRMS, this survey capability was used effectively to support a number of research projects that contributed to important and high profile personnel decisions. Decisions on the issues in question would have been made whether or not the CFPARU HRMS and its capability to support survey research existed. However, with more complete information, better decisions were undoubtedly made than might otherwise have been possible. In any event, being able to contribute in a significant way to the decision-making process certainly enhanced the status and future influence of CFPARU and its staff. A review of the studies presented in Wiskoff and Rampton (1989) indicates that these Canadian examples are paralleled in the research efforts of other western military forces.

3.7 — Summary

Human resources practitioners have not generally been very good at cost-justifying what they do. This has put them at a disadvantage with other functions more experienced at demonstrating their worth in operational and/or economic terms.

One of the most significant challenges facing human resources practitioners today is the justification of costs associated with the purchase and implementation of an HRMS. Most organizations already have a policy of cost-justifying new technology, and today's tight economy dictates that this be done for every new investment of this nature. This chapter has discussed various ways in which the cost of acquiring an HRMS may be justified, using actual examples.

3.8 — References

Abella, R.S. 1984. *Equality and Employment: A Royal Commission Report.* Ottawa: Ministry of Supply and Services.

Agarwal, N. 1988. "Pay Equity in Context." In *Human Resources Management in Canada.* Scarborough, Ont.: Carswell.

Beaman, K., ed. 2002. Boundaryless HR: Human Capital in The Global Economy. Austin: IHRIM Press.

Berry, W.E. 1993. "New Role for HR Requires a New Vision for Management Systems." *HR Focus* 70, no. 3 (March): 22.

Bloom, N.L. 1991. "Corporate Needs for HR Information." In A.L. Lederer (ed.), *Handbook of Human Resources Information Systems.* New York: Warren, Gorham and Lamont.

Broderick, R., and J.W. Boudreau. 1992. "Human Resource Management, Information Technology, and the Competitive Edge." *The Executive* 5, no. 2 (May): 7-17.

Brogden, H.E., and E.K. Taylor. 1950. "The Dollar Criterion-Applying the Cost Accounting Concept to Criterion Construction." *Personnel Psychology* 3: 133-54.

Cascio, W.F. 1991. *Costing Human Resources: The Financial Impact of Behaviour in Organizations*, 3rd ed. Boston, Mass.: PWS-Kent.

———. and J.W. Thacker. 1994. *Managing Human Resources*. Toronto: McGraw-Hill Ryerson.

Codega, K. 1991. "Compensation Applications." In A.L. Lederer (ed.), *Handbook of Human Resources Information Systems*. New York: Warren, Gorham and Lamont.

Cronbach, L.J., and G. Gleser. 1965. *Psychological Tests and Personnel Decisions*. Chicago, Ill.: University of Illinois Press.

Cronshaw, S. 1986. "The Status of Employment Testing in Canada: a Review and Evaluation of Theory and Professional Practice." *Canadian Psychology* 27: 183-95.

Fitz-Enz, J. 1980. "Quantifying the Human Resources Function." *Personnel* 57, no. 3: 41-52.

Fitz-enz, Jac 2000. The ROI of Human Capital. New York: Amacom.

Foulkes, F.K., and H.M. Morgan. 1980. "Organizing and Staffing the Personnel Function." *Harvard Business Review* 45: 107-13.

Gutteridge, T.G. 1988. "The HRPD Profession: a Vision of Tomorrow." *Human Resource Planning* 11, no. 2: 109–24.

Hunter, D.R. 1989. "Aviator Selection." In Martin F. Wiskoff and Glenn M. Rampton, eds., *Military Personnel Measurement*. New York: Praeger.

Jain, H.C. 1989. "Human Rights: Issues in Employment." In *Human Resources Management in Canada*. Scarborough, Ont.: Carswell.

MacPherson, D.L., and J.T. Wallace. 1992. "Employee Benefits Plans." In *Human Resources Management in Canada*. Scarborough, Ont.: Carswell.

Meade, J.G. 2003. The Human Resources Software Handbook, San Francisco: Jossey-Bass/Pfeiffer.

Rampton, G.M. 1978. "The Role and Function of the Personnel Applied Research Unit: Past, Present, and Future." Paper presented at APA 19 Symposium: "Research Programmes for the Canadian Forces," American Psychological Association Annual Convention Toronto (28 August-1 September).

Stright, J.F. 1993. "Strategic Goals Guide HRMS Development." *Personnel Journal* (September): 68-78.

Walker, A.J. 2001. Web-Based Human Resources, New York: McGraw-Hill.

Walker, J.W. 1980. Human Resource Planning. New York: McGraw Hill.

Watson, G.H. 1993 Strategic Benchmarking. Toronto: John Wiley & Sons.

Wiskoff, M.F., and Rampton, G.M. 1989. *Military Personnel Measurement.* New York: Praeger.

———. 1979. *Canadian Forces Personnel Applied Research Unit: Bi-Annual work report.* Fall report for fiscal year 1979/80. Toronto: Canadian Forces Personnel Applied Research Unit (October).

———. and J.A. Doran. 1994. "A Practitioners Model for a New Human Resources Management Information System." Paper presented at the annual Canadian Human Resources Systems Professionals' Conference. Toronto (October).

CHAPTER 4: PLANNING A NEW HRMS

4.1 — Introduction

Sound planning at the beginning of any HRMS project is critical, yet this step is often overlooked or given little attention in the rush to upgrade an existing system or to develop a new one. Too often such projects have been initiated and are well underway before there is a realization by those involved that key issues have been overlooked, whether through the lack of an adequate needs analysis to identify systems requirements, the need to gain the commitment of key stakeholders, or in limitations in hardware or software.

This chapter discusses important considerations in planning an HRMS project including:

- Planning process
- Elements of project management
- Steering committee
- Project team
- Planning communications strategy
- Identifying and building in critical success factors
- Planning for the management of change
- Options: repair and refine, build, or buy
- Implementing the plan
- Training and documentation

4.2 — Planning

The authors have found it useful to conceptualize planning for an HRMS in three distinct phases:

- Design and development
- Implementation
- Maintenance

Although they are related, the planning for each of these phases differs somewhat and must be coordinated carefully. Design and development planning, for example, involves defining requirements, investigating and deciding upon options, and then developing the action plan by which the project will be made a reality. Implementation planning involves deciding how the action plan will be carried out, including who will be responsible for each step in the plan, where each step will be carried out, and what resources will be needed. Maintenance planning involves developing a strategy for ensuring that the system remains dynamic in terms of being continually updated in response to changes in user requirements and evolving technology.

These plans must include provision for users and systems maintenance personnel to have access to up-to-date and user friendly documentation and training (see the discussion on documentation and training later in this chapter), so that they may use and maintain the system to best effect, and are able to make recommendations for improvements. Detailed planning of each phase of an HRMS project will not guarantee success, but it will make success much more likely.

Project plans are established to meet strategic, tactical, and operational goals. The objectives on which a plan is based define the scope of the project, which in turn defines the project specifications. Plans can be too broad, or too detailed.

Overplanning, or taking too much time to plan, can doom a project as can jumping into developing a system without a plan. Kerzner (1989) reports that project managers suggest that 10 hours per week is a reasonable amount of time to plan and replan.

Planning is a pragmatic process, with the aim of developing plans that are effective and efficient, but not all-inclusive or perfect. Plans, like their financial counterparts, budgets, represent the planner's best estimate at a specific point in time. If they are to be successful, plans should be flexible. It is the realization of the plan, through sound management, including adjusting for intangibles and reacting to resource changes, which yields success.

4.3 — The Planning Process

Planning is not a new activity. Twenty-five hundred years ago, Sun Tzu, General for the King of Wu, wrote:

> The general who wins a battle makes many calculations in his temple before the battle is fought. The general who loses a battle makes but few calculations beforehand. Thus do many calculations lead to victory, and few calculations to defeat; how much more no calculation at all! It is by attention to this point that I can foresee who is likely to win or lose. (as reported in, Clavell, 1983, 12)

The detailed steps of a planning process will of necessity vary by organization. However, most of the common steps, in a rough time order, are outlined in Figure 4.1.

The major steps illustrated are as follows:

1. Recognition of one or more needs for better human resources management (HRM) information.

2. If there is an existing system in place, determine whether it can be modified to produce the information at a reasonable cost.
3. If no system currently exists, or if the cost of modifying an existing system is not reasonable, conduct an analysis of whether buying a system or building one is preferred.
4. Prepare a detailed needs analysis.
5. Prepare a Request for Information (RFI) or Request for Proposal (RFP) and send it to selected vendors.
6. Analyze the results, reducing the short-list until only one or two options remain, and select finalist product and vendor.
7. Negotiate price and conditions, while conducting final vendor references, and financial review.
8. Receive a "GO" decision and select a project implementation team.

4.4 — Project Management

Project management combines planning with a controlled use of resources to develop and implement specific end results, or projects, such as designing and implementing a new HRMS.

The techniques used in project management are not new. Most are applicable to and have been applied in management in general. Some authors, in fact, have argued that the primary distinction between project management and other kinds of management is the duration of the task. This distinction has met with some resistance, since it challenges traditional organizational management structures, which tend to be vertical, with multiple organization levels rather than the few which are more typically found in project management. In project management, work is generally accomplished by flatter organizational teams led by a "functional leader" who may or may not have the formal designation of manager.

Every unique task, like every project, has at least one specific objective as well as resource limits and specifications:

4.4 Human Resources Management Systems

Figure 4.1 Steps in HRMS Planning

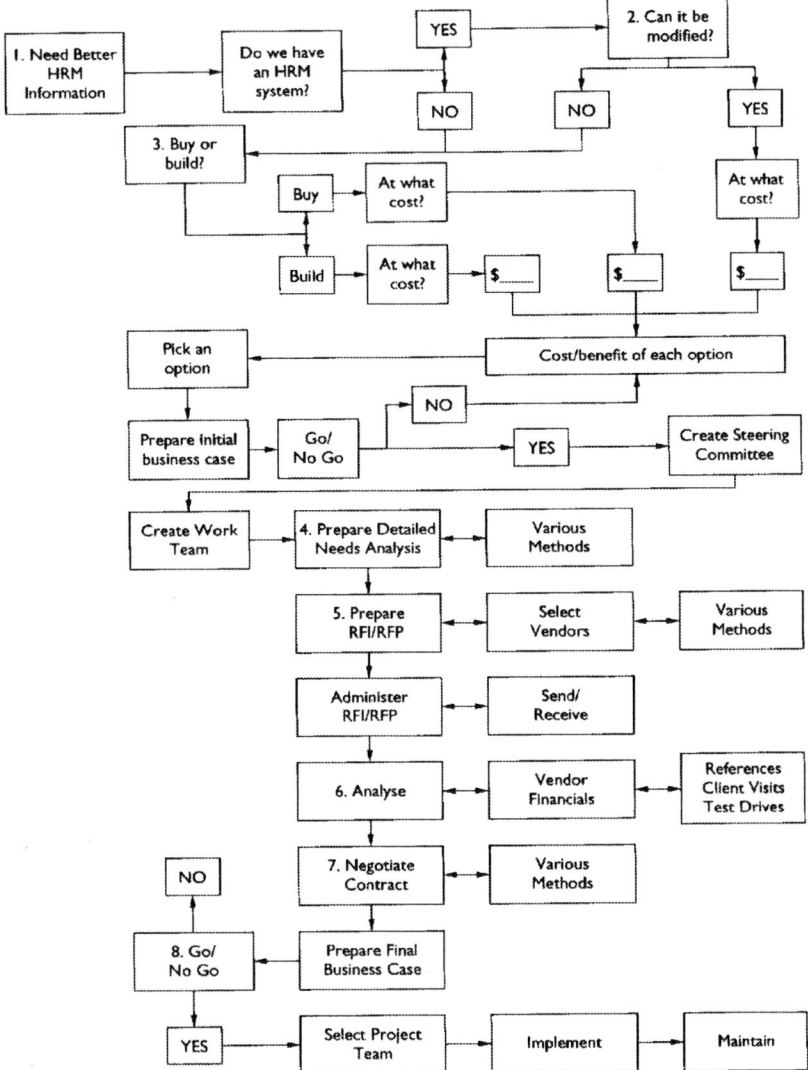

- Time (start/end dates)
- People (identification, specific skills they bring to project, availability, cost)
- Tools (equipment, software)
- Money (budget)

Project management adds in a familiar general management issue, performance appraisal, by monitoring progress against the plan, analyzing the gap and impact thereof, and adjusting the plan accordingly. Building or changing large and complex systems lend themselves to the project management process, in part because of the complexity, but also because of the sheer volume of activities that must occur, and occur in a particular sequence.

Project management adopts a planning and scheduling methodology that includes both conceptual framework and techniques to manage and track each component. It is the ongoing tracking and recording of activities and results that most distinguishes the project management approach from general management.

Various software tools exist that help document each step, balance and price resources, offer analysis models, and produce reports. Users may find some specific tools more useful than others, but all of the current project planning software known to the authors have limitations. Many of the more popular packages provide so much detail that over management of the project becomes a potential problem. Constantly updating the plan does not equate to managing the project.

These software tools support project activities by offering such features as:

1. *Tasks definition.* Each unique activity in the project must be clearly defined.
2. *Project scheduling.* Every task/activity is integrated into the project schedule by listing an estimate of its start and end dates.
3. *Milestones.* These are events that signify some specific and significant progress or an important time.
4. *Resource assignment.* Every person and piece of equipment, together with the cost of each, must be assigned to specific accomplishment of tasks. Downtime or, in Finance terms, indirect labour (e.g., vacation, union business, maintenance) is included where it is predictable.
5. *Costs and budgets.* Resource costs are calculated and amalgamated over the expenses estimated to be required to accomplish each task.
6. *Visual representations.* There are between 30 and 40 different visual methods for the representation of activities. Each one provides a different way of looking at project data, and different methods provide different levels of information. There are entire books on these techniques, and those interested should consult the literature (see References at the end of this and other chapters). Some of the more common techniques are:
    a. GANTT Chart — a bar chart that graphically displays the status of a task based on time or money (see Figure 4.2).
    b. PERT (Program Evaluation and Review Technique) — PERT charts

4.4 Human Resources Management Systems

illustrate the relationships and depen- dencies between different activities.

c. CPM (Critical Path Method) — CPM was developed around the same time as PERT, and performs the same function.

Figure 4.2 GANTT Chart

ID	WBS	O	Task Name	Duration	Start	Finish	2002 Qtr 1 Qtr 3	2003 Qtr 1 Qtr 3
1	1		PHASE I - IMPLEMENTATION	366.4 days	Mon 02-01-21	Wed 03-10-22		
2	1.1	✓	HIGH LEVEL IMPLEMENTATION PLAN	100.8 days	Mon 02-01-21	Mon 02-07-15		
3	1.1.1		Planning	100.8 days	Mon 02-01-21	Mon 02-07-15		
4	1.1.1.1	✓	P/S IPSW (Implement Planning & Strategy	13.4 days	Thu 02-04-04	Fri 02-04-26		
8	1.1.1.2		Fit/Gap	32.2 days	Fri 02-04-26	Fri 02-06-21		
14	1.1.1.3		Key Project Plan Iterations (+ regular wkly	100.8 days	Mon 02-01-21	Mon 02-07-15		
21	1.1.2	✓	Module selection	0.16 days	Thu 02-03-14	Thu 02-03-14		
24	1.2		Administration	336 days	Thu 02-03-14	Wed 03-10-22		
73	1.3		P/S Draft Implementation	259.2 days	Tue 02-03-12	Fri 03-06-06		
74	1.3.1		Draft 3 Module Order (as per SOSs 02/03/29)	259.2 days	Tue 02-03-12	Fri 03-06-06		
75	1.3.1.1		Core Operating Decisions	53.6 days	Thu 02-03-14	Fri 02-06-14		
76	1.3.1.1.1		Security	16 days	Mon 02-05-20	Fri 02-06-14		
80	1.3.1.1.2		Audit	16 days	Mon 02-05-20	Fri 02-06-14		
84	1.3.1.1.3		Other	0 days	Thu 02-03-14	Thu 02-03-14	♦ 03-14	
86	1.3.1.2		GROUP I	167.2 days	Tue 02-03-12	Fri 02-12-27		
87	1.3.1.2.1		Core HR	0 days	Thu 02-03-14	Thu 02-03-14	♦ 03-14	
90	1.3.1.2.2		Core PR	140 days	Mon 02-04-29	Fri 02-12-27		
91	1.3.1.2.3		Time & Labor - Section A	18 days	Tue 02-03-12	Thu 02-04-11		
120	1.3.1.2.4		e-Modules INQUIRY ONLY	165.6 days	Thu 02-03-14	Fri 02-12-27		
125	1.3.1.2.5		Enterprise Portal	16 days	Mon 02-04-29	Fri 02-05-24		
126	1.3.1.2.6		HRMS Portal Packs	16 days	Mon 02-04-29	Fri 02-05-24		
127	1.3.1.3		GROUP II	159.2 days	Tue 02-09-03	Fri 03-06-06		
128	1.3.1.3.1		HRMS Warehouse & Analytics	72 days	Mon 03-02-03	Fri 03-06-06		
129	1.3.1.3.1.1		Interim - Variable Comp to Wareh	72 days	Mon 03-02-03	Fri 03-06-06		
131	1.3.1.3.1.2		Interface to Hyperion	16 days	Mon 03-02-10	Fri 03-03-07		
132	1.3.1.3.2		Directory Interface (PI?)	72 days	Tue 02-09-03	Mon 03-01-06		
133	1.4		Software Development	96 days	Mon 02-06-24	Fri 02-12-06		
134	1.4.1		Design	12 days	Mon 02-06-24	Fri 02-07-12		
135	1.4.2		Create Test Plans	8 days	Mon 02-07-15	Fri 02-07-26		
136	1.4.3		Configure	16 days	Fri 02-07-19	Thu 02-08-15		
137	1.4.4		Build & Unit Test	48.8 days	Fri 02-07-19	Fri 02-10-11		
138	1.4.4.1		Build	44 days	Fri 02-07-19	Thu 02-10-03		
139	1.4.4.2		Unit Test	44 days	Fri 02-07-19	Thu 02-10-03		
140	1.4.4.3		Conversion	48 days	Mon 02-07-22	Fri 02-10-11		
144	1.4.4.4		Interfaces	44 days	Mon 02-07-22	Fri 02-10-04		
145	1.4.5		Integration Testing	12 days	Mon 02-10-14	Fri 02-11-01		
147	1.4.6		System Test	12 days	Mon 02-11-04	Fri 02-11-22		
148	1.4.7		Parallel Testing	24 days	Mon 02-10-28	Fri 02-12-06		

These tools combined with project management software, such as Microsoft Project or Harvard Project Manager, can facilitate the management and communication of the project. They assist the project manager in defining, tracking, and communicating tremendous numbers of project details. Scheduling the multiplicity of activities and tasks can be a nightmare, but a system that tracks dependencies, highlights staff availability, and allows for adjustments as required, makes the job easier and the results more professional. Whether or not a project planning tool is utilized, each step in the project should be planned.

The most important responsibilities of a project manager are planning, integrating, and executing plans. Almost all projects, because of their relatively

Planning a New HRMS 4.5

short duration and often prioritized control of resources, require formal detailed planning. (Kerzner, 1989, 37)

To that list of responsibilities may be added communicating.

4.5 — The Communications Process

The communication of plans and project status, both within a project team and throughout the organization, requires an inordinate amount of project time. Communication is not just telling; it is listening too. Peters (1987) suggests that managers and team members listening to one another, formally and informally, is one of the critical components of successful management. The project manager in particular, should be a strong communicator, speaking, listening, and writing effectively. These skills are critical to the project's success. One model for communication is presented in Figure 4.3.

Figure 4.3 Five R's of Reception

RECEIVER	Five Rs of Transmission	SENDER
What is the purpose of the message?	REASON	Know your reason for the message; motivational or instructional.
Do you know all the elements?	REDUCTION	Reduce the message to meaningful and understandable bits.
Have it repeated if necessary.	REDUNDANCY	Say it two or three different ways.
Repeat it back.	READBACK	Ask receiver to repeat it back.
Write it down, or ask for it in writing.	RECORD	Put it in writing if necessary.

Five Rs of Reception

Source: Adapted from D. Slevin, *The Whole Manager*. New York: American Management Association, 1989.

Planning encompasses both strategic and operational decisions, and requires the involvement of all groups concerned with the implementation. The involvement of all concerned, project manager, project team, primary client, and senior management, is a key component of success. Not all need to be equally involved, but the commitment that comes from participation and being part of the communication process is invaluable and irreplaceable.

This communication process encompasses the project team, the steering team, and the organization as a whole. Each must understand the project and have a sense of how the results will be integrated into the organization's business processes.

Kanter (1989) suggests that, in most projects, too little time is spent in selling ideas, keeping all participants up-to-date, and ensuring that each understands how the project fits with regard to his or her interests and responsibilities. Time spent ensuring that participation is offered and occurs is time well spent.

Kerzner (1989) points out that successful project managers are heavily dependent on the line managers who supply the human resources to a project, and on project employees who must operate in a matrix organization structure, reporting to their line managers even as they work on the project. Knutson and Blitz (1991) suggest some guidelines for developing effective team members:

1. Involve key members of the project team in developing a communication plan.
2. Work with each team member to define how and when communication will take place and how the team will work together to solve problems that might arise on the project.
3. Devise a strategy with each team member to help ensure that information does not get lost, and to prevent ruffled feathers that often occur when messages are miscommunicated or omitted.
4. Begin developing a communication plan as soon as a new project is undertaken, and update it as needed. Players often change in the project universe. Develop new communication strategies when this happens. Newcomers or replacement project team members are often left out and cannot fully contribute unless one takes time to involve them. (p. 24)

4.6 — Critical Success Factors

A number of factors can be critical in producing success or failure for a project. The management of each factor reduces the risk of negative events and their effect on the project. The critical factors are described below:

1. *The organization's financial health.* The degree of financial health is less important than a realistic appreciation of it. However, an organization in a serious financial crisis will rarely fund an HRMS (or any) project properly, cutting corners in a rash attempt to achieve results.
2. *The organization's structure.* An organization's structure and recent or proposed changes to it, such as restructuring and downsizing, can affect the organization's climate.
3. *The organization's culture.* Projects should be accepted as formal activities well supported by the organization. If this is not the case, it will be difficult to recruit, keep, and return project staff to the organization successfully. An organization that does not have many projects or that may have problems integrating this different type of activity should carefully consider how to ensure a climate for success.

4. *The existence of a "mission champion".* Even if the business need for an HRMS is clearly understood, the project will stand a much better chance of success if there is an identifiable champion prepared to advocate it. The better the champion(s) is/are regarded within the organization, the smoother the project's road to approval and success is likely to be.

5. *The status and involvement of the project manager.* Is the project this person's sole responsibility? Many organizations make the mistake of giving a competent but already busy person the job of project manager, in addition to his or her regular responsibilities, and find their project failing as a result. The size of project is an important factor, but generally speaking, a project manager should be detached from ongoing operational responsibilities that fall outside of project scope.

Project management requires many different areas of expertise. Competence as a manager in human resources, payroll, or systems is not a guarantee of success. Because an HRMS should be an organization-wide system, the project manager should be seen as unbiased, favouring no particular group, but working towards a functional system for all stakeholders.

Project champions and project managers are not always the same person. In fact, as noted below, the qualities requisite for each may be quite different. Some of these differences are summarized in Table 4.1.

Table 4.1 Project Managers vs. Project Champions

PROJECT MANAGERS	PROJECT CHAMPIONS
• Prefer to work in groups	• Prefer working individually
• Committed to managerial & technical responsibilities	• Committed to the technology
	• Committed to the profession
• Committed to the organization	• Seek to exceed the objective
• Seek to achieve the objective	• Are unwilling to take risks; try to test everything
• Are willing to take risks	
• Seek what is possible	• Seek perfection
• Think in terms of short time spans	• Think in terms of long time spans
• Manages people	• Manage things
• Committed to & pursue material values	• Are committed to & pursue intellectual values

Source: Adapted from D. Slevin, The Whole Manager, New York, American Management Association, 1989.

6. *The existence of project and steering committees.* At some early point in the process of planning for a new HRMS, the organization should establish a project team and consider the establishment of a steering committee as well.

A steering committee is often used as a strategic body for guiding the overall process by setting the scope and goals of the project. If established, it should be comprised of senior policy makers representing key organizational areas: human resources, finance, systems, and operations, and should champion the project when funding and approvals are sought. Steering committees normally meet periodically throughout the project to receive status reports from the project team and to make policy decisions as required.

A project team is also normally comprised of representatives of key organizational areas: human resources, finance, systems, and operations. The project team is the working group responsible for performing the day-to-day tasks of defining requirements, assessing current systems, determining whether to repair and refine a current system, or build or buy a new HRMS, and all other activities. Project team members are normally responsible for implementing the final system. They may also have ongoing responsibility for the subsequent management and maintenance of the system.

7. *Whether clearly defined business needs have been identified.* The requirement for the HR/Payroll system must be understood at senior management levels.

8. *Whether a formal documented plan has been developed.* HRMS projects cross functional boundaries, making great demands on all operational departments. The complexity of the task demands that a detailed documented plan exist and be used.

9. *Whether planning has been coordinated across departments.* Each department should have a strategic plan that exists as part of a larger organization plan. If not, it will be difficult to link project decisions to the global strategic and operational plans that it must support.

10. *The extent and quality of systems support.* The quality and extent of support provided by management information specialists directly affect the project, be it technical or functional in nature. If the department expresses a preference to build the system or to buy one already programmed (neither choice is inherently better than the other), the HRMS project should be consistent with the preferred approach, or the departure must be clearly resolved in advance.

11. *The age of and satisfaction with the current system.* In today's technological volcano where change is incremental, a system of five + years is approaching obsolescence. This focuses importance on keeping your systems current, adding in fixes and updates as received. An older system that works well is nevertheless in danger of holding the organization back if it does not offer the same degree of functional or technical flexibility as do other, newer systems. It can be harder to replace a system that is meeting current needs, but must be replaced to meet rapidly evolving requirements.

12. *Business process integration.* Implementation of a new computer system such as an HRMS provides an opportunity to re-examine the organization's human resources practices, processes, and systems, and to ensure

that these are integrated with other organizational systems and processes. A number of authors have pointed out that, in order to compete effectively in today's rapidly changing world, most organizations need to fundamentally "reengineer their processes and systems". Doing this, and then ensuring that the result is reflected in the design and implementation of a new HRMS, will lead to the most effective and efficient system.

13. *Realistic project budget.* Many organizations that embark on a systems project allocate as much as 90% or even 100% of the budget to software acquisition, leaving insufficient funds for many of the critical areas mentioned above. The actual requirement varies widely, but a good rule of thumb would be that a maximum of 25% should be allocated for system acquisition alone.

Whether or not a factor is critical will, to some extent, depend on circumstances in the organization.

4.7 — Dealing With Change

The implementation of a new computer system, while presenting challenges, also provides a wonderful opportunity for the organization to introduce larger measures of change than it might otherwise be possible to do. Organizations have different tolerance levels with respect to change. Most companies in the computer industry, service industries, and in aerospace are thought to have a high tolerance for change. Other organizations — perhaps those that reside in Beck's (1992) "old economy" — are less likely to have a climate in which change is a constant.

No matter what the nature of organization, it is important to remember that employees are individuals, individuals whose capacity for change varies enormously, and even fluctuates considerably within one person over time as various life events intrude. Change occasions emotional responses that cannot be overcome by the logic of an engineered business process or detailed project plan.

These processes of change and communication imply an understanding of individual and group interests and power structures; anticipating their concerns and objections; and involving them in exploring "what's in it for them."

4.7 Human Resources Management Systems

> **EXAMPLE**
>
> Prior to the implementation of a new HRMS in one organization, employees wishing to change personal information such as mailing address, contact, or emergency phone numbers in their automated human resources files were required to complete a personal information change form and have it approved by their supervisor, who would then forward it to Payroll, who would enter the information in the payroll system, photocopy the originating document for their files, and send the original on to HR for entry in the HR system and filing in HR files.
>
> Only Payroll and HR could enter the data into their systems due to the rigorous security for each. A new integrated HRMS with enhanced security permitted individual employees to directly input their changes into the system. Not only were the non-value-added supervisory activities stopped, but so were the duplicate data entry and filing activities.

Process re-engineering, and related concepts are, of course, not unique to human resources processes, or to HRMSs. Re-engineering business processes have wide application for organizations that wish to remain competitive in today's rapidly changing world (see the discussion of business process re-engineering in the next chapter for more detail). To illustrate this, another real-life example is provided below, demonstrating how concepts useful in human resources can have wider application.

> **EXAMPLE**
>
> A large mine suffered through a strike that left the nearby town ravaged. With many of its residents on strike, retail activity dropped below subsistence levels and the entire region was in peril.
>
> Management and union alike realized that significant changes had to be made if the emotion generated by 18 months of hardship were to be overcome. The change they came up with was considered radical for the mining industry.
>
> Previously, mechanics had to fill out a work order listing parts they required to complete repairs. Once approved by their supervisor, these paper requests would be forwarded to supply to be filled. Now, mechanics would be allowed to use computers to order directly from supply. Elimination of paper and time delays were two benefits, but by far the largest was the sense of trust that the new process engendered. In addition, supervisors, freed from their non-value-added paper approvals, were able to concentrate on further process improvements. Union, employees, management, and the town all became aware of and agreed on the success of this initiative.

Many organizations today are trying to "empower" their employees to assume responsibility and to act on their own in the best interests of the organization, often utilizing special training and cultural change programs, while ignoring the opportunities offered by making fundamental changes in day-to-day business processes. But organizations often understate the degree of change that a new system makes possible, and overstate the readiness of their employees to embrace that change, as the following example illustrates.

> **EXAMPLE**
>
> An HR department had two secretaries, both of whom typed 100 words a minute with almost no errors. At their request, the supervisor acquired new word processing equipment which would allow them to perform various time-saving activities. Training was delivered and the two secretaries willingly went to work on their new machines. But within the week both were staying late "to catch up" on their old machines, and then used the new equipment less and less. When questioned by their supervisor, they reluctantly admitted that they were not as productive on the new equipment, being neither as fast, nor as error free. Their dedication to getting the work done and their own self-images about their speed and skill with the old equipment made continued use of the old equipment more appealing.

While this example is over 25 years old it is as current today as it was then. The nature of the technology may have changed but the principles have not.

The nature of the system being implemented, and how different it is from that which existed previously will dictate how significant the change will seem to be by most stakeholders, including those responsible for using and maintaining it. Clearly a choice of technology that is new to the organization will impose more change than the continuation of current technology would. Similarly, a decision to substantially alter the underlying business processes through such techniques as process re-engineering activities could result in significant change. Senior management may, in fact, use the need to implement a new system as a strategic opportunity to make radical change, modifying organization culture, eliminating processes and/or positions, or excising entire departments.

Fossum (1989) states:

> There are many different models for different aspects of change. It does not matter at what level change is occurring, there is a series of stages, or phases, that will be encountered in implementing the change. While the length of time spent in each stage may vary, each will occur while coping with change. The stages are: denial, resistance, adaptation, and involvement. (pp. 63-66)

Thus, individuals may respond differently to the decision to develop a new HRMS. Examples might be as follows:

Denial:	*"We don't need a new system; the old one works just fine."*
Resistance:	*"We aren't going to share in its advantages, why should we cooperate? ... besides it will cost too much."*
Adaptation:	*"Well, if we are going to get a new HRMS we should ...."*
Involvement:	*"Let's get on the project team and make sure that ...."*

Each model of change is useful and applies to certain components of project management. The project must be planned in such a way as to deal with the organization's stages of change.

4.8 — Planning Implementation

The scope and schedule of each step must be coordinated to ensure a timely process. A common mistake is to work blindly backwards from management's desired implementation date, making the plan fit the expected end-date. Of course, it is necessary to respect management's priorities and operational requirements for information and the systems designed to gather, maintain, analyze, and provide it. The plan must, however, be realistic, not merely designed to fit the time that has been allotted for it. Acceding to an unrealistic timetable may result in a plan that easily gains management acceptance, but is difficult or even impossible to manage.

The integration of a well-developed system into the organization will dictate how the organization reacts to the system, and its ultimate usefulness. A complete, documented plan is key to the successful implementation of any information system.

4.9 — Training and Documentation

Deadlines and cost constraints are given higher priority over user comprehension in the planning, development, and implementation of many HRMS applications. In planning for the development and implementation of a new HRMS, the two related functions of documentation and training are often overlooked or given insufficient priority. Overriding concern for getting the system "up and running," often leads to putting documentation and training off to another time when there "will be more time and resources to devote to them." Unfortunately this means that, for many systems, these important functions are never dealt with effectively. For reasons discussed below, the critical need to plan for systems training and documentation should be identified early in the planning process for any HRMS.

The project team responsible for planning a new HRMS may produce a state-of-the-art product tailored to the needs of the organization. Whether it will be used effectively within the organization, and therefore be successful, will depend on how well users understand and accept it. This, in turn, may depend on the effectiveness of how users are introduced to the system and are trained to use it. Some of the requirements of effective systems documentation and training are outlined below.

(a) — Purpose of Documentation and Training

There are various levels of documentation and training required depending on whether the individual will be primarily concerned about procedural or technical aspects of the system. Different levels of documentation and training may be required for managers with access to the system, specialist users such as human resources personnel, and management information specialists (MIS) responsible for maintaining technical aspects of the system.

The purpose of systems documentation is to ensure that there is a complete and up-to-date record of the system's technical details, and how it operates. Training for MIS personnel is most often aimed at imparting an understanding of the technical details of the system, while the training for other users is aimed at teaching why and how the system operates. Therefore, training must be tailored to the requirements of the particular target group. It is unlikely that one course will satisfy the needs of all groups requiring training.

Systems documentation involves making a complete and accurate record of the technical underpinnings of the system, as well as how the system may be used. Such documentation forms the basis of technical and operational reference material for both users and maintenance personnel.

Documentation is generally done in both technical and users manuals. Training needs analysis is used to determine which content in the manuals needs to be taught, how, to whom, and using what teaching methods. Teaching has traditionally involved classroom presentations with practical hands-on laboratory demonstrations and the opportunity to practice specific applications, perhaps supplemented with audio-visual presentations. More recently, other methods, including self-paced, video-disc based, and computer-assisted applications have gained prominence.

(b) — Training Phases

Well-developed training programs fall into the following phases.

1. *Training needs analysis.* In this phase the task to be performed, the standard of performance required, and the skills needed to perform at this level are identified. In gathering this information, one may use such data-gathering strategies as:

    - Focus groups
    - Structured interviews

4.9 Human Resources Management Systems

- Questionnaires/surveys
- Direct observations
- Analysis of documents such as technical manuals or job descriptions

2. *Identification of training media and methods of training.* In this phase the project team training specialist determines the most appropriate training media and method of training for imparting the required knowledge and skills, to the given standard. Training media may include standard manuals, video-tape, video-disc, or various kinds of computer aides. Method of training might include standard classroom presentations, laboratory experiential learning, self-paced computerized adaptive teaching, or combinations of these.

3. *Training program development.* In this phase the training program is developed using the media and method(s) selected.

4. *Training conduct.* This phase involves the scheduling and conduct of training.

5. *Training evaluation.* This critical phase is often overlooked or given short shrift. It links back to the needs analysis phase, and involves ensuring that the training program actually does what it was designed to do. The purpose is to identify and implement improvements.

6. *Skill maintenance.* This is another phase that is often overlooked. It involves developing and implementing the means of maintaining the required knowledge and skills on the system as time goes on. Ongoing training and development may be needed to get new people started on the system, raise individuals to higher levels of expertise, and refresh skills.

7. *Continued support for post-implementation documentation and training.* As time goes on, after the system is up and running, amendments will be required, whether as a consequence of up-grades provided by the vendor, or changing in-house requirements. It is important that allowance for both of these be planned for.

(c) — In-House or Off-the-Shelf Systems

If the system is being developed in-house, all aspects of systems documentation and training must be developed from scratch. In such cases it is advisable to have a training specialist on the project team from the start. Systems purchased off-the-shelf, from external suppliers, as sets of pre-developed modules, usually come with documentation and training packages.

In fact, the adequacy of these documentation and training programs should be included as an important set of criteria to be considered when deciding to purchase HRMS systems off-the-shelf. Among the criteria to be considered are:

Planning a New HRMS 4.9

- Comprehensiveness, relevance, and "user-friendliness"
- Any additional costs
- Number of people to be trained and what level of training is required
- Any differentiation in training depending on the needs of the various "users"

(d) — Timeliness of Documentation

Those responsible for planning and developing the system have unique insights into its capabilities, limitations, and peculiarities. Once they get away from it, they will progressively lose touch with specific details. It is very difficult for anyone else to learn the system sufficiently to do an effective job of documentation later. Whether the system is developed in-house or purchased off-the-shelf, therefore, planning for systems documentation and training must begin when the HRMS needs analysis is initiated and must carry on through all phases of the project. Every system has subtle changes or modifications arising from unforeseen problems. Accurate and timely documentation ensure that one can maintain a clear picture as to whether the system ends up doing what it was intended to do, and the rationale and potential impact of any changes.

As time goes on after systems implementation, modifications will be necessary to keep up with user requirements, including those resulting from technological advances and legislative changes. If system documentation is not complete and up-to-date, the progressive overlay of these modifications can render system maintenance very complicated and time-consuming.

The distinction between documentation and training has become less pronounced with the advent of such innovations as:

1. User friendly database management information systems that do not require much technical sophistication to program and maintain data menus, input screen, and reports;
2. User instruction documentation and tutorials built into the system to guide database modification, and data input and retrieval; and
3. Graphical user interface (GUI), which on the one hand makes the purpose and use of various functions more evident and, on the other, has readily available help facilities to provide assistance when problems arise or clarification is needed.

Some systems utilizing combinations of these innovations have evolved to the point that a user with some familiarity with data management information systems, human resources systems, and graphical user interface can begin to use the system with little or no formal training by following the on-line aids and instructions provided. Formal training programs are still required with such systems, but should be coordinated with the built-in documentation and aides.

Written technical manuals for I/T professionals, and procedures manuals for such users as line managers and human resources professionals are still required. Each of these manuals must have a table of contents, a comprehensive index, and a method for updating. All must be clearly written. The managers' manual, in particular, should explain how the system can enhance the individual's role as a manager, in simple terms. These manuals, normally accessed on-line, should be consistent and integrated with tutorials, aids, and explanatory information resident in the system.

(e) — Timeliness of Training

Training should be timely so that the individual can apply what was learned as soon as possible after the training was provided. Too often, for economic or other reasons, individuals are scheduled for training when the course is available, rather than when it is needed. This means that individuals may be given a course, but have no need to use it for some considerable length of time later. In the meantime, the individual's knowledge and motivation to apply what was learned wanes. Other individuals may be given training months after they begin working on the particular application in question. In such cases the individual must "learn by doing." Although many people have done very well under such circumstances, this process can be wasteful. Individuals are forced to flounder, learning things by "trial and error." Sometimes training is provided that is no longer required. Those responsible for using and maintaining the system become demotivated and give up when they could have succeeded with appropriate and timely training and development.

Readers are referred to Belcourt and Wright (1995), Goldstein (1974) and Birnbrauer (1988) for more detailed overviews of the technical aspects of training needs analysis and course development.

4.10 — Summary

The cross-functional nature of an HRMS makes it one of the more complex and sensitive projects to manage. Project management is a discipline of its own and is not easily done by the inexperienced. Plans should not be made for their own sake, nor should they become all consuming, but plans and other project management tools are essential to manage the complex and detailed processes of an HRMS. Just as planning and project management are key success factors, so too is a complete communication plan and an honest assessment of the organization as measured against the critical success factors.

This chapter provided an overview of the training and documentation issues that need to be considered when planning for a new HRMS. Conducting an effective needs analysis, and then successfully developing and implementing the requisite training programs calls for a considerable degree of skill and experience. For this reason, it is generally advisable to have training specialists included as integral members of the HRMS project planning, development, and implementation team(s), or at least to have ready access to them.

4.11 — References

Beck, N. 1992. *Shifting Gears, Thriving in the New Economy*. Toronto: HarperCollins Publishers Ltd.

Belcourt, M., and P. Wright. 1996. Managing Performance Through Training and Development. Toronto: Nelson Canada.

Belcourt, M. and McBey, K.J. 2004. Strategic Human Resources Planning. Toronto: Thomson Nelson.

Birnbrauer, H., ed. 1988. *ASTD Handbook for Technical and Skills Training* (2 vols.). Alexandria, Va.: American Society for Training and Development.

Clavell, J. 1983. *Sun Tzu: The Art Of War*. New York: Doubleday Dell Publishing Group, Inc.

DeMarco, T. 1979. *Structured Analysis and Systems Specification*. Englewood Cliffs, N.J.: Prentice-Hall.

Easton, T.S., and E.D. Easton. 1988. "HRIS Documentation: a Road Map to Application and Maintenance." *Computers in Personnel* (Fall): 38-40.

Fay, C.H. 1988. "Educating Old and New HR Managers." *Computers in Personnel* (Summer): 20-25.

Fossum, L. 1989. *Understanding Organizational Change: Converting Theory to Practice*. Los Altos, Cal.: CRISP Publications, Inc.

Goldstein, B.L. 1974. *Training: Program Development and Evaluation*. Monterey, Cal.: Brooks Cole.

Gueutal, H.G., S.I. Tannenbaum, and M.J. Kavanagh. 1988. "Where to go for an HRIS Education." *Computers in Education*, 22-25.

Gueutal, H.G. and Stone, D.L. 2005. The Brave New World of eHR. San Francisco: John Wiley.

Horsfield, D. 1987. "Home-grown Documentation." *Computers in Personnel* (Summer): 51.

Kanter, R.M. 1989. *When Giants Learn To Dance*. New York: Simon and Schuster.

Kerzner, H. 1989. *Project Management: A Systems Approach to Planning, Scheduling, and Controlling*, 3rd ed. New York: Van Nostrand Reinhold.

Knutson, J., and I. Bitz. 1991. *Project Management: How to Plan and Manage Successful Projects.* New York: American Management Association.

MacAdam, M. 1991. "Training HRIS Users." In A.L. Lederer, ed., *Handbook of Human Resource Information Systems.* New York: Warren, Gorham and Lamont.

Martin, M.P. 1987. "The Human Connection in System Design: Part VI. Designing Systems for Change." *Journal of Systems Management* (July): 14-18.

Meade, J.G. 2003. The Human Resources Software Handbook, San Francisco: Jossey-Bass/Pfeiffer.

Peters, T. 1987. *Thriving On Chaos.* New York: Alfred A. Knopf.

_____. 1988. "The Human Connection in System Design: Part VII. Prototypes for User Training." *Journal of Systems Management* (July): 19-22.

Pfeffer, J. 1998. The Human Equation. Boston: Harvard Business School Press.

Plantamura, L.M. 1990. "Automated Project Management." *The Review Human Resource Systems Professionals* (October/November): 19-21.

Schein, E.H. 1978. *Human Resource Planning and Development: a Total System.* Boston, Mass.: MIT, Sloan School of Management.

Tomasko, R.M. 1993. *Rethinking the Corporation: The Architecture of Change.* New York: AMACOM.

Turnbull, IJ and Delaney, R, ed. 2006. CHRP National Knowledge Exam Study Guide. Toronto: Canadian HR Press.

Walker, A.J. 2001. Web-Based Human Resources. New York: McGraw-Hill.

Weiss, D.S. 2000. High Performance HR. Toronto: John Wiley & Sons.

Chapter 5: Designing and Developing a New HRMS

5.1 — Introduction

This chapter discusses concepts that are relevant to designing and developing a new HRMS. Some questions addressed include:

- What are the components of an HRMS?
- What steps are needed to develop one?
- What is the best way to acquire a new HRMS — to develop one internally or to acquire one from an external software supplier?
- If acquiring, should you buy, lease, or outsource?
- What's better — the best possible HRMS module regardless of whether this module works well with other organizational software, or, a HRMS module that is well coordinated with other organization-wide software packages like finance, manufacturing, or student information?

Other important considerations addressed in this chapter include:

- Language and Currency Requirements
- Security and Privacy
- Business Process Engineering
- Tools:
  - Flow Charts
  - Benchmarking and Best Practices
  - Human Resource Metrics (and the Business Case)
- Options:
  - Repair and refine
  - And, as mentioned, build, buy or outsource.

Information technology has changed considerably over the last four decades. We have gone from carbon paper and Gestetner machines to scanners and high speed colour photocopiers; from cutting and pasting with scissors and glue to cutting and pasting digitalized images on a computer.

Computer systems design has also undergone considerable change. Many organizations that formerly built information systems now build information management structures instead. Into these structures they insert the appropriate software applications, to communicate through networks of electrical, telephone, and various kinds of cable connections.

Whether the decision is made to build an HRMS internally, or to acquire an already developed system from a software supplier, the design of the system can facilitate or restrict the uses to which it is put. Many systems both facilitate and restrict, depending on the functional area or application involved.

5.2 — General Design Considerations

The design of any software package requires both functional and technical decisions, and it should be predicated on the uses to which the system will be put. A computer software company determines the components of the HRMS it is building by developing its own concept of what an HRMS should be, and by taking into account market conditions — that is, what potential clients want and what competitors offer.

5.3 — Applications: Breadth and Depth

The degree to which an HRMS is useful to potential clients can be measured by what are termed its "breadth" and "depth." The breadth of a system indicates how many different applications or functions are covered by the software. Some of the most common HRMS functions or applications were outlined in Chapters 1 and 2 and expanded on in Chapters 8 – 12; they include human resources planning and development, staffing, training, occupational health and safety, compensation and payroll, benefits, and pension.

The depth of a system may vary by functional or application area. A system that provides a lot of detail in one functional area (benefits administration, for example), may provide less detailed coverage in another area, such as health and safety. Another system will offer a different breadth and/or depth. These differences in software packages provide users with options by which to evaluate packages depending on their specific requirements.

The payroll function has one common purpose across all organizations — to pay people accurately and on time. However, a comparison of different payroll systems will show a surprising number of differences in how the functions are performed, and many ancillary payroll functions, such as retroactive payments or mass updates, may exist in some systems and not in others.

The manner by which systems offer breadth and depth will also vary. Some systems are totally integrated, while others offer a core or main module, along with a number of other optional modules. In these cases, the core module often has limited capability in every area, with the additional modules offering much more depth in specific areas. Thus, the buyer can pick and choose both the breadth and depth of system depending on the needs or finances of the organization.

Designing and Developing a New HRMS

Most systems offer at least some capability in all areas, but the manner in which they appear may vary considerably. They may be contained within a core module, a secondary module, or both, to varying degrees.

Table 5.1 and Figure 5.1 show the relationships between HRMS core and application modules design. Table 5.1 shows how the applications modules relate to the core HRMS/payroll module, while Figure 5.1 demonstrates the relationship between a training module and the counterpart segment on the core module.

Table 5.1 Comparison of Core & Secondary Training Module

CORE SYSTEM – TRAINING SECTION	SECONDARY TRAINING MODULE

Individual employee education/training history, referencing:
• Table of training classes
• Table of degrees
• Table of licenses
• Table of education providers:
    • Universities
    • Colleges
    • On-line (i.e., eCornell, etc)
	Full Administrative Model with:
	• Session & class scheduling
	• Room assignments
	• Expenses
	• Materials management
	• Audiovisual & other equipment tracking & booking
	• Salary costs of students
	• Expenses of students

Normally the core modules can operate independently of the secondary modules, but are required for the secondary modules to work. Systems designers usually have extremely detailed flow diagrams of their systems. These data diagrams act as maps to the system which can be used by functional and technical users alike.

A data dictionary accompanies the data diagram and lists every data element (e.g., "surname") together with its definition and characteristics. Characteristics include the nature of the field (alpha, numeric, or both), the size of the field (i.e., 28 characters — although this factor is becoming less important), and sometimes, the screens on which that particular data element appears. Data diagrams and dictionaries are key parts of system design documentation and can be of great help to prospective purchasers in understanding the conceptual framework of the system.

Tracking the movement of people is a primary HRMS function. This function is usually spread among several sections or modules. Beginning with documenting an application for employment (usually recorded in the applicant tracking section of the staffing module), most HRMSs will record hiring an employee and subsequent employee movement (transfers, promotions, demotions, termination). Associated activities, such as additional salary on promotion, are recorded in other modules, in this case, compensation and payroll. These salary changes will, in turn, effect changes in the benefits module, the pension module, and perhaps even the training or health and safety modules (cost of employee time based on salary cost).

5.3 Human Resources Management Systems

Figure 5.1 Modular Design

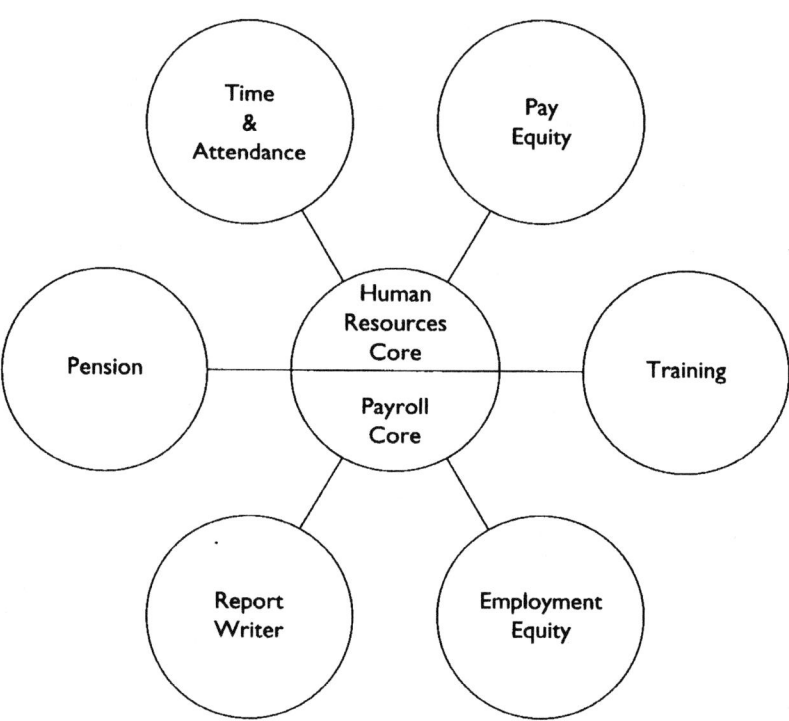

An HRMS should be designed to inform users about themselves, and management about all workforce participants. As noted in previous chapters, modern organizations require human resources management systems rather than personnel or human resources information systems. The former have all the capabilities of the latter, but in addition, provide managers at all levels with information reporting, analysis, and modelling capabilities for the effective management of human resources, rather than just collecting, storing, and reporting human resources information.

Thus, HRMSs are not merely buckets into which data is poured and retrieved, but tools to manipulate data into usable information. A theme throughout this text is that HRMSs are no longer restricted to "employees," whatever that term may imply; rather, a modern HRMS is a critical tool in the strategic and operational management of the total workforce of the organization. Whereas systems of a decade ago referred to "employee databases" and contained information on employees only, those being designed today include contractors, consultants, and all significant others.

Huva (1995) has pointed out some of the shortfalls in the design of current HRMS programs measured against Walker's (1993) principle of total workforce inclusion:

> Very few HR systems can track membership in teams. We have a hard enough time tracking the department to allocate payroll costs, let alone something as ephemeral as teams. We cannot track the historical relationships between people to discover if our team members had worked together within the last three years. We cannot track the outcome of work such as the 18% profit margin on the last project. We cannot track the competencies that our people have gained through the work experience. Even if we could track contractors, which very few HR systems can do effectively, we know even less about a contractors competencies than we do our employees. (pp. 29-30)

5.4 — Language and Currency Requirements

Organizations building or buying an HRMS should begin by examining what current and future requirements the HRMS should be satisfying for the organization. To do this effectively it might be necessary to analyze, in turn, the effectiveness of the human resources processes that the system is being designed and developed to support.

In Canada an additional and highly significant design feature is whether or not the system will be bilingual (English/French), unilingual (just one or the other), or whether two unilingual systems (one each of English and French) are desired. The Province of Quebec has a Charter of the French Language that places very strict requirements on employers with respect to the language of software in the workplace.

The issue of language has long been recognized in European software, and it is currently gaining prominence in the design of systems in the United States due to the increasing Spanish influence in that country.

Another issue that is gaining prominence is that of multiple currencies. Only the larger software packages on the market as this text is being written, provide for a "home country currency" and other currencies. For example, with many current systems, organizations based in the United States with employees in the United Kingdom and other countries, may be faced with keeping a record in U.S. dollars or U.K. pounds, but not both. Either choice places severe restrictions on management's ability to use the system effectively.

The introduction of the "Euro" by the European Union (EU) has complicated the issue of multiple currencies but has also helped simplify this issue. Regulations in EU member states will require the use of the Euro in addition to, and then instead of, their own national currencies. Thirteen (13) countries have adopted the Euro: Belgium, Germany, Greece, Spain, France, Ireland, Italy, Luxembourg, the Netherlands, Austria, Portugal, Slovenia and Finland.[1] It remains to be seen if the United Kingdom, Denmark and Sweden will reverse their decisions to opt out of the use of the Euro.

5.5 — Security and Privacy

Data security is a very important aspect in the design of any HRMS. A system's security features should permit the organization to group individual users by various and multiple criteria such as job function, organization structure, level within an organization, union (of both user and employees accessed), and geographic location. Ideally, security profiles, which should be date effective (start and end dates), would be defined by position (e.g., Director HR vs. Director Finance), and the employee movement portion of the system would then link the position's security profile to the user identification of the current incumbent(s) of that position. Linking security profiles to position level rather than to individual users makes the day-to-day administrative elements of the system as simple as possible; employee movement in and out of positions does not require extensive administrative intervention.

Flexible security structures within a system usually indicate that the system will satisfy concerns regarding system control and privacy. System control is often offered through audit trails that allow users to analyze system usage and to review processes for a variety of purposes. Audit records after the fact can be used to analyze system activity by type of transaction or by user. The proper use of audit trails and system security can replace various traditional control mechanisms, such as the requirement of multiple authorization signatures before an action can be taken.

In most states and provinces (to varying degrees) privacy is a legislated right of anyone whose personal data resides within an HRMS. Privacy rules usually address the "need to know," and require that access to data that is considered to be of a particularly personal nature (racial characteristics and medical information for example) be restricted to those who require it as part of their job. Thus a supervisor may be permitted access to an employee's home phone number in order to call that person to return to work, but denied access to that same employee's employment equity declaration.

(a) — Privacy

Data privacy is very much a moving target today. Three factors, or drivers of changes, emerged during the mid-1990s that compelled democratic societies around the world to pay more attention to the protection of personal information:

---

1 Gathered 07/02/24 from <http://ec.europa.eu/euro/entry.html>.

1. The long-heralded arrival of the Information Age, marked by ubiquitous and economical digitization of almost all forms of information;

2. The convergence of computational and communications technologies that brought about the Internet and e-commerce; and

3. The European Union Data Protection Directive. The first made personal information easily accessible and capable of manipulation. The second substantially increased its availability and commercial value. The third challenged any nation wishing to do business with Europe to take seriously the need to protect privacy when dealing with personal information.

The CSA Model Code for the Protection of Personal Information, the drafting of which was initiated in the early 1990s, reflected Canada's initial response to the first two of these factors. The Code established a comprehensive voluntary standard that private sector organizations could adopt, as well as a standard with respect to which organizations could gain independent certification of conformance.[2]

However, as the EU Data Protection Directive came into effect between 1995 and 1998, it exposed the lack of North American legislation and regulation in this area. In 1999 both the United States and Canada were assessed as "not adequate" with respect to meeting EU guidelines on the transfer of data to/from the EU.

The prospect of not being able to legally transfer personal information about customers and employees out of Europe commanded the attention of multi-national companies headquartered in Canada, the U.S. and elsewhere, and their governments as well. The options were limited: either the recipient nation had to provide a level of protection judged to be adequate by the European Union, or one of the Article 26 conditions, or derogations, had to be satisfied.

The government of Canada realized that such a self-regulatory approach to privacy protection would not meet European standards. This recognition led to the incorporation of the Model Code into the legislation known as PIPEDA, transforming what had been a voluntary standard into a mandatory requirement for organizations subject to its provisions.[3]

(b) — Privacy in Canada

PIPEDA — the Personal Information Protection and Electronic Documents Act — came into full effect in January 2001, applying to all commercial activities in the provinces where no substantially similar legislation had been passed. As of the writing of this book, only Quebec, Alberta and British Columbia had substantially similar legislation.

---

2 Privacy in the Workplace – the Employment Perspective, pp. 38-39.
3 Privacy in the Workplace – the Employment Perspective, pp. 38-39.

Since PIPEDA applies to situations unless the applicable province has "substantially similar" legislation, this means in essence, that PIPEDA's standards represent the minimum Canadian standard. Any organization or person who wonders what a specific province's legislation may require can thus assure itself that meeting PIPEDA's standards will go a long way to satisfying similar legislation.[4]

(c) — Privacy in the U.S.A.

While Canada initiated legislative action at the national level in order to satisfy the EU's adequacy requirements, the U.S., on the other hand, ruled out national privacy legislation and instead began what proved to be an extensive period of negotiation with the European Union that ultimately culminated with the November 2000 establishment of the bi-lateral Safe Harbor Program.[5]

As this book is being written the U.S. Federal Government has been confronted by numerous identity theft problems involving millions of people. Most states, California in particular, have been churning out a wide variety of laws attacking some aspect of data privacy and/or security and the maze has become more of a quagmire:

> The growing focus on privacy at both state and federal levels has resulted in an increasingly rapid adoption of well-intended privacy laws that are at times overlapping, inconsistent and often incomplete. This is not only confusing for businesses, but it also leaves consumers unprotected. A single federal approach will create a common standard for protection that consumers and businesses can understand and count on.[6]

The international maze of data protection, especially as it relates to personal information, is changing and growing daily. Readers are warned to carefully review the legislation in the countries in which your organization operates or plans to operate. Legislation prepared to accommodate data transfers between countries will almost certainly affect internal legislative environments as well. Add to that mix the growing influence of the Internet and World Wide Web, which, to date, has resisted all attempts of individual countries to control it, and the one certainty is that the uncertainty will continue.

(d) — Date Effectivity

Date effectivity allows a system to have multiple versions of a table or event, with each occurrence having a start date and an end date. Thus, for example, a

---

[4] Privacy in the Workplace – the Employment Perspective, pp. 3-4.
[5] Privacy in the Workplace – the Employment Perspective, pp. 38-39. Note: An extensive amount of information about the program may be found on the U.S. Department of Commerce's Safe Harbor website at <http://www.export.gov/safeharbor/>, as well as on the European Union's website at <http://europa.eu.int/comm/internal_market/privacy/adequacy_en.htm>.
[6] Brad Smith, General Counsel & Senior Vice President Microsoft November 3, 2005 speech to the USA Congressional Internet Caucus.

system can hold many copies of a salary structure, each coming into effect within its own time parameters. Most systems now come with data effectivity but buyers should be sure to verify the nature and extent — the depth and breadth, of that functionality.

Many systems allow the user to rank actions that occur on the same date according to their priority. For example,

1. annual salary increase
2. performance pay
3. promotion to a different position at a new rate of pay.

Some systems also offer time stamps showing the time of day an action is processed.

(e) — Reports

We noted above that a HRMS should be much more than a bucket to hold data. It needs to be a tool that allows users to mix and match data to create information that is then actionable. "Information" that is generated from a software application may be thought of as a "report", but it need not be a traditional hard copy document.

In fact most "reports" today are most likely not printed. They can created, generated (with effective dates), viewed on-line, and then discarded, only to be regenerated at the touch of a few buttons. Since (we hope) your organization has good data backup and recovery methodology there is no need to print and store the report.

Many who shop for systems spend huge amounts of time collecting every report currently created, and then "test" the potential new systems against those criteria.

The intent is good but the approach is flawed. Presumably your organization does a number of things now, including the creation of reports, that a new system will make redundant, or at least different.

Most software packages come with some predefined or "standard" reports, but for a system to be truly usable, it must have an easy-to-use report writer to generate new reports as required. The key questions then are:

- What ad hoc tool(s) is/are used?
- Are they sufficiently flexible, powerful and easy to use for your user group?
- Does HRMS security govern the ad hoc report tools?

5.5 Human Resources Management Systems

(f) — Technical issues

There are numerous technical issues that need to be considered regardless of whether you build, buy, or outsource. There are no absolute "right" answers as to what the hardware configuration should be, only that the hardware required by the software is compatible with that used in your organization.

If your organization has settled on the (for example) IBM AS400 platform, don't go looking for software that doesn't run on that platform, and so on. The technical setup shouldn't overpower your functional requirements, but each piece must be considered.

In Chapter 4 we suggested the makeup of an ideal HRMS Project Team that included one (and sometimes more) I/T person. This is their time to make their largest contribution, so let them do their thing.

Questions can include:

- What platform?
  - Type of server?
  - Web-enabled or designed?
  - Tiered architecture?
- What operating system?
- What programming language(s) (do you want to acquire software written in a code type you know)?
- Database(s)
  - Relational (most should be)
  - Object?
  - Proprietary?
  - Type offered (if your organization is already "an xyz shop" then integrating a xyz-based software package will be easier
- Tool sets
- Transaction methodology (workflow) type
- User device (dumb terminals, work stations, PCs (IBM standard), Macs (Apple standard), or some combination. Are there minimum requirements in order for the software to function?
- Interfaces (existing and available for Finance systems, for example)
- Connectivity to Microsoft desktop products
- etc.

Just as functional requirements will vary by organization, so too will technical requirements. As you move further through the selection process the technical questions may get more detailed.

(g) — The Internet

In the 1990s THE technical approach that everyone wanted was the client server approach made famous by PeopleSoft. Today it is the World Wide Web, or Internet. Walker (2001) states that:

> Human Capital has become the last competitive advantage in business. As management of this critical resource grows in importance, the nature of Human Resources management is changing dramatically. Human Resources management is no longer just a single entity, but an array of disciplines, plans, processes, products, and services each with its own opportunities for adding value, and each with its own inherent risks.
>
> Providing this vast array of services and products is no longer possible without web-based technology.[7]

5.6 — Analysis of Business Processes

Too often in the past, new systems have been developed based on existing organizational requirements. This has greatly limited the life span of such systems. Some were obsolete even before being implemented.

Acquiring/developing and implementing new computer software without considering how it can best be applied to achieve organizational goals is likely to be, at best, a costly exercise, and at worst a complete waste of resources. The automation of inefficient work flows will simply produce the wrong result more quickly. Even more important, automation of current processes can mean that totally unnecessary activities are being codified.

It is important to ensure that the human resources processes being automated are effective. The following paragraphs outline a number of concepts that have recently gained prominence as a means of analyzing and improving business processes, including human resources processes.

In their landmark work, Re-engineering the Corporation, Hammer and Champy (1993) argued that American corporations had to radically change the way they did business, or go out of business. The arrival of this work coincided with an extended economic downturn throughout the Western world, a downturn that had managers at every level and in every industry worrying about the future of their businesses and their careers. Industry and nonprofit organizations alike searched for ways to improve productivity and financial performance. Nurtured by other concepts, such as customer service, total quality management and continuous

---

7 Web-based HR 2001, p. vii.

improvement, organizations examined the value of every employee and every task with a new intensity.

The concepts of re-engineering and "restructuring" were wholeheartedly embraced by business, although the emphasis has been on evolution rather than revolution as encouraged by Hammer and Champy (1993).

The term "re-engineering" implies that business processes in the corporation have already been engineered or designed, but that is rarely the case. Organizations have evolved over time, one step at a time. New tasks are identified as necessary and new employees are added to perform them. Davenport (1993) considers the term "re-engineering" to be too narrow in scope for the techniques that have come to be included in this general area, and prefers "process innovation" as the more inclusive and descriptive term. A more accurate term, might even be "business process engineering."

Whatever descriptor is chosen, the common theme is "if it ain't broke, break it" in a stark contrast to the catchphrase of just years before "if it ain't broke, don't fix it." In fact, Burrus and Gittines (1993) suggest that one of the shifts we have seen in business is the understanding that breaks may exist even if they cannot be seen.

The core steps in business process re-engineering are:

(a) — Analysis Phase

1. Identify WHAT tasks are being done.
2. Determine WHY those tasks are being done.
3. Analyze HOW they are being done.
4. Identify WHO is doing them.

(b) — Problem-Solving Phase

1. Identify what tasks should be done, along with why they should be done.
2. Determine how the tasks should be done.
3. Determine who should do the tasks, along with where and when the tasks should be done.

   In conducting these steps,

1. Develop a strategy and scope for the re-engineering plan.
2. Ensure that management at all levels are convinced of the value of project, and committed to supporting it.
3. Chart process flows and analyze current high or low level tasks.

Designing and Developing a New HRMS 5.6

4. Consider what supporting application software will be required.
5. Conduct value for money audits to ensure that you can justify your project in terms of dollars and cents (see Chapter 3).
6. Develop benchmarks for the projects to be used as standards to be met (or exceeded) by the project.
7. Develop new effective and efficient tasks and processes.
8. Prepare an implementation plan (see Chapter 6).
9. Implement the plan.
10. Develop a plan for maintaining the system.

The degree of change to effect this restructuring may vary, within the human resources department, between departments, across the entire organization, and even between organizations, on a continuum ranging from dramatic radical innovation to small incremental change. Both strategic and operational goals can be addressed as part of business process re-engineering.

It should be noted that business process re-engineering and related concepts are not without their critics. Tomasko (1993), for example, has characterized business process re-engineering as "another useful but narrow and potentially static path to organization improvement." (p. 13)

Using tools improperly, or depending on any one tool or set of tools to provide "the answer" has never been successful. Nor is jumping on a new solution or "fad". But properly implemented, business process engineering can pay big dividends.

Once it has been decided that the human resources processes in the organization are the "right ones to automate" attention can then be turned to designing the HRMS to automate the processes in the "right way."

Ceriello (1991) outlines the steps to be followed in designing an HRMS:

1. Design a database with the capacity to handle the relevant populations.
2. Label each field and each data element to create a complete data dictionary.
3. Create tables of values that can be drawn on by data fields as appropriate.
4. Establish data relationships, including all algorithms and routines, to optimize editing and validation of fields.
5. Create menus and screens to assist users in navigating through the HRMS.
6. Create operator messages that specify action options.
7. Build in error-checking routines.

5.7 Human Resources Management Systems

8. Build in data security, including audit trails.
9. Define standard reports.
10. Include a tutorial module to assist new users. (p. 142)

5.7 — Tools to Assist in HRMS Design and Development

(a) — Flow Charts

The graphic depiction of the activities and sequence of business processes can be useful in designing and developing an HRMS. Additional data, such as the amount of time per process, can be added to charts or to supplementary text. Flow charts highlight duplication, roadblocks, and process gaps and make the job of designing new processes easier. Existing processes should be mapped to determine the strategic principles you want to ensure will exist in the new ones.

The level at which flow charting is done can be a factor. Extremely high level processes will not provide enough detail to make significant changes in the day-to-day processes, but too low a level can create mountains of detail that obscure rather than enlighten.

Whether charting large and/or complex processes, or getting ready to assess current or future software, a data dictionary with a set of standard terms and definitions could be useful. Information systems professionals may already have developed flow diagrams and/or data models with data dictionaries, which should be made available to you.

As with any tool, flow charts have their limitations. Harrington (1991) states that: "Many business people have used flowcharting techniques with enviable results. Others, however, have been less successful. Generally this happens because they view their flowcharts as the end of, rather than the means to, what they are seeking" (p. 9).

Several new systems use a concept known as "work flow". Work flow is a method and tool that allows the user to map out and to integrate the entire business process with the computer support system.

Traditional HRMSs have used the technique of sequencing a number of screens to simulate the flow of paper in a process. Systems with work flow take this concept a step farther by automating much of the paper flow. This is accomplished by linking the HRMS to other application tools such as spreadsheets, word processors, e-mail systems, and schedulers.

Thus, for example, the need to do a performance appraisal, is triggered by a flag in the HRMS and the responsible supervisor is reminded automatically by e-mail. The supervisor does the evaluation, and then he or she and the employee put notes together on an electronic form and complete the "paperwork" by e-mailing the form back to Human Resources where it becomes part of the HRMS.

Box 5.1 Software Attributes For Happy Users

- Easy to establish contact with software (sign-on process; security)
- Uses icons, menus, or both to guide user choices (no need to use code or learn mnemonics)
- Software easy to learn and use (windows, scrolling, and other features)
- Users are guided through various processes; help to correct mistakes is easily available
- Error messages are fully explanatory
- Data dictionary is available on-line
- Software has edit checks to verify syntax, semantics, and overall data integrity (i.e., The Canadian Social Insurance Number has nine digits; the software should require nine before data entry continuation is permitted)
- Downloads/uploads to/from PC products such as word processors, spreadsheets
- Effective use of graphics

(b) — Benchmarking and Best Practices

Even as organizations are flow charting, analyzing, and engineering processes, many are casting glances both internally and at other organizations to determine if there are any standards or benchmarks with which to compare or aim for.

Benchmarking is a process for continuously measuring and comparing an organization's business processes against the processes of business leaders elsewhere in the world to help the organization improve its performance.

As noted in Chapter 3, contrary to popular belief it is possible to quantify the value of human resource management. Fitz-Enz (1995) writes:

> A mythology has developed around personnel work. It has to do with the nature and purpose of the work. More important, it deals with the outcomes or results of the labour. The fundamental belief was that the true and full value of personnel's work could only be judged by those who perform it. There was a belief that business-type measures could not be applied to this function. (p. 7)

Fitz-Enz (1995) then offers some principles in performance measurement:

The productivity and effectiveness of any function can be measured by some combination of cost, time, quantity, or quality indices:

1. A measurement system promotes productivity by focusing attention on the important issues, tasks, and objectives.
2. Professional and knowledge workers are best measured as a group.
3. Managers can be measured by the efficiency and effectiveness of the units they manage.
4. The ultimate measurement is not efficiency, but effectiveness. (pp. 261-263)

5.8 — HR Metrics

You manage input, but you measure output. All output can be quantified by at least one and often more than one of: Quality, Quantity, Cost and Time. By producing measures of results — actual costs, you can then project benefits of any proposed action — like automation with an HRMS, and produce a rational, believable, saleable business case.

Many HR practitioners argue that many aspects of HR cannot be measured in that way; that HR has many soft values that contribute even if not measurable. Others disagree, suggesting that ALL activity by an HR department can and should be measured. There is no question that some activities are more difficult to measure, but that makes it all the more important to apply some measures against them.

What kind of HR metrics should be applied? The list will vary by organization, but interested parties should consider participating in comparative surveys such as that produced annually by the Saratoga Institute (now part of Price Waterhouse Coopers — see <www.pwc.com>).

Saratoga surveys in five subject areas (Organization Effectiveness, Compensation, Benefits, Separations and Staffing) for a total of 33 measures, including their top nine measures: Revenue Factor, Human Investment Ratio, Compensation Revenue Factor, Total Compensation Expense Factor, Healthcare Factor, Voluntary Separation Factor, Turnover Cost, Cost per Hire and ROI for Training. This is by no means a complete description or list of Saratoga's measures, nor a total list of metrics that can be applied to HR.

An example of one particular Saratoga metric is the HR Expense Percent. HR Expense Percent includes: total HR department expenditures, internal and external, including salary and benefit costs (of the HR department only; not all salaries), facilities, equipment (excluding depreciation), outsourcing, consulting, legal. It excludes: training, security, payroll, medical, childcare, relocation, cafeteria and safety. HR Expense Percent is affected by two other metrics: HR Separation Rate and HR Headcount Ratio. High HR separation will result in higher costs and instability in departments, overstaffing will increase HR costs, understaffing will reduce costs in the short run, but cost more in the long run because key initiatives won't be effective.

Here are two views of the HR Expense Percent. The first shows the HR Expense based on the number of employees by organization. The second shows HR Expense Percent by industry (both samples have been drawn from the Saratoga Institute's 1997 report — note: since metrics build on and compare historical data, ten-year-old metrics are still very useful). For example, on the first chart, organizations under 500 employees spend approximately 1% of total expenses on the HR department.

The first message is that there is clearly a difference here, depending on size and/or industry and also on several other distinctions. But, while size and industry make a significant difference in some measures, they do not in others. Each measure needs to be looked at independently. Furthermore, while "industry" may be significant in some measures, your organization's industry should not be a barrier to you looking for best practices outside of your industry.

The best time to establish a program like this is well before you need to produce measures as part of a business case; the more history you have, the better. But it is never too late. One dilemma faced by many organizations is that their current information systems are so poor that they are unable to successfully track or report on measures of any kind. That is a valid concern, but some annual measurement should still be possible. Turnover, number of staffing actions, and costing information should be available through payroll.

Performance measures can be very useful in day-to-day management and can make all the difference in selling a business case for automation. But, after all is said and done, it should be emphasized that there is such a thing as "analysis paralysis". It isn't very useful for an HR department to get so wound up in establishing measures that it forgets its *raison d'être*. In the end result, if the distinction must be made, people are more important than measures.

5.8   Human Resources Management Systems

Figure 5.2 HR Expense By Number of Employees

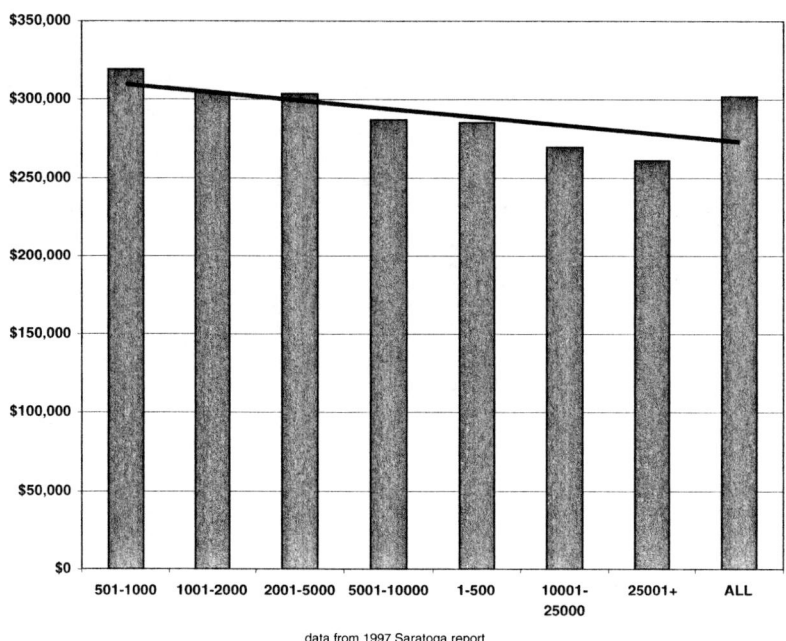

data from 1997 Saratoga report

Figure 5.3 HR Expense By Industry

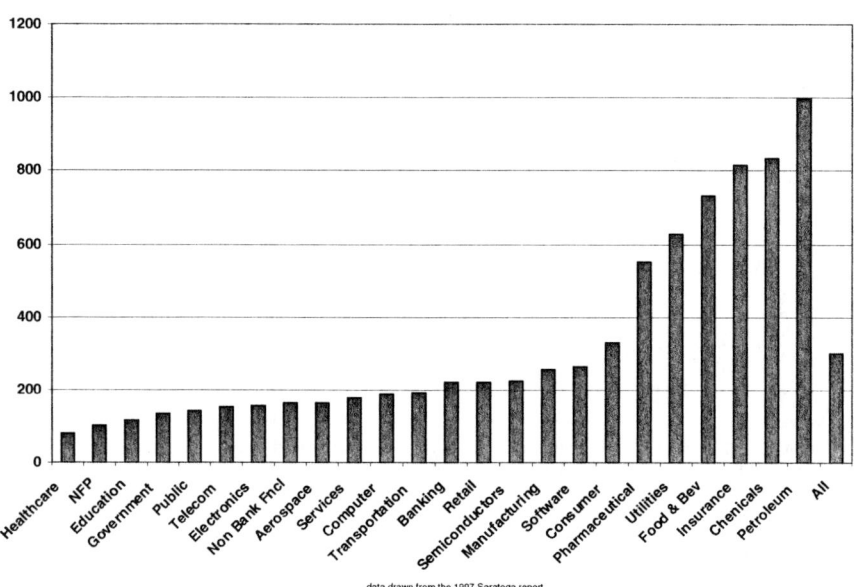

data drawn from the 1997 Saratoga report

5.9 — To Build or Buy

Should an organization design and build its own HRMS, or acquire one that has already been developed by an external supplier? The answer to this question can perhaps be sought in the importance the organization attaches to human resources in achieving organizational goals. Donovan (1991), for example, states that strategic applications should not be purchased "off the shelf" from external suppliers because strategic applications must be designed to reflect internal re-engineered business processes.

Are human resources management systems strategic? Donovan defines an information system as strategic when: "it enables an organization to meet its highest goals, giving that organization a competitive advantage, be it survival, profit, or increased business" (p. 3). In today's business and political environment, with downsizing and right-sizing occurring in almost every organization, it seems clear that human resources, and the systems that manage them, do fit that definition.

So, does this imply that all organizations should build their own HRMSs from scratch? No. We do not believe that this is necessarily the case. The rate of change for most organizations has increased to the point where commercial developers of HRMS software produce new versions of their software annually or even more frequently. Donovan (1991) points out that the goals and environment of organizations change, and that taking years to build strategic applications will produce outdated systems.

Organizations must understand that the strategic advantage of good information systems comes not from building some unique tool, but by ensuring that the tool has all of the capabilities that the organization requires, and by using these capabilities well. Selecting the correct system, installing it properly, ensuring that converted data is accurate and complete, designing complimentary and efficient business processes, and then using the combination of processes and software efficiently and effectively are all important.

If analysis of the organization's needs compared to systems available on the market indicates that no system will meet them, then building a system internally may be necessary. If there is a close match between needs and a system off the shelf, from an external supplier, buying the system and amending it to meet the requirements of the organization may be the better option.

The amount of fit that is desirable before a buying decision is made is a matter of debate. Ceriello (1991) suggests that a 75% fit is sufficient for the buying decision, while others suggest as much as 95%. The less fit there is between user requirements and a software package, the greater the change that will be required. This may be a combination of changing business processes, and therefore user requirements, and modifying or customizing the system. Modern systems offer tools to make many changes, ranging from screen colour to the addition/deletion/re-sizing of data elements. However, the more a system is modified or customized, the

5.9 Human Resources Management Systems

more difficult it may be to maintain, especially when updates must be made frequently or when new versions have to be loaded.

Meade (2003) suggests that the degree of variability is minuscule, quoting Jim Spoor (President of a HRMS software company) that:

> What is important to recognize today is that the HR systems industry has matured substantially... Systems from all of the well-established and longer term vendors have now reached a mature state and content is no longer a differentiating factor. (p. 15)

This is simplistic. First, even the best-known vendor products — i.e., PeopleSoft, go through changes, and not all are customer driven or focused. In the case of PeopleSoft it's acquisition of JD Edwards, followed closely by Oracle's takeover of PeopleSoft is perceived by the marketplace to have made differences in the company's software and services offerings.

Second, while a cursory glance will suggest that the same breadth of product is available from most vendors, a more thorough analysis of various software products will demonstrate a considerable range of offerings, both functional and technical. Most organizations that take the time to investigate complete the process glad that they did so.

Third, HRMS projects have similar results to other technology initiatives.

Building a custom HRMS has operating implications as well. Most external software suppliers offer training and maintenance services to compliment their products. As outlined in Chapter 1, legislation has considerable impact on both the human resources and payroll elements of an HRMS. Program developers regularly update their software to meet legislative requirements. These updates are released at least annually, and sometimes quarterly. An organization that undertakes to build some or all of an HRMS must determine how it will meet these legislative imperatives.

In the early 1990s the feeling was that every organization should search out the best software solution (or, "best-of-breed") in each functional area — human resources, payroll, finance, purchasing, distribution, and manufacturing. Let the information systems people worry about the technical issues involved; just make sure that you have THE best functional software available for each functional area, regardless of any other issue.

Today the emphasis has shifted so that more coordinated, more global, "enterprise-wide," software is being developed — that is, some companies are now more interested in purchasing a broad variety of integrated software modules (e.g., human resources, payroll, finance, purchasing, distribution, and manufacturing) from the same vendor.

Why this move to enterprise-wide systems? Organizations are working hard to escape the functional business process silos of the last few decades. The popularity of business process engineering (BPE) — a recent survey indicated that of 600

North American and European organizations, 70% were involved in some form of BPE — indicates that solutions, which work only within one functional area, are losing their appeal.

If (as they do), engineered/re-engineered business processes often cross functional lines, how can the software that supports those functional areas and processes be far behind? Organizations — public and private — want to plan and model organization/enterprise-wide.

What is/are the major strength(s) of enterprise-wide solutions? From a functional perspective, everyone throughout the organization sees exactly the same information. The concept of entering data once, at source, saves time because there is no or very little duplication of data entry, and ensures that data can be treated as a corporate resource, used by any and all who need (and have authorized access) to it. Through this horizontal integration of information, issues about whose/which data is correct are avoided, time is saved and the organization as a whole benefits.

In most organizations, few users have traditionally accessed multiple systems. In addition to business processes getting engineered and crossing functional lines, the tendency to extend the use of HR/PR systems to all line management means that more and more users will access multiple systems. There is no question that a common look and feel, a shared report writer, and common technology would be desirable, and enterprise solutions provide an umbrella for work flow.

What are the major strength(s) of enterprise-wide solutions from a technical perspective? Enterprise-wide solutions offer a standardized foundation, which greatly simplifies the information systems process. Information systems staff can focus on one primary technical approach, including common hardware, database, communications, security, and report writers. Training is less costly, backups are easier to find, and a range of software interface-based problems fade away.

Best-of-Breed (BoB) systems require interfaces between each to be developed and maintained often adjusted several times a year when new releases and/or upgrades are many to any and all software. While these costs are largely hidden in information system's budgets and maintenance costs, they do directly effect the return on investment (ROI) of any and all BoB software implementations. Enterprise-wide software greatly simplifies these technical issues.

Having a common technical framework opens the door to easily use inter/intra/extra-net applications in concert with internal software applications.

What are some of the weaknesses of an enterprise-wide software? Enterprise-wide solutions come with their own levels of complexity. Implementing any major software application is time-consuming and complex. Determining which functional area is best implemented first, and assessing how decisions in one functional area effect others is not easy, and implementation of a full enterprise solution will be complex and costly. Individuals who have experience with both "enterprise-wide" and "best-of-breed" systems generally indicate that the cost of enterprise solutions is more than offset by increased savings and effectiveness.

Of course, the very process of selecting software becomes more complex since all modules in an entreprise-wide solution will have to meet the demands of many diverse functional areas, as well as overall corporate technical requirements. Traditional capital planning/approval by functional area may no longer be appropriate because phased purchasing and implementation of individual modules may be more expensive than more coordinated acquisition and implementation of the same modules.

There are a number of software requirements that are not met by any one vendor's product offerings. Many specialized industry software needs, such as patient care software or student information systems, are not part of the core set of enterprise systems — that is, they are "left out". But enterprise systems can be developed over time to accommodate demand for more specialized systems. Further, even if 100% of an organization's needs are not met by the implementation of a software package containing a number of integrated software modules, the addition of other, less coordinated modules later can still be more cost effective than implementing a diverse group of more or less independent systems across major functional areas.

In adopting an enterprise-wide system, the process of needs analysis and software selection is critical. Choosing the wrong software package for a corporate-wide enterprise-wide system can be more problematic than having just one module not meet one's expectations (which could be traumatic enough).

Enterprise solutions lower the cost of software ownership and maintenance. They offer flexibility and standardized approaches at the same time. They support business process engineering and the reduced paper burden that results. Global requirements (i.e., multiple currencies and linguistics) are much more easily dealt with. Are enterprise-wide solutions preferred in all cases? The answer is not absolute. Careful assessment of an organization's needs must always be done. BoB may well be the best option for many, but there is no question that enterprise solutions have become a major option when selecting software.

5.10 — Typical HRMS Components

A review of the various available guides to HR Technology will invariably lead you to ask what vendors really mean when they publish their system specifications. Just as the word "Human Resources" means different things to different people, HRSM software programs may consist of different modules, including:

- HR (no Payroll)
- Payroll (no HR)
- Core HR and Payroll (core administration)

- Full-suite HR and Payroll

Full-suite HR packages normally include benefits, and/or flex benefits, and some mix of: training administration (and/or skills/competencies), health and safety, WCB administration, position management, labour relations and performance management. All will offer some form of report writer and all will claim that they can interface to almost anything else.

In addition, many offer automatic links to various word processing, spreadsheet and organization charting packages and most will claim some features to enhance productivity and work flow.

The best known software packages cost many hundreds of thousands of dollars to purchase, and many more to implement effectively, while the smallest can cost less than $2,500. How do small (under 250 employees) and medium (under 2,500 employees) organizations sift through this morass of data to come up with a reasonable number of software candidates?

Here are some key questions that the human resources specialists who are responsible for making a case for a new HRMS package should consider early in the planning process:

1. Can you state a business case in terms that your organization's senior management will appreciate? This should be based on your understanding of one's organization's overall strategy, and HR's place in it. If your case rests on automation of current tasks, do you have reliable criteria on which to base your analysis?

2. Do you have an organization-wide list of needs (versus wants) in order of priority? The process used to do this can build user anticipation and acceptance. Lack of participation now to develop a list quickly can significantly reduce buy-in later on. **WARNING**: Spend lots of time doing this before you look at commercial software systems. Shopping first and developing the list later will almost certainly result in problems.

3. Do you know how the software you want to acquire will fit into your organization's technical framework? Hopefully your organization has a strategy in place regarding communications' hardware. New software should be able to run on the existing and possible future hardware. Creating a new technical infrastructure is costly and can do nasty things to an HR cost/benefit analysis.

4. Do you understand the relationships between human resources (especially benefits) and payroll? Studies show that integration between the two result in:
    - fewer mistakes occurring in employee file setup and pay processing
    - elimination of politics between Accounting and HR

- employees' satisfaction with the new arrangement — one stop shopping!
- easier and quicker implementation of new benefit programs, pension plans and downsizing programs, as one group controls the whole administrative process
- fewer mistakes occurring on insurance carrier remittances

5. If you want to outsource some or all of your processing (Payroll, benefits, pension, . . .), do you know:
   - the complexity and nature of the interfaces with internal systems?
   - the services the vendor provides (installation, training, etc.)?
   - the processing deadlines and, how well those match your needs?
   - if the vendor provides a consistent contact for each client company?
   - the cost of the service (by cheque/employee, claim, report, interface, annual maintenance costs, upgrade costs, software costs)?
   - if the vendor can accommodate all the business needs (retroactive payments, casual or contract staff, benefits for part-time employees, . . .)?
6. And, have you conducted reference checks and visited a current client?

Finally, when assessing systems, don't forget about data connectivity, report/output requirements, security, support and services, hardware requirements, development language, price, flexibility for the future, performance requirements, technical support requirements, user and integration requirements, training requirements, methods and formats of data input, significant operating constraints, and costs of converting existing data.

And remember, software often represents the smaller portion of the costs, sometimes only 10% of the total. Investing in proper implementation, i.e., planning, business process engineering, and training, will pay big dividends.

5.11 — Screening and Selecting Software

If you've decided to "buy" software, comparing different HRMSs can be difficult because they may have been developed with different organizational assumptions and requirements in mind. The traditional approach to software selection involves the following steps:

1. Defining user requirements.
2. Developing a request for information (RFI) or request for proposal (RFP), which is then sent to appropriate software suppliers. The requests list

functional and technical requirements and ask suppliers to compare their systems against that list.

3. Assessing supplier responses, screening out systems or suppliers that do not match sufficient criteria.

4. Viewing demonstrations of short-listed products to get the "look and feel" and to confirm that stated capability does exist.

5. Assessing vendor and software reliability.

(a) — Definition of Requirements

The definition of an organization's requirements can be simple or detailed and complex, depending, again, on the organization's requirements.

Requirements are generally defined according to three categories: functional, system operations, and technical requirements. Functional requirements include determining the depth and breadth of each functional area necessary to successful operation. Organizations use various methods for establishing functional requirements.

Systems operations issues include such matters as how the user moves around within the system and ease of use of the system. Ceriello (1991) lists some attributes of "user-friendly" systems:

- It is easy to establish contact with software (sign-on process, security)
- Icons, menus, or both are used to guide user choices (no need to use code or learn mnemonics)
- The software is easy to learn and use (windows, scrolling, and other features)
- Users are guided through various processes; help to correct mistakes is easily available
- All error messages are fully explanatory
- The data dictionary is available on-line
- Software has edit checks to verify syntax, semantics, and overall data integrity
- Downloads/uploads to/from PC products such as word processors, spreadsheets
- Demonstrates an effective use of graphics

(b) — Development of an RFI/RFP

A request for information (RFI) or request for proposal (RFP) can contain very similar information. The primary distinction is considered to be that a software supplier's response to an RFI is not binding, whereas a response to an RFP forms part of the information that the parties may use as the basis of a subsequent contractual arrangement.

Determining the criteria for selecting and comparing suppliers and products is a critical step in the process. There are tools available to reduce the work required in the selection process. For instance, the HR Matrix compares information on many HRMSs in a grid. What applications are included, their capabilities, options and/or modules, and various other information are laid out in a large checklist for buyers to assess products. This comparison of vendor-supplied data against the organization's needs can help to narrow the number of systems/suppliers to be contacted. Their responses should consequently be of higher quality and the time required to assess them may therefore be used more effectively.

Unfortunately, the detail available in a matrix such as is produced by this software is somewhat limited. The same terminology used by two different software suppliers may imply system capabilities that are considerably different in breadth and depth. This may not be possible to determine these differences from information in the matrix. In addition, the warning of *caveat emptor* (buyer beware) should be heeded. No buyer should rely on this kind of tool alone to make a "buy/no buy" decision.

Developing an RFI/RFP is a complex task. The RFI/RFP should be designed in a way that will facilitate comparative analysis of several software supplier's responses. Open-ended questions invite open-ended answers, which are very hard to compare. To the extent possible, questions should be specific. One method of achieving this is to offer multiple choice responses followed by a "comments" section for the software supplier to elaborate as required, thus providing comparative data and allowing for an explanation of variances.

(c) — Assessment of Vendor Responses

Where the RFI/RFP has been designed well, the analysis of results should be easy, if often time-consuming. The purpose of the analysis is to weed out unsuitable systems or suppliers, leaving only the best options for further review.

Through the process of acquiring and using an HRMS you will deal with a number of software vendors and probably some consultants as well.[8] In assessing your organization's need for a new HRMS you likely dealt with the current vendor of whatever system(s) you had. You also probably used an external consultant to

---

[8] Selecting the Right Software Vendor, Laird & Greer Management Consultants, 2004.

help you to assess opportunities to fix or upgrade existing systems with the relative Return on Investment (ROI) of acquiring new systems.

If your organization followed the acquisition path outlined in Chapter Five – Designing or Developing a HRMS you would likely:

- Sent a RFI or RFP to multiple vendors
- Read and assessed their responses
- Asked questions to clarify those responses
- Contacted them regarding dates and approaches for demonstrations
- Attended demonstrations
- Conducted reference checks, and
- Negotiated contract terms.

Then, as described in Chapter Six — Implementation, when you implement your product of choice you get exposure to many more of the vendor's staff than just the salesperson. You would meet, or at least have phone and e-mail interaction with the vendors software installers, implementation specialists (functional and technical), trainers, product managers and help desk.

Some vendors assign a particular individual, or even a group of individuals as your primary points of contact. This/these "account manager(s)" can play a key role in ensuring your satisfaction with the new purchase.

User organizations should likewise assign responsibility for contact coordination with the vendor to a specific person or group.

It is a very rare occurrence when selection and implementation do not raise some issues between the user (buyer) and vender (seller). One of the common complaints from users is that the implementation process has exposed issues where the software either does not handle an issue, or handles it in a way that one of more users don't like, or at least in a way that is different from what they — the users — thought, based on the demo and/or documentation.

A typical comment at this stage in the process is for one or more users to curse the vendor's salesperson for "lying".

Do vendors, and specifically salespeople, lie? Yes and no. Certainly, *caveat emptor* — "let the buyer beware". There are salespeople, many, many salespeople, whose knowledge of the product(s) they are selling is somewhat (if not woefully) lacking. Their misstatements may not arise from dishonesty so much as from a true lack of knowledge of the truth. This is no more, or less true with respect to HRMS sales people than for any other group — car or furniture salespeople, for example. You, the buyer, have to take responsibility for managing the relationship, and for determining the veracity of sales materials.

But obviously there are times when some may stretch intentionally the truth a little. This "Warranty/Disclaimer was taken from a contract offered to a client in 2002. The emphasis is ours:

> Warranty/Disclaimer: For purposes of this Section, Information is defined as all information furnished by Discloser to Recipient, whether or not Confidential Information as defined in Section 1. Discloser hereby represents and warrants that it is entitled to disclose any Information it provides to Recipient. **Discloser provides all Information on an "as-is" basis** and, except as provided in the immediately preceding sentence, makes no warranty, either expressed or implied, concerning the Information including, without limitation, its accuracy or completeness. **Recipient assumes all risk in, and Discloser will not be liable for any damages arising out of, use of the Information including, without limitation, business decisions made or inferences drawn by Recipient in reliance on the Information or the fact of the disclosure of the Information.**[9]

The buyer who willingly signs that contract without considerable research is far braver than we.

It is also rare for an implementation to come to satisfactory completion without that dreaded words "customization" being uttered. If all of the steps outlined in the previous chapters have been followed this should not come as a surprise — you knew that some custom programming would be required. But an important part of being a customer is to understand that your vendor has many other customers.

(d) — Demonstrations

Potential suppliers should be asked to provide demonstrations of their products. Demonstrations of software can be as short as one hour, or as long as a week or more. Many software selection processes include at least two phases: a short (one to three hours), general, initial demonstration, followed by a more detailed and focused demonstration.

Organizations may ask suppliers to help them work through a detailed set of scenarios meant to simulate various functional and/or technical issues that are critical to the organization's success. These detailed "test runs" can be both complex and time-consuming, but they are well worth it. Time and money spent at this stage will help to ensure that the final decision and implementation have the maximum opportunity for success.

As an example, a forestry company in western Canada was concerned about the performance characteristics of a particular software product. The software vendor provided software and hardware and was present to assist in a multi-site simulation over a five-day period. The test results provided the company with new ideas

---

9 Vendors Lie?, Laird & Greer Management Consultants, 2004.

about the most desirable hardware and communications network configuration, and confirmed their business process design concepts.

(e) — Supplier and Product Reliability

Buying a software package, particularly an HRMS, should mean that you are buying not just the current software version, but future versions as well. This investment in a product and its supplier can be a marriage of five, ten, or even more years. It should only be made if the buyer is sure that the supplier and the product are reliable, that is, that both are a good investment.

The research should be much more rigorous than a simple reference check. Many suppliers have made arrangements with current clients to allow prospective buyers to visit. These visits can include watching the system in operation, and question and answer sessions regarding everything from the implementation process and training to ongoing maintenance.

Supplier reliability analysis can include a review of the supplier's products and its development plans (both HRMS and other product lines), financial stability, problem hot-line, maintenance costs and approaches, and software upgrade policy.

5.12 — Building an HRMS or Contracting Out

If the decision has been made to develop the HRMS in-house, the first question that must be asked is what the breadth and depth of the system will be? Perhaps more fundamentally: Will the HRMS contain a payroll module as well as other human resources management modules? As Figure 5.1 suggests, the core human resources and payroll functions can exist separately.

Today, the decision to build an HRMS is most often based on the assessment that existing commercial HRMS software does not have all of the HRMS capabilities that the organization requires. There is another option, however. Rather than relying on external suppliers for HRMS software products, some of the services typically provided by an HRMS can be contracted out.

(a) — Contracting Out Example: Payroll Services

There are several components to the pay process:

- Determining employee entitlements (as derived from union and/or individual employee contracts and policy)
- Basic pay
- Secondary pay (overtime, shift differential)
- Calculating employee deductions (statutory, mandatory, company policy)

5.12 Human Resources Management Systems

- Tracking time worked/not worked
- Making gross to net calculation of pay
- Generating cheque/electronic deposit
- Generating/delivering pay slip to employee
- Generating annual report calculations (T4, PAs, etc.)

A payroll service usually performs only the last four functions, based on data drawn from the organization regarding the other components: entitlements, deductions, and time worked/not worked. This is a significant portion of the work, but it does not relieve an organization of its legislative responsibilities. Too few payroll systems include or are linked to automated systems for capturing employee schedules, time worked (direct labour) or not worked (indirect labour costs). The steps generally performed by payroll service bureaus (the last four mentioned above) are those that are most heavily reliant on computers.

Many payroll professionals who use a third party service argue that the use of a service ensures employees are paid on time. This presumably reflects past use of internal systems that were so unreliable as to be "crashing, or going down" at some crucial point in the payroll process on a regular basis. Regardless of the relative perfection of a third party's processing, the responsibility for paying employees correctly and on time continues to reside with the organization's payroll staff.

The payroll application software and the computers available today would seem to make this kind of problem highly unlikely. However, if an organization's internal computer resources are sufficiently unreliable, payroll service bureaus are an option well worth considering. The primary advantage to this process is that no in-house system expertise is necessary. But there are risks. Sookman (1994) warns that contracting out may lead to rigid costing structures, licensing and security problems, and a loss of control over key organization data. Some payroll service bureaus, for example, control the generation of management reports and charge for each line of each report (a particularly non-service-oriented approach). The cost of other payroll service bureaus is based on the number of employees being processed, with secondary pricing for a number of variables, including generation of reports.

Since the initial cost of contracting out is much lower than purchasing and implementing an internal payroll system, it is often considered a cheaper solution. Over the longer term, however, contracting out payroll services may not be as cost effective, particularly for larger organizations. Those thinking of using a payroll service bureau should analyze all costs over a period of at least three years before making a decision.

Some organizations have multiple payroll software applications and many other applications, often available to only one person, such as PC-based statistical packages for compensation. These applications can range from an internal payroll system or a payroll service system to a complete HRMS. In between these options lie various mainframe programs that were written in response to specific requirements, or PC software purchased to meet a functional requirement.

5.13 — Summary

This chapter has pointed out the need for those undertaking to design and develop a new HRMS to begin by answering the following questions:

1. Are there new and/or different business requirements that require a change in functionality? The current system may be fine for today's needs, but inadequate for those of tomorrow.

2. Are new or different legislative requirements expected? If a software supplier has a good track record with respect to keeping pace with legislative change, one can be reasonably assured about the future. However, it must always be remembered that the host organization, not the software supplier, has the legal responsibility to ensure compliance with legislation in the day-to-day operation of the HRMS.

Existing HR, payroll, and time and attendance computer systems (whether mainframe, mini, or PC-based; integrated or stand-alone) should be assessed to determine which functions should be retained or replaced, and how to interface/integrate any of these systems that remain with the HRMS.

Designing an HRMS, whether the design is for the internal development of a system, or the preparation to buy and install a system, is a complex task. Functional and technical issues must be dealt with, and occasionally compromises must be accepted.

Acquiring a software package, whether buying or outsourced, is by far the most common solution today. Chapter 3 — Return on Investment illustrates the costs of such a choice, the most important part of which is that the software license is only a limited part of the total cost.

The effective contribution of human resources management to an organization's success is directly related to the effectiveness of underlying human resources management systems. Organizations that spend time considering all aspects, including supporting technology, of the work they do will surely perform better than those which do not.

Every computer system works in support of a set of business processes. Engineering or re-engineering those processes is an important piece of the system design and development puzzle.

5.14 — References

Albrecht, K., and R. Zemke. 1985. *Service America: Doing Business in the New Economy.* Homewood, Ill.: Dow Jones-Irwin.

Belcourt, M., A.W. Sherman, G.W. Bohlander, and S.A. Snell. 1996. *Managing Human Resources.* Toronto: Nelson Canada.

Broderick, R., and J.W. Boudreau. 1992. "Human Resource Management, Information Technology, and the Competitive Edge." *The Executive* 5, no. 2 (May): 7-17.

Burrus, D., and R. Gittines. 1993. *Technotrends: How to Use Technology to Go Beyond Your Competition.* New York: Harper Business.

Campion, M.A., and L.L. Campion. 1995. "A Practical Checklist for Content and Organization." *HR Focus* 72, no. 1 (January): 12-13.

Ceriello, V.R. 1991. *Human Resource Management Systems: Strategy, Factors, and Techniques.* Toronto: Maxwell Macmillan.

Champy, M. 1995. Re-engineering Management: the Mandate for New Leadership. Toronto: HarperBusiness.

Davenport, T.H. 1993. Process Innovation: Re-engineering Work through Information Technology. Boston, Mass.: Harvard Business School Press.

Donovan, J.J. 1996. Opportunities in Technology. Cambridge, Mass.: Cambridge Technology Group.

Farquhar, C.R., and C.G. Johnston. 1990. Total Quality Management: A Competitive Imperative Report. 60-90. Ottawa: The Conference Board of Canada.

Fitz-Enz, J. 1993. Benchmarking Staff Performance. San Francisco, C.A: Jossey-Bass.

Fitz-Enz, J. 1995. How To Measure Human Resources Management, 2nd ed. New York: McGraw-Hill.

Forrer, S.E., and Z.B. Leibowitz. 1991. Using Computers in Human Resources. San Francisco, C.A.: Jossey-Bass.

Hammer, M., and J. Champy. 1993. Re-engineering The Corporation: A Manifesto for Business Revolution. New York: HarperCollins.

Harrington, H.J. 1991. Business Process Improvement. New York: McGraw-Hill.

Heinen, J.C. 1994. "Automating the Process for HRIS Selection." Employment Relations Today 21, no. 4 (Winter): 371-80.

Huva, W. 1995. "Globalization and the HRMS." RESOURCE 4, no. 3 (September): 29-30.

Johnston, C.G., and M.J. Daniel. 1991. Customer Satisfaction Through Quality: An International Perspective. Report 74-91-E. Ottawa: The Conference Board of Canada.

Lasden, M. 1985. "Fad in fad out." Computer Decisions (May): 74-88.

"Privacy and Security Measures in Computing." 1994. Personnel Journal (November): 9-10.

Rampton, G.M., and J.A. Doran. 1994. A Practitioners Guide for a New HRIS. Paper presented at the 9th Annual CHRSP Conference (October): 4-7.

Slofstra, M. 1994. "A Positive New Image in the Works." Computing Canada 20, no. 16 (August): 27.

Sookman, B. 1994. "The Legal Issues Abound." Computing Canada 20, no. 16 (August): 29.

Tomasko, R.M. 1993. Rethinking the Corporation: The Architecture of Change. New York: AMACOM.

Turnbull, I.J., The Canadian Privacy Institute, 2004. Privacy in the Workplace – the Employment Perspective. Toronto. CCH.

Turnbull, I.J. 1994. Let the great world spin. London, England: The Interactive Group Softworld Report and Directory, "Alphabet Soup - RFIs, RFPs, etc." Paper presented to the Greater Toronto Chapter of IHRIM, March 7, Toronto.

Walker, A.J. 1993. Handbook of Human Resource Information Systems. New York: McGraw-Hill.

Weizer, N., G. Gartner III, S. Lipoff, M.F. Roetter, and F.G. Withington. 1991. The Arthur D. Little Forecast on Information Technology and Productivity. New York: John Wiley and Sons.

CHAPTER 6: IMPLEMENTATION

6.1 — Introduction

This chapter deals with the most complex and potentially the most expensive phase of an HRMS project: implementation. At this point the customer takes the HRMS from the design state to an operational state. Where the organization has purchased a pre-programmed HRMS, this could be described as taking the product out of its shrink-wrap and making it work.

Implementing an HRMS can take three months, or from one to two years — or even longer — depending upon a number of factors. For a smaller organization, installing a PC- or LAN-based HRMS, this time frame may be much shorter, particularly if the requirements of the HRMS are limited and well defined. But even for a small organization with simple needs, the impact of implementation can be significant. In the case of a large organization implementing an HRMS using a mainframe or a client/server network, the cost of implementation can be three to five times that of the original software purchased from the software supplier. Realizing this from the start of the project, and planning accordingly, will increase the chances of successful implementation.

6.2 — Change

One of the more significant challenges facing an organization implementing a new HRMS is the resistance that many people have to change. In most situations, the implementation of the new system will necessarily mean change for many people. Some potential examples are described below.

1. *Technology.* Moving, for example, from a mainframe to a client/server environment could affect:

    - technical personnel having to learn to use new tools;

    - traditional users of the system having to familiarize themselves with new tools and new procedures; and

    - additional users who may be given access to the new system because of its increased capabilities.

2. *Business.* Implementing an HRMS could affect:

    - the way information is captured and used in terms of:

        (a) a move to decentralized data capture;

        (b) users now being responsible for the quality and timeliness of data;

        (c) the elimination of procedures through the use of modern business techniques such as process re- engineering; and

(d) the provision of management information to users, including ready access to flexible, and easy-to-use reporting tools.

To determine the extent of the changes that may be involved, we need only go back to the basic reasons for moving to a new HRMS. These may include a change in computer technology that may or may not be a result of an overall organizational change. Such technological change will not necessarily have a significant impact on the HRMS or those that depend on it. If an organization is reasonably comfortable with its existing HRMS but wants, for example, to standardize its computer technology, it may be possible to buy a version of the current HRMS that will work on the new computer technology. If this is the case *and if* the organization is satisfied with existing procedures, the technological change may only affect those involved with the transition to the alternate software programs.

More than likely, however, a change in technology will be associated with some degree of "re-engineering" of work processes. For example, the move away from large mainframes to client/server or LAN-based systems generally results in a degree of decentralization of information gathering and use, as well as increased accountability for the entering, accuracy and use of information by the users of that information.

One of the most common reasons for implementing a new HRMS is the need to increase HRMS capabilities. If the old HRMS was essentially a centralized record-keeping system, one that only met the most basic HR information requirements of the organization, the push for a new system may have been linked to the need to have the new HRMS take on more strategic human resources management functions (see Chapter 1). This may or may not be coupled with a move to new technology. Whatever the circumstances, and regardless of the extent of change involved, planning how to manage that change is an integral part of HRMS implementation.

6.3 — Pitfalls in HRMS Implementation

A number of problems have been identified as leading to failures in HRMS implementation. Some of these include:

1. insufficient planning;

2. lack of management commitment, leading to inadequate resources and personnel;

3. failure to assign a project team for the duration of the project (it is imperative that the core project team members stay with the project from inception to implementation);

4. political intrigue, conflict, hidden agendas;

5. poorly written, incomplete needs analysis reports, leading to incorrect

decisions and a costly system that does not meet the needs of the organization;

6. failure to include key personnel on the project team; this can exacerbate political problems and reduce perceived ownership to a small group; and

7. failure to include key groups in the organization in various steps in the process.

6.4 — Implementation Phases

A successful HRMS implementation requires that many people in various parts of the organization cooperate effectively with the shared goal of implementing the HRMS successfully. Good communication and project management are crucial to each stage of project implementation.

During an HRMS implementation a number of overlapping processes occur:

- Implementation planning
- Input of the steering committee
- Ongoing communications to all interested parties
- Policy and procedure development
- Project team training
- Installation
- Fit analysis
- Modification
- Interfaces
- Conversion
- User (and technical support) training
- Unit and integrated testing
- Parallel testing

6.5 — Implementation Planning

When the software program has been chosen and finally arrives on-site, a great deal of time must be devoted to planning the HRMS implementation. Before beginning the planning process, a number of things must be known, including the scope and goals of the project. If the needs analysis was thorough and the successful software vendor represented the capabilities of its product realistically, this task will be simpler. The team entrusted with the implementation must have

6.5 Human Resources Management Systems

very good project management skills, as well as some knowledge of the HRMS product and the technology base to be used. If the latter two are new to the project manager and to team members, some training may be in order before a proper plan can be developed.

An effective project plan will include:

- Project Goals
- Timetables
- Responsibilities
- Resources
- Monitoring and Reporting Mechanisms

Some project management tools that the project manager may find useful include: Gantt Charts, CPM, PERT, and Project Management Software (see Chapter 4 for details).

(a) — Priorities

During the development of the overall implementation plan, key resources from Human Resources and from the Information Technology area must work together to ensure that all of the expectations of both areas are met. If, in fact, users are going to be greatly affected (through new duties, responsibilities, re-engineering) they too should be involved in the initial planning. In all cases, the priorities of Human Resources, Information Technology, and the user area must be addressed. Quite often an outside consultant or neutral third party expert is used to facilitate the development of the implementation plan and to ensure the needs of all areas are addressed.

Items for consideration during the development of the implementation plan include the following:

1. the technical environment: what equipment or technology must be acquired/expanded/reconfigured;
2. the priority assigned to individual HR modules; whether to implement all at once, or in a specific sequence;
3. the expectations of new users, such as moving to a decentralized system;
4. the availability of resources, including whether Human Resources or Information Technology expertise will be provided by internal resources, contract resources, or external consultants; and
5. the availability of training for the project team.

(b) — Implementation Schedules

Once priorities have been reviewed and a consensus reached, the HRMS project manager must work with the team leaders to schedule each task in the plan. This is a critical component of success and the only way to control costs and resources effectively.

The implementation schedule must include estimated completion dates, as well as the elapsed time or duration of each task. Again, it is very important to obtain input from everyone with a significant interest in the effective implementation and use of the HRMS. The time estimated to complete each task will be based on experience in this area as well as the planned availability of key resources to complete the work. This will include knowledge gained during the selection of the software program(s), including knowledge of the supplier's ability to provide support in key areas. If consultants are going to be used on the project team, they must have input into this planning process and be able to clearly communicate their knowledge and abilities in related areas, as well as the availability of resources in the time frames being discussed.

Once the implementation plan has reached the draft stage, it must be circulated to all members of the HRMS project team, the steering committee, the software vendor, and consultants (if applicable). All of the individuals involved in the project should have input into the development of the schedule. Many projects have found it wise to give a thorough presentation of the project schedule to all affected individuals, to explain what the plan means, and point out areas on which each individual may want to concentrate before final input is reviewed. A follow-up presentation to explain the final plan will go a long way toward building a solid project team, whose members understand that this is their plan.

6.6 — The HRMS Project Implementation Team

During the earlier stages of the HRMS project, the key people involved have been functional experts from Human Resources, Information Technology, line management, a consultant (if applicable), and the project manager (often from Human Resources). Quite often many of these people have already worked as a team in the ongoing maintenance of the HRMS to be replaced. During the implementation phase, the number of people involved frequently increases. In some cases, almost the entire Human Resources department becomes involved, particularly if important new applications will be included, or if work processes are being re-engineered. Certainly, anyone in Human Resources who will eventually be using the new system should have some role to play in the implementation.

Quite often, Information Technology resources are also expanded at this time. If a stable HRMS has been in place, a few knowledgeable individuals will have been maintaining the application. During the upcoming implementation phase, additional ones are often required. Several specialists may be added, depending

6.7   Human Resources Management Systems

upon the scope of the project. These may include additional application programmer/analysts; DBAs (Data Base Analysts); technical support: communications experts, software experts, and security specialists; a project manager (for project or information technology staff); or documentation specialists.

Other members on the implementation team may include:

1. *Implementation specialists.* Quite often an external consultant who is an expert in the implementation of HR systems, and in particular of the specific software purchased by the organization, is hired to provide important technical and planning guidance.

2. *Internal or information systems auditor.* This individual would be responsible for reviewing the new HRMS from the point of view of its acceptability on behalf of the corporation, ensuring that it meets all of the expectations of such a system. The effective auditor monitors progress on the project and provides sound advice on how to avoid potential pitfalls. Ultimately, the auditor must ensure that the system is accurately performing all calculations, deductions, and payments correctly.

3. *Training coordinator/adviser.* Training on an HRMS project takes place at various intervals, including up-front technical training by the software vendor. Sometimes it is advisable and more cost effective for the software vendor to train only the key people and allow them to train the remainder of the team. The training coordinator may actually deliver some of that training, but at the minimum required to ensure that those who will be training others in their turn have the support they need to deliver it correctly. Once the system is nearing readiness for testing, the training coordinator may assist in the training of the end-users who are currently using the system, and/or new users who may be using the system, so that they will know how to perform their work using the new system during the test phase. During final implementation, the coordinator will be involved in training the user community who may or may not be taking on new or different responsibilities. The actual training is often given by members of the user community, but with guidance from the training coordinator.

4. *User representatives.* If the new HRMS is going to be extended to a variety of users, line management, etc., representatives from these groups must be on the project team. If this is a new area of responsibility for particular groups, the representative/s of these groups must be chosen even more carefully. An important role of these representatives is to provide input into the implementation of the new HRMS. At least as important is their role in serving as a focal point of communication between the project team and the functional area that they represent.

6.7 — The HRMS Manager

Quite often the overall HRMS project manager is in fact the HRMS manager from Human Resources, if such exists. Even if this is not the case, it is the HRMS manager who effectively takes over the new system once it is implemented. Where the HRMS being implemented is the first such system acquired by the organization, the HRMS project manager may, in fact, become the HRMS manager once the system is in place. This is not always the case; the interests and skills of the project manager may lean towards project planning and to working as a systems administrator. Nonetheless, the HRMS manager is a key player in the implementation phase of an HRMS and needs effective skills in three main areas:

- Strong knowledge of main functional areas of human resources
- Automated systems
- Organization management

6.8 — Policy and Procedure Issues

The implementation of a new HRMS generally has a significant impact on the policies and procedures of functional and technical aspects of human resources information management. To implement the new system effectively, and to integrate the new procedures into the organization, close attention must be paid to any impact on these policies and procedures. Quite often, it will have been made clear during the initial stages of an HRMS project that one of the reasons for implementing a new system is to make way for change, to make things easier, more effective. Throughout the implementation process, new and different problems/ opportunities will be encountered that must be addressed.

During the implementation of a new HRMS, an organization will usually take the time to revisit its policies, procedures, workflow, and goals, and to re-engineer the business. If this is done in advance of the HRMS implementation, that implementation will be delayed; an organization will therefore sometimes undertake to do this work in parallel, or it will wait until the implementation is completed before trying to effect any significant change. There are many arguments for doing this re-engineering work first, but quite often, once a decision on a new HRMS is made, it must be implemented and as quickly as possible. In these cases, the re-engineering work generally comes later.

An organization might review its policies and procedures for any of the reasons outlined below:

1. *Workflow.* Using evolving business process re-engineering tools, organizations determine whether current processes can be eliminated, replaced, or made easier.

2. *Regulatory requirements.* If the new HRMS cannot meet all of the regu-

latory requirements imposed on it, alternatives must be reviewed. Usually, the new HRMS will enable the organization to more easily address those requirements, but in some cases the old system was modified to handle unique requirements. Will the new system be similarly modified?

3. *Data capture.* Will the organization move the responsibility for data capture out to line management? Will new technology be used to capture information closer to the source?

4. *Business cycle.* Will the organization change any of its deadlines (e.g., payroll cut off dates), or the way that it processes information, in order to take advantage of the new system's capabilities?

5. *Security.* If a variety of users are given direct access to the system (e.g., through their office PCs), what data will they be able to add, to see, to change?

6. *New technology:* New tools, such as the Internet (or Intranet for companies considering internal web sites) raise many questions about security, accountability and training.

6.9 — The Role of the Steering Committee

Ostensibly, dealing with policy and procedure issues is the role of the HRMS steering committee. A steering committee may or may not have been set up to guide the requirements definition and software vendor selection phases, but in most cases, it will have been established just prior to the implementation phase.

6.10 — Corporate/Executive Sponsor

The HRMS steering committee will generally be made up of a minimum of the following:

- Chair (corporate/executive sponsor (see below) or other senior executive)
- Vice-president or director of Human Resources
- Vice-president or director of Information Technology
- Executive level representative(s) from line management

A steering committee will sometimes include:

- Vice-president or director of Finance
- Change agent (senior person responsible for business process re-engineering)
- Representative from the board of directors
- Director of Internal Audit

The following individuals are generally not included on the steering committee:
- HRMS project manager
- HRMS manager
- Information Technology manager
- Other HRMS project team members.

The HRMS Project Manager and HRMS and Information Technology managers report to the steering committee.

Generally speaking, every project of any magnitude will have corporate or executive sponsor. This will be the person who takes the case to the CEO and/or board of directors of the organization to obtain approval and funding for the project. It is usually this person to whom the HRMS steering committee will report. In some cases, this individual, will be chair of the steering committee.

6.11 — Project Team Training

The best HRMS in the world will only work if users know how to use it effectively. Human Resources can foster that knowledge by providing explicit training and ongoing support as part of the HRMS.

Training is one of the keys to a successful HRMS implementation. At one time, many organizations ran their business systems on one main computer system. Although upgrades were made from time to time, the basic hardware and software technology did not change nearly as quickly as it does now. In most cases today, however, technology is changing so fast that with each new implementation, new skills must be developed.

Traditional HRMS implementations have had to address the way in which the system will be used during the project, and how key users and others will use the system after its implementation. Today, an HRMS implementation may require an extensive training program because of the large changes in technology and user-requirements. In some cases it will be necessary to hire new resources and/or consultants to assist during the implementation.

(a) — The Training Plan

The HRMS project manager will work with the training coordinator and team leaders to develop a training plan that will address all areas of training related to the project. The time taken to plan, develop, and deliver the training must be built into the project plan. An effective training plan will include:

1. identification of the actual kinds of users requiring training;
2. identification of the type of training needed;

3. an estimate of the number of individuals to be trained on each topic;
4. an inventory of specific information and skills each group requires;
5. decisions on training media;
6. identification of the trainers;
7. a schedule for the training; and
8. a development plan for the training materials.

If the organization is adopting a whole new area of technology and if it also plans to extend access to a broader variety of users, many levels of training will be required. These will include:

1. technical training on the new technology;
2. computer equipment, databases, programming tools, communications tools, and security;
3. key user training on the HRMS software;
4. technical training for Information Systems personnel; and
5. specific user training for Human Resources personnel, including benefits, payroll, reporting, and staffing applications.

Every person on the project and every person who will eventually be a user will require some level of training. The HRMS Project Plan should allocate time and staff to address training issues, both to deliver the training and to receive it.

(b) — Technical Team Training

Technical training must take place early, especially if the organization is changing technology. In particular, the HRMS project team, the nucleus of the project, must receive thorough training on all aspects of the new product to assist others on the project with its use. This training must be delivered at an early stage in the project or the team will waste a great deal of time trying to figure out things that would have been clear if proper training had been received.

Most software vendors offer training in the streams mentioned above: technical, human resources, benefits, payroll and reporting. As this training is usually expensive, careful thought must be given as to who will receive the training, and when. When training resources are scarce, (and they usually are), it is advisable to prioritize training so that key personnel get it first (they may then share what they know on return), and when it is needed.

In the case of other users, it is often beneficial to provide some hands on experience with the application, and time to review the user manuals, before official training is provided. Taking the training course and then waiting two months for the application to become available on the work stations is a waste of time and money.

(c) — Extended Team Training

Once the project is well underway and the core project team is well trained, time should be set aside to train the extended members of the team, including for example, the employees in Human Resources, Payroll, and Benefits who will be using the system as soon as it is ready. This training can generally be done in-house by members of the core project team, usually from Human Resources. Training addressed during these sessions will relate to the way in which the new system works and any new procedures that may have evolved during the early phases of the implementation.

The training coordinator will be of great use in setting up formal training for those who require it. Just because these employees are busy and already know most of the business side of the application, their training should not be glossed over. Training should be formal; it must be provided in a proper training environment, where the correct tools are available.

(d) — Training of other Users

During the early phases of the project, the project team will have identified who in the organization should be trained on the new HRMS. This may extend from the current users in Human Resources to a new group of users in the general community (e.g., line management). During the various phases of the project, this user community would have received regular updates informing it that this training was coming, and why. Again, this training should be formal, and given in a proper setting, using professional equipment. The staff providing it should be the experts in the area, generally Human Resources employees who work with the data on a regular basis. Before this training takes place, the new user group should be surveyed to determine if any additional technological training is needed and to determine access requirements. Once trained, this group should have access to a Help Desk support group that can not only assist them with the basics of the technology, but more importantly, provide information about the functional aspects of the system being used.

6.12 — Installation

The installation of new HRMS software involves much more than just removing the shrink-wrap from the packages and loading the software. In many cases a new system means new technology. By the time the software is ready to be loaded and run on real data, in a test mode, the project team should have done a great deal of groundwork. In addition to the steps outlined above, this will mean ensuring that the old system and the new one may run in parallel until the new system is running smoothly. Sizing and evaluating different computer options or testing new communications technology may be necessary.

Generally speaking, the support team responsible for running the new system along with the old one does not have to meet on a regular basis for any length of time with the HRMS project team; however, it will require clear direction as to what equipment and peripherals to set up. Once that environment has been established and stabilized, the new software can be loaded and testing can begin.

After the software is loaded, the technical support group and the information technology application staff work in parallel to test out various aspects of the software. It is accepted practice to set up one or more test environments with all of the software loaded and accessible to the project team. Once it is clear that the software has been loaded successfully, access can be extended to the remainder of the project team for future project work. This stage generally involves becoming acquainted with the software. If timed correctly, the users on the project will already have received their manuals, and will have some time to play with the system before taking their initial training.

6.13 — Fit Analysis

Once the software has been installed and users have been trained, fit analysis can begin. During the earlier phases of the project, when needs were being identified and analyzed, good documentation was developed to enable the fit analysis to be conducted. Sometimes called gap analysis, a fit analysis is basically the determination of the differences between the delivered system and what the client wants to do with it.

It is often said that the amount of time spent early on a project saves 10 times this amount later on: this is most true of fit analysis. If the team has done a thorough job of recording the details of requirements, this phase will be significantly easier to complete.

At the beginning of a fit analysis, the project team divides up the various requirements to be tested. Generally a two- to three-person team works on each task, each of which is modelled or trialed on one of the test databases. Often, several hundred examples of real data or data that have been created to have the characteristics of real data are loaded into the test database for the project team to work with. Each task to be evaluated is reviewed fully, with notes taken on any gaps. A simple example of a task to be reviewed would be to simulate the hiring of a new part time casual worker. All of the steps involved will have been well documented. Using this information as a guide, a team member could try and create a "new hire" on the new system: any difficulties or anomalies experienced would be documented in the fit analysis notes. If the new system would not enable the team to follow through with HRMS requirements or support the test case to their satisfaction, the deficiencies are reviewed with the project team. In some cases the software vendor may have to be contacted to help fix the anomaly, or to offer an alternate solution to the problem. If the new system will not handle a requirement, the team is faced with either modifying the system, changing corporate procedures, or a combination of the two.

Once the project team has come up with a recommendation on how to handle the problem, it is usually documented and submitted to the HRMS steering committee for approval. If the recommendation is a modification to the delivered system, a cost estimate of the fix and the benefit it will deliver if completed must be included. If the recommendation is to leave the system as is and change some corporate procedures, the impact of this change must be fully documented as well. Once all the gaps have been identified and fully documented, the project plan can be modified to reflect the additional work.

(a) — Reliance on Vendor

It is a very rare occurrence when selection and implementation do not raise some issues between the user (buyer) and vendor (seller). One of the common complaints from users is that the implementation process has exposed issues where the software either does not handle an issue, or handles it in a way that one of more users don't like, or at least in a way that is different from what they — the users — thought, based on the demo and/or documentation.

A typical comment at this stage in the process is for one or more users to curse the vendor's salesperson for being misleading.

Do vendors, and specifically salespeople, purposefully mislead? Yes and no. Certainly, *caveat emptor* — "let the buyer beware". There are salespeople, many, many salespeople, whose knowledge of the product(s) they are selling is somewhat (if not woefully) lacking. Their misstatements may not arise from dishonesty so much as from a true lack of knowledge of the truth. This is no more, or less true with respect to HRMS sales people than for any other group — car or furniture salespeople, for example. You, the buyer, have to take responsibility for managing the relationship, and for determining the veracity of sales materials.

But obviously there are times when some may stretch intentionally the truth a little. This Warranty/Disclaimer was taken from a contract offered to a client in 2002. The emphasis is ours:

> Warranty/Disclaimer: For purposes of this Section, Information is defined as all information furnished by Discloser to Recipient, whether or not Confidential Information as defined in Section 1. Discloser hereby represents and warrants that it is entitled to disclose any Information it provides to Recipient. **Discloser provides all Information on an "as-is" basis** and, except as provided in the immediately preceding sentence, makes no warranty, either expressed or implied, concerning the Information including, without limitation, its accuracy or completeness. **Recipient assumes all risk in, and Discloser will not be liable for any damages arising out of, use of the Information including, without limitation, business decisions made or**

inferences drawn by Recipient in reliance on the Information or the fact of the disclosure of the Information.[1]

The buyer who willingly signs that contract without considerable research is far braver than we.

It is also rare for an implementation to come to satisfactory completion without those dreaded words "customization" being uttered. If all of the steps outlined in the previous chapters have been followed this should not come as a surprise — you knew that some custom programming would be required. But an important part of being a customer is to understand that your vendor has many other customers and in Chapter 7 we discuss ways that you can cooperate with other users to reduce your customization costs.

6.14 — Modifying the System

Making modifications to the system after it is delivered can have very significant long-term costs. Traditionally, such modifications meant that with each subsequent official software release from the supplier, the modification had to be redone or carried over. This is changing, with modular systems and new tools designed to track these modifications. Software vendors today try and deliver systems where the changes made to the original version can be tracked and accounted for relatively easily with vendor supplied updates (releases). If a modification is made to a system that is not easily tracked, the cost of maintaining that modification over the life cycle of the system can be considered. For example, if it is estimated that the modification will cost 20 person-days to make, and 10 person-days with each subsequent release, the total estimated cost over five years (and four more releases) will be 60 person-days. If there are 20 modifications of this type, the estimate will be 1,200 person-days to perpetuate the maintenance of the modifications over five years. This gives pause to approving modifications that do not absolutely have to be made.

Fortunately, many new systems being developed today permit some modifications that are not labour intensive over time. Where this is not the case, the cost of the modification over time must be weighed against the savings to the organization from having a system more responsive to its needs. Once all of the modifications have been documented, costed, and approved, they must be added into the project schedule. Generally these modifications can be made during unit testing of the system.

6.15 — Unit Testing

To some extent, the system has already been heavily tested. Unless your implementation is an alpha (first) or beta (second or third) time this product has ever

---

[1] Vendors Lie? Laird & Greer Management Consultants, 2004.

been implemented, there are likely dozens (or more) clients already using the same software. And during the fit analysis, every possible requirement should have been tried. Shortcomings will have been noted and corrections made or fine-tuning of the system completed. By now, the system should be running almost as it will when it is fully implemented. But to ensure that all components are working properly, unit testing of each function within the system is required.

Unit testing involves a review of every major process planned for the system and the testing of outputs. Hiring a hypothetical employee to ensure all deductions can be set up properly; terminating a hypothetical employee to ensure all the final calculations are correct; or calculating pay for a hypothetical employee and comparing it to an actual pay are examples of simulations that might be set up as part of unit testing.

This testing will reveal any obvious problems or "bugs" in the system. Any problems detected are discussed with the project team and corrective action planned. When the correction is made, the system is tested again. Once the system is working well, the team will move on to testing more of its integrated features, such as a full payroll simulation using the test database.

Another method of testing is to attempt to enter incorrect data into the system to ensure the edits are working correctly. Testing of the system is a "user-driven" activity, with all of the project team working together and coming up with test cases. Each function within Human Resources (including Payroll) must come up with a test for every conceivable item to be tested. Apart from validating the system, this accomplishes several objectives. First, users have an opportunity to practice what they have learned in training and thus become more familiar with the system. Second, the test reassures users that the HRMS functions correctly.

6.16 — Conversion

Often underestimated in project planning, conversion is a very important phase in the project, and one that is potentially very time-consuming. Seldom is enough time set aside for converting information from the old system to the new one. In most cases, there will be data to be converted, unless the HRMS implementation takes place in a very new company without any history.

In many cases, the information currently in the existing HRMS is an accumulation of a succession of HR systems that have in turn been converted. Why is conversion so difficult and time-consuming? In most cases, design of the new HRMS will be significantly different from that of the old one, and data elements will not translate to the new HRMS exactly as they appeared in the old system. As well, each successive software package may handle data a little bit differently. Older, character-based systems retained information in longitudinal files, while modern systems use relational database technology and virtually all data is stored in tables

6.17   Human Resources Management Systems

(see Chapter 1). To this end, data from the old HRMS may have to be split up to be stored in the newer system.

During the "requirements definitions" phase, the organization will have documented all details sufficiently to know how much data from the old system must be converted. During the fit analysis, just how the new system would handle that data would have been determined. Where changes are necessary, decisions will have to be made on how to effect that change. In some cases, an organization may simply choose to key in the data in the new format manually. But in most cases, an algorithm (program) may be written to convert the data from its old format to the new. After each data element is converted and transferred to the new system, one of the most common ways to check the new information is to run reports displaying the information, and checking these manually. Another test is to run calculations or cross tabulations on the data and compare the results to the current system.

Once the conversion process, and as much checking as possible, have been completed, it is time to conduct parallel tests of the new system.

6.17 — Parallel Testing

When all of the steps described above have been completed, a significant amount of testing has been done on the new system. During the fit analysis and unit testing, however, test data (not real data) may have been used. Once real data from the existing HRMS has been converted and copied over to the new system, it is time to test the system using real data.

Following the final conversion of all the data from the current system, the project team may decide to run a test based on the last few months of activity. For example, if the conversion is completed at the end of October, the system may be tested by actually running a test of payroll processing for September and October. This kind of testing provides an immediate and realistic indication of potential problems. In this example, if the payroll is run for each of September and October, and the results are the same as from the existing system, there is every indication that the system is working properly. In most cases there will be some differences, and fine-tuning of the new system may be required. Each new system calculates things a bit differently and often small differences occur as the result of the way in which the systems round fractions/decimals. These are generally easy to fix.

Once the system has been stabilized with all the new data on it, the project plan will call for a parallel test that may vary from one to several months. During this time period, corporate information will be entered into both systems and the results compared. Generally the old system will be used to actually pay employees, but the new system will be handled exactly as it would during full live production. The results from the payroll runs, reports, and other activities will be carefully compared during the parallel trial period and adjustments made to the new system, if necessary.

During the parallel period, not only will input be duplicated on both systems, but both systems will be used to:

1. produce cheques;
2. print pay advances;
3. print payroll distribution;
4. calculate and print regular reports;
5. generate pay transactions for bank deposit, which may then be tested with the bank;
6. generate carrier transactions for insurance providers, which may be cross-checked live with the carriers;
7. generate interfaces to other systems, including:
   (a) the general ledger; and
   (b) other sub-HR subsystems.

During the parallel testing, Human Resources should monitor the system very carefully. Once HR has determined that the system is operating to its full satisfaction, the project team will work out an actual cut-over date, where the old system will be shut down and the new system will be used in full live production.

6.18 — Summary

Implementing a new HRMS can be complicated and time-consuming. As HRMSs become more important in the strategic management of critical organizational resources, and a broader range of users access the HRMS from their offices, individuals at all levels in the organization are finding that they have a stake in the effective implementation of such systems.

This chapter has described the steps required for the successful implementation of a new HRMS, as well as the pitfalls to avoid. The *who*, *what*, and *when* of each step has been explored, along with various governance issues, such relationships between executive sponsors, steering committees, project committees, project members, and user representatives. The importance of training was documented, as was the need for systematic testing at each stage of implementation.

6.19 — References

Ceriello, V.R. 1991. *Human Resource Management Systems: Strategy, Tactics, and Techniques.* Toronto: Maxwell Macmillan.

6.19 Human Resources Management Systems

Doran, J.A. (1996). "Human Resources on the Internet." Unpublished paper presented at the Annual HR Technology Conference, Canadian Institute. Toronto (March).

_____. 1996. "Implementing HRMS Client/Server at York University." Unpublished paper presented at the Annual HR Technology Conference, Canadian Institute. Toronto (March).

_____. L. Magagna, and S. Busse. 1994. "HR Applications Plan. A Project Document for York University." Toronto (June).

_____. L. Magagna, N.L. Rankin, and D. Willamson. 1994. "Training Project Plan. A Project Document for York University." Toronto (June).

Drechsel, D. 1995. "Principles for Client/Server Success: the Difference between Winners and Losers." *The Association of Human Resource Systems Professionals Review Magazine* (September): 26–29.

Eckhert, G. 1996. "How to Define Needs and Requirements for an HRMS." Unpublished paper presented at the International Association for Human Resource Information Management Conference. Toronto (February).

Eizen, M. 1996. "Business Modelling: a Technique for Implementing Your PeopleSoft HRIS." Unpublished paper presented to The PeopleSoft Eastern Canada Regional Users Group Toronto (March).

Hughes, P. 1995. "Marrying Technology to the Business of Human Resources." Unpublished paper presented at the annual Canadian Human Resources Systems Professionals Conference. Vancouver (October).

Huntington, G. 1995. "Electronic Survival Guide for Human Resource Managers: Using the Information Highway." Seminar workbook used at the 1995 Annual Human Resource Systems Professionals Conference. Reno Nev. (June).

_____. 1995. "The Internet for *HR: To be or not to be?*" *The Association of Human Resource Systems Professionals Review Magazine* (September): 36-42.

_____. 1996. "Less than a Second: Using the Internet to Revolutionize the Way You Work." Unpublished manuscript.

Iorfida, R. 1996. "Implementation and Change Issues: HR System Challenges, the Vendor's Experience." Unpublished paper presented at the Annual HR Technology Conference, Canadian Institute. Toronto (February).

Johnston, J. 1995. "Coming to a Company Near You: Purchasing and Installing an HRIS is a Complex Process. To be Successful it must be Well Planned." *The Canadian Association of Human Resource Systems Professionals Resource Magazine* (March): 18-19.

Kavanagh, M.J., H.G. Gueutal, and S.I. Tannenbaum. 1990. *Human Resource Information Systems: Development and Application*. Boston, Mass.: PWS-Kent.

Kucharsky, P. 1995. "Re-Engineering the Personnel Action Form." Unpublished paper presented at the annual Canadian Human Resources Systems Professionals Conference. Vancouver (October).

_____. and I.J. Turnbull. 1996. "Human Resources and Technology at York University." Unpublished paper presented at the Annual HR Technology Conference, Canadian Institute. Toronto (February).

Meade, J.G., 2003. The Human Resources Software Handbook. San Francisco: Jossey-Bass.

Small, D. (1995). "Why it Didn't Work ... HRIS Projects that Fail." *The Canadian Association of Human Resources Systems Professionals Resource Magazine* (December): 14-15.

Tapscott, D.C. 1993. *Art Paradigm Shift: The New Promise of Information Technology.* Toronto: McGraw-Hill.

Thompson, C. 1995. "HRMS Implementation – Approach and Process." Unpublished paper presented at the annual Canadian Human Resources Systems Professionals Conference. Vancouver (October).

Walker, A.J. 1993. *Handbook of Human Resource Information Systems.* New York: McGraw-Hill, Inc.

Winter, Robert W. 1996. "HRMS Project Management: The Basics are Essential to Success." Unpublished paper presented at the 1996 Greater Toronto Chapter Vendor Show, International Association for Human Resource Information Management. Toronto (March).

CHAPTER 7: MAINTAINING THE HRMS

7.1 — Introduction

The reasons for investing in an HRMS should never be overlooked. As outlined in various ways in Chapters 1 through 4, an HRMS provides information about the organization's most important resource — its human resources — that they and thereby the whole organization can be managed more successfully. An HRMS is not merely a place where information is collected and stored.

Successful implementation of a new HRMS is often regarded as the conclusion of a project and, indeed, it is. But it is not the end of the larger issue of managing human resources data, or of ensuring that the system remains up-to-date and effective. Implementation marks the beginning of an ongoing and continuous maintenance process.

Not the least of the ongoing process is the costs. Annual maintenance fees from the vendor are normally required to be paid to the vendor in order to maintain your organization's right to have software updates and new versions.

There is no set annual fee but typically the range is from 15% - 25% of the then market list price of your software configuration. For example:

Consider only the list price, purchase price, and maintenance (no hardware, additional software, implementation, training, or customization costs).

Year	0	1	2	3	4	5	6 YR Total Paid
List*	$200,000	$210,000	$220,500	$231,525	$243,101	$255,256	---
Purchase	$150,000	---	---	---	---	---	$ 150,000
Maintenance of 20%	$ 40,000	$ 42,000	$ 44,100	$ 46,305	$ 48,620	$ 48,620	$ 221,025

*assumes 5% increases per year

	Total Paid Over 6 years	$371,025

Of that total of $371,025 just 40% was purchase, the rest was maintenance. In this (not untypical) example the maintenance paid equals the purchase price after just three-and-a-half years, and after six years the organization will have paid 50% than the software cost ($150,000) for maintenance ($221,025). This is a simple example to illustrate the extent to which maintenance costs are part of the equation. For a more detailed view of costs see Chapters 5 and 6.

The maintenance/support picture is also more complex than one simple fee. Many vendors offer a series of support options: bronze, silver, platinum, or some other ranking.

Costs increase proportionately with the number and/or extent of services offered. Services are most offered remotely although some include visits to your site (but expenses will probably be at your cost).

Determining what mix of services is best for an organization has to take into account both the functional and technical support available, whether in house or through consultants or a hosting service. For example, in the case of either an I/T department that is not technically up to speed on the new platform, or too busy on other projects, the solution is to outsource some support, to a consultant or to the service side of your software provider.

More importantly though, once an organization has implemented an HRMS, focus must turn to the day-to-day use of the system in support of human resources management processes and organizational goals. No matter how good the hardware and software contained within an HRMS are, or how well the project team has completed its responsibilities, problems and issues will arise. Maintenance issues include continually monitoring the effectiveness of the system, and upgrading or replacing hardware, software, communications (networks) and business processes.

The entire system is dynamic: new users emerge and others cease to use it. Usage patterns may shift within a day, or over a week; processes change as user needs change (or as organizations reorganize/downsize); and files vary in length and in complexity. Unlike many software systems, HRMS products are often updated quarterly to accommodate legislative changes. Each new update, or "release" as they are commonly known, brings the potential for problems.

Compounding these problems is the fact that most HRMSs are being used continuously, so that it may be difficult or impossible to shut the system down for any length of time during the process of upgrading. Therefore, issues/problems are generally tried out in a test environment before they are implemented in the actual HRMS. Further, the project team dedicated to the implementation probably no longer exists; its members have either moved on to other projects or returned to whatever job they held prior to the commencement of the project.

7.2 — Shared Services

Walker (2001) states that: "Many believe that the Web will soon eliminate the need for an HR service center, it has become clear that some human support will still be needed to address complex issues and to assist users as they navigate through a Web transaction." (p. 212)

What is a "service centre"? Centralized services, such as technology, functional assistance, clerical assistance (the scope is as broad and deep as your HR, and Payroll, services) that are intended to offer a gain in efficiency and/or effectiveness over each organization operating on its own. A Service Centre can be internal, outsourced, or some mix of both.

The benefits (Weiss, 2000) can include:

- Less expensive than outsourcing;
- Can customize better than outsourcing;
- Knowledge gained is retained. (p. 49)

"Organizations are asking the HR personnel function to become administrative experts, taking costs out of HR systems while imposing the quality of services" (Ulrich 1997, p. 72). "The result has led to the reengineering of HR processes, to shared services, to centers of excellence, to organization development" (Ulrich 1997, p. 72).

Regardless of how the Shared Service function is structured the key characteristic of shared services is centralization, either physical and/or virtual, and both technological and functional. Some organizations pull all services into one physical location while others use different departments/locations to create "centres of excellence". In either case the hope is that the synergy created will result in knowledge and technology being leveraged, thus being cost effective.

Delivery methods can be the Web, the telephone, e-mail (and instant messaging), hard copy, and even the old standby, physical contact. Each method offers its own access issues, but what matters is not the mix of deliverable methods but **[author – missing text]**.

7.3 — Vendor Relations

In Chapter Five we (and others) recommend a detailed, thorough review of requirements with a detailed and fully documented comparison to the software product(s) that you are considering/acquiring. Through the process of acquiring and using a HRMS you will deal with a number of software vendors (probably including your current vendor of whatever system(s) your organization may currently operate).[1]

You also probably used an external consultant to help you to assess opportunities to fix or upgrade existing systems with the relative Return on Investment (ROI) of acquiring new systems.

If your organization followed the acquisition path outlined in Chapter Five — Designing or Developing a HRMS, you would likely have:

- Sent a RFI or RFP to multiple vendors
- Read and assessed their responses
- Asked questions to clarify those responses

---

[1] Selecting the Right Software Vendor, Laird & Greer Management Consultants, 2004.

7.3 Human Resources Management Systems

- Contacted them regarding dates and approaches for demonstrations
- Attended demonstrations
- Conducted reference checks, and
- Negotiated contract terms

Then, as described in Chapter Six — Implementation, when you implement your product of choice you get exposure to many more of the vendor's staff than just the salesperson. You would meet, or at least have phone and e-mail interaction with the vendors software installers, implementation specialists (functional and technical), trainers, product managers and help desk.

Some vendors assign a particular individual, or even a group of individuals as your primary points of contact. This/these "account manager(s)" can play a key role in ensuring your satisfaction with the new purchase. Your organization should likewise assign responsibility for contact coordination with the vendor to a specific person or group.

If your requirement for customized functionality is logical (as opposed to being intended to work around existing internal practices that should be changed instead), then it is reasonable to assume that other users might also require the same functionality. Enter the "User Group".

(a) — User Groups

If an organization has acquired an HRMS from an external software supplier, other organizations will have acquired the same software. Most software suppliers encourage their clients to join together in "user groups." User groups allow those who use the same system to network and exchange ideas about the software, its foibles and follies, its strengths and opportunities.

Active participation in such organizations, from both technical and functional perspectives, allows organizations to gain from each other's experiences and to approach the vendor with joint requests for significant modifications or customization. In addition, most vendors look to the user group to set future development priorities.

Traditionally structured along product lines, these groups usually meet at least annually to trade functional and technical war stories. The degree to which vendors direct or support their user group(s) varies widely. Some fund all meeting expenses; others offer optional user group attendance as part of maintenance contracts; others pay some support while expecting users to contribute the bulk of the cost; and some vendors have no formal user group program at all.

Elaborate multi-product user conferences are held in various desirable travel destinations, with key note speakers and numerous functional and technical sessions on everything from minute detail to the future vision of a particular product line. At the other end of the scale, small groups of users borrow meeting rooms to discuss joint concerns.

Regardless of the degree of financial or administrative support provided to user groups by vendors, the user group is a very useful tool for vendors and users alike. Users can compare notes on problems, solutions, or new desirable functionality. This latter activity can be a major money-saver. Instead of each paying for unique customization, user organizations can combine their requirements and focus on convincing the vendor to make the changes or provide the new functionality within the core product at no cost. For one organization, this resulted in a saving of almost $200,000, which had been earmarked for custom programming.

Vendors, too, like the user group concept. It gives them one or more opportunities to reinforce their clients' purchase decisions. It gives them a captive audience to sell new products to, and provides an opportunity to hear and diffuse or act on complaints before they get out of control. Many vendors use the annual user group meeting to survey clients on new perceived requirements.

Clients may be asked to complete a survey form or to vote on their most desired changes to the system. From the client's perspective, this should require some planning. Attendees at the conference may not represent the full range of knowledge about problems or the relative priorities for future development, and should always try to prepare "at home" before venturing forth to represent their organization in this way.

Other tools that vendors utilize to maintain communications between themselves and users, or between users and users, are electronic bulletin boards, group-ware products such as Lotus Notes, and Internet e-mail and home pages. All of these tools offer opportunities for geographically separated people to exchange ideas electronically. Electronic bulletin boards are being replaced with "chat groups" on the Internet, but the concept remains unchanged. Each user can access a common file where they can read other's thoughts and add their own. File topics may be very general or very specific, and depending on the technology used, comments may be relatively private, or very public.

7.4 — Coordination with Other Clients/Users

(a) — Internal

There is an ongoing requirement to ensure that the HRMS is operating effectively, in terms of meeting the needs of its main client groups and the organization at large. As noted in earlier chapters, access to an HRMS, formerly restricted to HR and Payroll, is increasingly organization-wide in scope. Executives, line management, and employees at all levels are being given direct access to information on the system, and to reports prepared by it, on a need-to-know basis that is defined more and more broadly over time.

Some progressive organizations have adopted a steering committee to coordinate human resources issues, including those associated with the maintenance and use of human resources information. Others recognize the interdependence of all of their major operating systems and give long-standing information systems steering committees more focus on data management and software integration, instead of the hardware and communications issues that more normally occupy their time.

7.5 — Hardware and Communications Maintenance

Hardware and communications network(s), the physical body and neural links of the HRMS, require maintenance like any other electrical or mechanical device. They suffer from wear and tear, and must be maintained regularly or they lose their effectiveness. In addition, it is a rare organization indeed that requires neither expansion nor change of the hardware or the network. The mere moving about of furniture in a single office can require the computer connections to be moved. Wholesale reorganizations can place heavy demands on those who maintain the physical network.

7.6 — Software Maintenance

Lientz and Swansen (1980) categorize software maintenance into three types:

- Corrective (60%)
- Adaptive (25%)
- Perfective (15%)

Corrective maintenance is defined by the authors as fixing problems that prevent the system from working as intended. An important aspect of maintenance for the earliest computers was to keep moths and other flying insects that were attracted to the light of vacuum tubes away from critical components, and to repair the damage caused when such bugs caused "shorted out" electrical components. Then, when a computer broke down, or would not work as it should, the operator or technician would often say: "it must be a bug," and to this day software problems are known as "bugs." These are not just "bugs" (programming errors), but also include poor definition of requirements, design flaws, coding flaws (true bugs), and various other problems. Adaptive maintenance refers to modifications to the HRMS made in response to changes in technology, government regulations, or external forces. Perfective maintenance is the term used to describe modifications to the system in response to user and/or technicians' requests.

This last area can consume considerable time and expense. Organizations tend to want to make extensive changes to software products to make them "fit" better. These fit issues may be minor changes to the name of a data element, "Surname" to "Last Name," or the color of a screen, for example. But they may also involve major restructuring of several screens, addition of data elements, or changing the properties of existing elements.

7.7 — Business Process Maintenance

"Managing for excellence requires process thinking. A process can only lead to excellent results when it is managed as a series of flexible, repeatable tasks that are continuously improved, and the variety removed" (Brimson and Antos, 1994, p. 45). Just as software must be maintained, so must the business processes of an organization. In North America today people see themselves as customers and expect a high level of service from every supplier, be it government or pizza delivery. To become and remain competitive, organizations must constantly enhance service, improve productivity, and control (if not reduce) costs.

The target of excellence is not static or absolute. Brimson (1991) defines excellence as the cost-effective integration of activities within all units of an organization to continuously improve the delivery of products and services that satisfy the customer. This trend is confirmed by Spencer and Spencer (1993) whose book, *Competence at Work: Models for Superior Performance* underlines the need for individual competence in order to achieve excellence.

The last few decades have seen many management improvement philosophies come into favour: Quality Management Systems (QMS), Total Quality Management (TQM), Continuous Improvement (CI), Business Process Engineering/Re-engineering/ Improvement (BPE, BPR, BPI), ISO9000, and Activity-Based Costing among them. These philosophies have significantly affected the way that many organizations conduct business. It is wise for HRMS personnel to have a strong understanding of these concepts because those individuals will often be called on to assume critical leadership roles in the implementation of these new philosophies in their organizations. (See the discussion in Chapter 4 on business process re-engineering.)

Total Quality Management (TQM) is the single management philosophy having the most longstanding impact worldwide. TQM's avowed focus, "to delight the customer," is achieved through continuous process improvement. To find the source of the continuous improvement process, Martin (1995) directs us to the Japanese management philosophy of "kaizen." Kaizen, which, roughly translated means everybody improving everything all the time, can be seen in Deming's and Juran's work during and after World War II.

TQM's prominence has recently receded, as is typical of many such popularized management concepts over time; probably because it has either lost favour or organizations have absorbed the concept into their culture and daily life. Less than successful TQM programs have been reported and publicized. The reasons for such failures have many causes, including a lack of top management leadership and/or commitment, unrealistic expectations of quick (or easy) results, lack of true employee empowerment, failure to recognize the need for cultural change, too restricted a scope, or emphasis on internal customers at the expense of the paying, external customer.

Each new "management philosophy" offers its own perspectives on business processes and how to improve them, but students of these philosophies will realize that few are mutually exclusive. The message is generally consistent. Change, however radical or slight, is normal, not exceptional. And in our modern era of rapid change, no process, however recently created or blessed, should be assumed to be inviolate. This continuous change reflects a need to regularly maintain business processes.

Juran (1988) proposes that a process of "value analysis" be used to focus the desire for excellence on value-added activities that will supply functions needed by customers at minimal cost. Martin (1995) agrees, and suggests that "value stream," an end-to-end set of activities that is collectively valuable to a internal or external customer, is a much more precise and useful term than "process."

Planning for quality, establishing an organizational framework for continuous improvement, a climate in which constant organization change is desired, encouraged, and supported, is not easy. Practitioners of the traditional HR functions of organizational design, development, behaviour (OD, OD, and OB) and human resources systems find themselves at the same table with accountants working with activity accounting, and management information systems staff responsible for business process engineering (BPE). Working at the detail level of modelling processes is very useful, but should never be taken as an "end unto itself." Ould (1995) stated that "many models can be drawn of a process, all will be wrong, but some will be useful (p. 210)." The individuals responsible for maintaining an HRMS must continually work to stay up-to-date with business, human resources, and technical trends and, in fact, be prepared to act as proactive change agents in their areas of specialty.

7.8 — Roles

What roles must those responsible for maintaining an HRMS play to ensure that it operates and is used effectively? To a large extent, these roles vary according to the way an organization has structured its business and computer processes, and the way it has defined the relationship between its technical and functional staff. Some organizations view the support of an HRMS as a technical function, with systems staff providing all expertise. Other organizations supplement or replace internal systems and/or functional expertise with consultants from the vendor of the system, or from a third party. Still others create a new function of HRMS specialist within the organization.

The last option (internal HRMS specialist) is growing in popularity, as evidenced by the growth in membership in HRMS specialty professional organizations, such as the International Association of Human Resources Information Management (IHRIM), which grew out of the Association of Human Resources Systems Professionals in the United States (HRSP), Canada (CHRSP), and elsewhere (IHRIM, 1996).

A 1994 survey conducted by the University of Sherbrooke and the Canadian Association of Human Resources Systems Professionals (Haines and Petit, 1994) states:

> One of the most important findings of this study is that satisfaction levels and usage of (HRMS) systems are much higher where there is a specialized HRIS unit than where there is no such unit. (p. 4)

The formation of a specialized HRIS/HRMS unit can be quite contentious. For example, the Management Information Systems department may feel threatened by users allowed to have system-management responsibilities that had previously been handled exclusively by their department. Also, if Human Resources and Payroll staff report through different organizations there may be turf wars, as each argues that they should be responsible for various aspects of systems maintenance.

7.9 — Responsibilities

A number of responsibilities that fall to those employed to maintain an HRMS (whoever they report to in the organization) derive naturally from the requirements to keep the HRMS operating effectively. Each organization's list may vary somewhat, but the core responsibilities are described below.

(a) — Functional Maintenance

No sooner than an HRMS is implemented, changes will occur. Union agreements will be settled, court decisions will require special reports or retroactive adjustments, and so on. Modern HRMSs are constructed with tables containing "date specific" information; for example, salary compensation (ranges, steps, etc.), benefit amounts, deductions and taxes, and performance criteria. Each of these tables may change annually, or more often, and will need to be updated and otherwise managed effectively, which in turn requires a degree of functional expertise.

In addition, a number of additional data management considerations must be taken into account. These considerations can be specific to a single application (e.g., payroll, human resources/strategic planning, pension and benefits, training and development, and occupational health and safety), or to many.

7.9 Human Resources Management Systems

EXAMPLE An organization of 60,000 puts in place a three point scale for employee performance:

3	2	1
exceeds expectations	meets expectations	below expectations

Employee X is rated as "2,' or average, her first year, and again in her second year. In year three the manager responsible for performance management systems changes; the new manager, determined to make her mark, recommends implementing a five-point scale:

5	4	3	2	1
Greatly exceeds expectations	Exceeds expectations	Meets expectations	Almost meets expectations	Far short of expectations

Once again employee X is rated as average, only now the code for this rating is "3." The HRMS has a performance appraisal report that graphs an employee's performance over time for bonus participation and promotional opportunities. Unless the system administrators have taken the proper steps to adjust for the change in the rating scale, the net result could make it seem that the individual's performance has increased, when, in fact, all that has happened is that the rating scale has changed.

(b) — Technical Maintenance

Computer structures are never static for long. Most organizations have several software systems using much the same sort of technology, often on the same computer. Even if a specific software package remains completely unchanged over a year, the computer that runs it, and the communications network that provides input into it and ensures that its output gets to where it is needed, may be shifting constantly.

Performance demands on the HRMS or other systems, backup, disaster recovery, the number and nature of central processing units, data storage units, and communications networks, all require constant management. This is true whether the organization is using its own staff or contracting someone external to maintain the system.

(c) — Functional/Technical Maintenance

If the HRMS in question has been purchased from an external software supplier or vendor, the vendor usually provides regular program "updates." These updates can contain not only changes in the way the system handles human resources issues, but also changes of a more technical nature. A human resources and payroll system update for example, may include changes in taxation from every applicable legislative jurisdiction. Such updates are often made available by the software vendor on a quarterly basis.

New versions (upgrades) of the software can come out annually or even more frequently. Implementing new software containing either specific updates or upgrades may not be critical. However, successive functional and technical changes will generally assume that prior releases have been implemented; without implementing them the system will rapidly become out of date.

7.10 — New Functional Requirements

At some point, perhaps a week or a year after the HRMS has been implemented, new functional requirements will be added to or turned on in the system. Each of these will itself be a mini-implementation project and should be treated as such, using the sorts of procedures outlined in the previous chapter.

7.11 — User Support

Ideally, as outlined in Chapter 6, an organization will have trained every user to operate the system as it is being implemented. However, the "users" of the system will change jobs, new responsibilities will appear, complex reports never before conceived will be required, and users will forget what they learned. Ongoing training and coaching on every aspect of the system will be required, as will documentation updates.

7.12 — Summary

The preceding chapter discussed concepts relevant to implementing a new HRMS. This chapter extended that discussion by outlining what is required to maintain the HRMS after implementation.

An HRMS is composed of many different parts, all of which must be maintained to keep the system functional and effective. Implementation of a software package or completion of a re-engineering project does not represent an end but a beginning: the start of using the system, and continually upgrading it to accomplish management objectives. Keeping an HRMS effective and up-to-date means fostering a culture of continual improvement.

7.13 — References

Bennett P., and Swansen, B. 1980. *Software Maintenance Management.* New York: Addison-Wesley.

7.13 Human Resources Management Systems

Brimson, J.A. 1991. *Activity Accounting*. Toronto: John Wiley and Sons.

Brimson, J.A., and J. Antos. 1994. *Activity-Based Management*. Toronto: John Wiley and Sons.

Ceriello, V. 1991. *Human Resource Management Systems: Strategies, Tactics and Techniques*. New York: Lexington Books.

Haines, V., and A. Petit. 1994. "Explaining HRIS Success." *RESOURCE* 4, no. 4 (September): 4.

International Association of Human Resource Information Management (IHRIM) Membership Statistics (January): Toronto, 1995.

Juran, J.M. 1988. *Planning For Quality*. Toronto: Maxwell Macmillan International.

Martin, J. 1995. *The Great Transition*. Toronto: AMACOM.

Ould, M.A. 1995. *Business Processes*. Toronto: John Wiley and Sons.

Spencer, L.M., Jr., and S.M. Spencer. 1993. *Competence At Work*. Toronto: John Wiley and Sons.

Ulrich D., Losey M.R., Lake G., 1997. Tomorrow's HR Management. New York: Wiley.

Walker A.J., 2001. Web-Based Human Resources. New York: McGraw-Hill.

Weiss D.S., 2000. High Performance HR. Etobicoke: John Wiley & Sons.

CHAPTER 8: HUMAN RESOURCES STRATEGIC & TACTICAL PLANNING

8.1 — Introduction

The general human resources model presented in Chapter 1 was designed to show the relationships between traditional human resources programs, the external and internal strategic context, and an HRMS. This chapter explores more deeply many of the concepts raised by discussing the uses of an HRMS in human resources planning, both strategic and tactical. Using variations of the general human resources model (see Chapter 1, Figure 1.4) this (and subsequent) chapters discuss HRMS applications in support of the following core human resources functions:

- Human Resource Management — strategic & tactical planning
- Staffing
- Training and development
- Compensation (including pension, benefits and payroll)
- Labour and employee relations
- Occupational health and safety

As noted elsewhere in this text, there are important distinctions between "human resources" and "human resource management" (HRM).

"Human Resource Management" (HRM) refers to all of the activities within an organization that have to do with managing people. This includes all managerial/supervisory as well as peer-to-peer activity.

"Human Resources" refers to the organizational unit — the HR Department (hereafter, "HR") — that is responsible for establishing and maintaining the framework within which HRM occurs. HR is most often thought of in tactical terms. That is, an organizational that focuses solely on administrative activities including:

- Organizational transactions
  - Defining, creating, evaluating positions and jobs
  - Establishing organizations made up of positions (and linking those organizations to organizational indicators, such as account codes)
  - Establishing HRM programs: benefits, pension, compensation, performance assessment, etc.
- People transactions

8.1 Human Resources Management Systems

- Staffing and employee movement (recruiting, selecting, hiring, promoting/demoting/transferring, terminating)
- Creating and maintaining records for employees and other human resources — contractors, consultants, applicants, students, etc.

These transactional administrative activities are critical foundation tasks that add immense value to an organization. Without these tasks being performed in a timely, complete and accurate manner an organization will founder, unable to manage the day-to-day routine that ensures that people can be acquired and employed appropriately.

Transactional administration is what HR is best known for. Much like the actor who has been type-cast,[1] HR struggles to escape this narrow definition of its capabilities.

There are many challenges that rise above these transactional activities. They include strategic planning and transformational activities that go to the heart of an organization's ability to acquire and employ people efficiently and effectively. While it is true that the jobs of some senior Human Resources personnel who do these transactional activities well do not evolve to the point of becoming involved in strategic planning for an organization, it is also true that unless these activities are done well, that HR has no chance of being seen as capable of being involved in higher level strategic functions.

There is no single definition of the line that separates strategic vs. transactional HR. There is wide-spread agreement, at least in HR circles, that the two co-exist, and that strategic HR is "essential in all major business activities and decisions".[2]

The existence of strategic HR within an organization can be seen as the moment when senior executives cannot conceive of ignoring people issues in the operation of their business.[3] Of course, in many organizations it has also been asserted that strategic people issues are of such importance that they cannot be left to HR; clearly an image problem.

Others define the awakening of strategic HR within an organization as the time when the senior HR manager is invited to join the "executive suite" with the CEO, COO, CFO and CIO. In either case, the rest of the executive suite will have accepted the proposition that HR is a key component of organizational success. To some extent the challenge to have the strategic aspects of HR recognized is the classic chicken/egg question; how can it be seen to exist until it does?

There is a strong comparison with another "back-office" function. "Accounting" is usually seen as transactional, while "Finance" is seen as strategic. It is the rare

---

1 Ralph Christensen, *ROADMAP to Strategic HR*, p. vii.
2 Report on the Society for Human Resource Management (SHRM) Symposium on the Future of Strategic HR, November 21, 2005, p. 3.
3 *Ibid.*, p. 4.

(and, one suspects, unsuccessful) organization that decides to have only Accounting functions, but not Finance.

8.2 — Internal and External Trends

It is a rare organization that does not, at least give "lip service" to the importance of its people to achieving success. Corporate annual reports commonly contain such phrases as: "our people are our most important asset".

Almost everything that organizations do has some people component. Shrinking markets and changing processes often means downsizing the workforce. Growth, whether through acquisitions, mergers, or general growth (including expansion to new countries and continents) means that more, and possible, different people must be acquired and used effectively. It may also mean that new or different organization structures have to be created, and so on.

An organization's ability to foresee and manage these changes effectively that greatly enhances its chances for success. The trends include:

1. Shortages of qualified workers. Most developed countries, including Canada and the USA, are facing shortages at all levels of the economy, most particularly shortages of "knowledge workers". These include systems analysts, engineers, database specialists, information/communications specialists. Many organizations are finding that alarming numbers of secondary and post-secondary school graduates do not have the literacy, numeracy and technical skills that they require. Some of these problems may stem from the fact that increasing numbers of employees are working in their second language, while technological and other changes are creating new demands that the educational system cannot respond to quickly enough.

2. A strong continuing emphasis on the requirement to foster management teams capable of "accomplishing more with less," and with a more diverse workforce. Most developed countries have increasingly diversified workplaces. Accompanied with a greater demand for knowledge workers of all types, along with a shrinking labour force (the baby bust), Canada and other developed countries must learn how to make best use of the new immigrants many of whom have the appropriate skills but not the proper certification for many trades and professions. Dealing with this challenge is currently a priority for many organizations and their host countries.

3. Pressure to contain human resources costs in the context of the trend by governments to off-load training /development, health, benefits and other costs onto employers.

4. Accelerating social and legislative changes (e.g., pay equity, privacy, identity theft, employment equity).

5. A need for better defined requirements in terms of skills and competencies, and the need to assess and keep track of them.
6. The complications of managing an international workforce, resulting from increased globalization.

Size used to be a predictor of complexity, but no longer. Small organizations — the huge majority of the North American economy — may have HR and HRM needs that are every bit as complex of the those of the largest organizations in the world.

8.3 — The Importance of Effective Human Resources Planning

With the support of tools such as an HRMS, human resources staff have increasingly been able to demonstrate that they can have an important contribution to corporate strategic corporate decision making. Consequently, Human Resources executives who can show that they have something important to contribute to the bottom-line success of the organization are increasingly being welcomed to sit on senior executive committees. The objective of Human Resources planning is to ensure that there are sufficient numbers of competent and motivated employees to meet an organization's current needs, and those of the foreseeable future. This is the direct link between the HR function and the organization/business's success.

The use of an HRMS in strategic corporate decision making can facilitate these goals by improving:

1. understanding of the human resources implications of business/operational strategies;
2. awareness of the experience, knowledge, and ability of the organization's employees;
3. productivity (as defined through goal setting, and measured through performance management and outcome indictors);
4. the selection of potential replacements for key/vulnerable positions; and
5. the development of existing staff to perform current and/or future roles.

8.4 — Demand and Supply Forecasting

The structure of an organization's workforce, including the number of workers (employees and/or others — such as contractors and consultants) that may be required, with specified skills, in defined positions, should be determined from the organization's strategic/business plans through *demand forecasting*. The availability of human resources to meet these demands, whether from within the organization, or from the external labour market may be determined through *supply forecasting*, as shown in Figure 1.4. The purpose of supply forecasting is to identify whether individuals exist to meet the needs of the organization. Supply forecasting is also meant to identify whether there are sufficient numbers of individuals with the potential to develop the skills that may be required for the future.

Human Resources, and its more specific component, succession planning are meant to ensure that qualified and competent individuals exist in sufficient numbers within the organization. Together, these functions constitute the employer's half of the equation, the mirror image of which is "career management", the process that looks at development and progression through the worker's perspective. Even if sufficient numbers of qualified people can be found within an organization, it can be a strategic decision to recruit a certain number from outside of the organization in an attempt to introduce fresh faces, new perspectives, a broadening of the corporate "gene pool".

Internal selection (whether through a formal succession planning process or not) and external recruitment combine to ensure that the organization will satisfy the requirement of having the "right number of individuals, doing the right things, in the right places, at the right time" (see Walker, 1980). Human resources and succession planning determine whether gaps exist in the demand and supply of human resources for the organization, and if so, how these gaps are to be dealt with.

In terms of staffing, this may mean determining first whether a vacancy exists, and then whether and how it will be filled.

Human resources and succession planning are sometimes confused. We have found the following rule of thumb to be useful in distinguishing between the two:

1. *Human resources planning* is aimed at resolving gaps that may exist with respect to human resources, either generally, or with respect to certain skills, whether across the organization, or in specific organizational units.

2. *Succession planning* is aimed at determining how specific key, and/or vulnerable positions are to be filled appropriately.

Thus, in operating specifically at the position or individual level, succession planning may be regarded as a subset or special application of human resources planning.

Globalization and other contemporary business trends have resulted in many organizations establishing a workforce world-wide making direct personal contact more difficult, and increasing the need for tracking tools. An effective HRMS will have, at minimum, modules for positions and employees. In addition, an "organization module" is often present to record how positions are structured within the organization. Using information contained in these modules, analyses can be done of such issues as:

1. the structure of the organization, as well as units within it, relative to defined organizational requirements;
2. the numbers of unfilled positions;
3. the qualifications and assessed performance of the workforce relative to present and future defined requirements;
4. the age distribution of the workforce (and therefore predicted retirements) across the organization, within organizational units, and within specific functions;
5. employment equity reports, including the distribution of women, individuals with disabilities, native people, and visible minorities in the workforce, relative to the distribution of such individuals in the population; and
6. turnover statistics (forced, unforced, etc.) by unit, function, qualifications, employment equity (affirmative action) category, etc.

Such analyses may be included in regular or ad hoc reports to executives or line management at various levels in the organization. They may also be necessary to fulfil legislative requirements such as employment equity reporting.

An effective HRMS will have the capability of creating reports that relate this information to organizational requirements in meaningful ways. Interpreted intelligently, these reports can serve as the basis of effective human resources planning.

The intent of a succession planning product is to have alternatives in place to fill gaps/vacancies in key positions, whether they occur tomorrow, or in a few years.

Many organizations, and particularly smaller organizations, do not have a formal succession planning process. It is seen as overly bureaucratic, particularly at senior levels where the CEO usually knows who she/he wants to place in a certain role if it becomes vacant. In such organizations there is little or no recognized need for any software tool since it is thought that the back of a napkin will suffice.

Larger organizations, and those that are geographically diverse regardless of size, may find a succession planning tool essential.

There are specialty software applications that facilitate both human resources and succession planning (and often career development as well). Since human resources planning pertains to very global organizational processes, most organizations find it necessary to develop reports tailored to the specific needs of the organization. Likewise, some succession planning functionality can be found in some generic HR software applications, but for the dedicated succession planner these applications generally are not sufficiently sophisticated. More sophisticated succession planning programs exist that may suit most organizations' demands.

8.5 — The Use of an HRMS in Human Resources/ Succession Planning

Figure 8.1 is a model showing demand forecasting, supply forecasting, employee information, and human resources succession planning processes that was implemented successfully by the authors in a large communications corporation and in a large forest industry research laboratory.

Human resources and succession planning are most effective when done by line management of the organizational areas involved, supported by human resources personnel.

Line (operational) management begins the process by asking the following questions:

1. Are there any special business/economic factors that are likely to have major effects on the organization over the next one to five years? For example, do foreseeable trends in the market and economic conditions lead one to believe that restructuring and/or downsizing may be necessary? What specific functions are likely to be affected? What strategic/ business plans exist to address these external influences?

2. What will the organizational unit look like one year from now? Two years from now? Three years from now? The HRMS should provide up-to-date organization charts as a starting point in this process, as well as the capability to support "what-if" modeling so that alternate organizational structures may be produced quickly.

3. What organizational problems are being experienced? This question gives the management team involved the opportunity to discuss any troublesome reporting relationships or communication problems that need addressing.

4. What human resources problems are being experienced — performance, skill, deficiencies, recruitment? How many people will be needed? When, where, and with what experience, knowledge, and ability?

8.5 Human Resources Management Systems

INPUTS

Demand Forecast	Supply Forecast	Employee Information
What are the requirements of all the positions in the unit?	What is the statistical overview?	How well are current staff performing (performance review)?
What are the key jobs within the unit?	What is the vacancy forecast?	What are the development plans, areas of interest, skills, strengths?
What human resources will be needed when, where, and with what knowledge and skills?	What resources are/will be available (using HRMS, job profiles, and career ladders)?	What are the assessment results?
What are the change plans?		

PROCESS

OUTPUTS

- Managerial review
- Human Resources/succession planning
- Implementation
- Progress feedback
- Human Resources planning
- Career development plans
- Succession plans

Answers to these questions should be documented in writing, as they may be used as the basis for the organization's business plans with respect to human resources.

Significant parts of the data required to answer the above questions (e.g., performance appraisal results, academic qualifications, skills inventories, applicant data, turnover data, job description and job requirements data) should be resident in the HRMS, as should an analysis capability, so that relationships may be drawn in the data and the results of these analyses reported in clear, "user-friendly" form.

Knowing what is on the system, as well as how to conduct the requisite analyses and report the results, provides human resources personnel with a golden opportunity for gaining credibility with line management in an area that is crucial to the long-term health of many organizations.

The human resources practitioner should be able to use the HRMS to provide statistical overviews for the whole organization, as well as each unit involved in human resources/succession planning. The overview should summarize flow data, such as recruitment, separations, promotions, transfers and turnover; and various personal data, such as gender, designated group for employment equity purposes, language(s), group and level, age, and years of service. A preliminary estimate of potential vacancies based on retirement projections should also be provided.

In the HRMS-vision of the world, where operational managers have information access directly from the system, this information would also be available for each manager with respect to the jobs and workers within their own organization.

The human resource plan of an organization, even if only to outline probable growth and metrics such as turnover, etc., would often be considered as key business information worthy of the highest security. Of necessity, most succession and/or career planning details containing individual possibilities such as transfers, promotions, terminations and retirements, raise not only the security flag, but also that of privacy.

As noted in Chapter 1, the vast inconsistent web of evolving privacy law in Canada, the U.S., and internationally makes every employer's task difficult. Regardless of the legislation in the jurisdiction(s) in which your organization operates, the rule of thumb should be caution. For example, it could be extremely disruptive should succession plan become widely known, so the security levels should be tight, and the highly personal nature of the data acknowledged and guarded appropriately.

Regardless of whether the data is in hard copy or in the latest HRMS, the key questions are: what is the "need to know", by whom, and why?[4]

The HRMS should contain, or at least have access to, job description information that can be related to its modules that have detailed information on the positions and organizational structure. It should possess the capability of presenting this information quickly, in user-friendly form.

While a fully operational Managerial Self-Service model would give line management access to this information directly it is likely that a human resources practitioner would do summary analyses including "what if" modeling as part of the planning process, providing line management information to review job descriptions/positions that will probably become vacant in the next few years and/or those that have significant operational impact. These analyses should not be

---

4 *Privacy in the Workplace – the Employment Perspective*. Toronto: CCH Canada, 2004, p. 123.

too conservative, since more than the identified positions may become vacant. The job description information should be examined to help identify the major qualities of experience, knowledge, and ability that will be required in successors to the present incumbent.

The HRMS can then be used to provide information on current employees, including the latest performance review and career development reports that have been entered on the system. Summary reports of this information prepared by human resources practitioners and supplied to line management beforehand can be used to refresh memories regarding individual strengths, areas that need improvement, career interests, and development plans.

While the human resources practitioner can help line management identify potential successors for all positions that have been identified as "key and or vulnerable," he or she can play a special role in using the HRMS to identify appropriate individuals in organizational units other than the one in question.

The human resources/succession planning module of the HRMS should have pre-established screens that allow those responsible for human resources/succession planning to document the additional knowledge experience, or formal training that is determined to be necessary for the identified individuals to qualify as candidates when each position becomes vacant.

The organizational charting function of an HRMS should be able to show the relation of such "key or vulnerable" positions to each other, and to other positions in the organization, thus providing a graphic overview of the health of management "depth" of the organization, as well as where there might be weaknesses.

Figure 8.2 provides an example of the documentation for succession planning of a single position. The methodology underlying this figure was adapted from Walker (1980) and has been used successfully in a number of organizations of various sizes over the last 25 years.

Figure 8.2 Succession Planning Chart

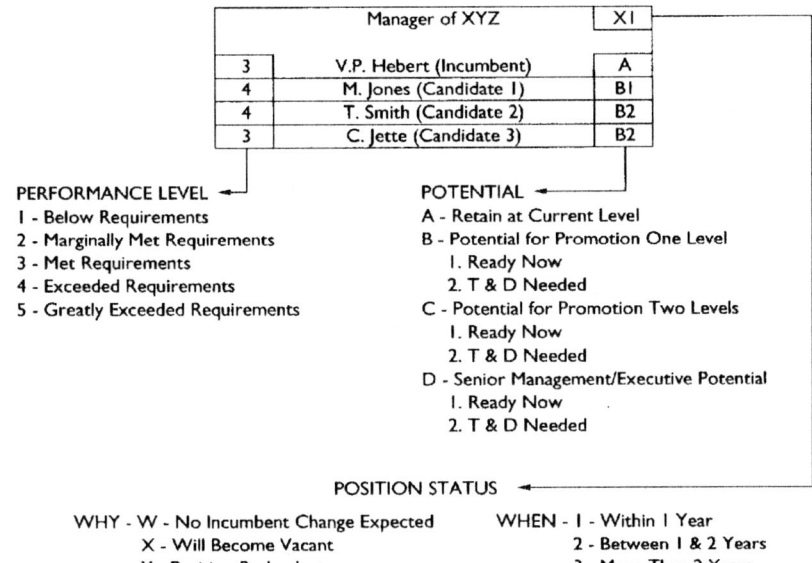

In medium and large organizations human resources/succession planning is often done by committees formed from the senior management team of the organizational unit concerned, with the head of the unit as chair and a human resources practitioner as a resource person. Such a committee attempts to reconcile the demand of workers with the required skill mix and the available supply reflected in the career planning and development information and summary reports available through the HRMS. The committee examines this information in the context of what the unit requires now and in the future, both generally and for specific positions (including employment equity considerations).

The main basis for human resources/succession plans are organizational requirements (as determined by the demand/supply forecasts outlined earlier). It is generally more effective and economical to develop human resources internally. When, however, it is evident that certain requirements will not, or may not, be met through such efforts, or when the strategy is to inject new blood into the organization, then the human resources plan must have contingencies to ensure that appropriate individuals are recruited externally.

8.6 — Case Study — Application of an HRMS in Human Resources Planning

An on-line, direct access HRMS was developed for a large communications corporation, during and after this organization made the transition from being a department of the federal government to becoming an independent corporation. Development of this HRMS was initiated within the human resources planning and development function in Head Office, so that the capability to do strategic human resources planning was a critical design feature of the system. This capability has provided the organization with the means of conducting human resources planning analyses and reports as input into corporate strategic planning processes since its implementation.

The foundations of the program are repeated here to illustrate applications of the sorts of analyses and reports alluded to above.[5]

1. A detailed analysis of the organization's business plan was conducted, with the focus on comparing estimates of natural attrition with forecasts based on past separation patterns and retirement eligibility. This study highlighted the importance of good attrition forecasts in determining person- year requirements.

2. Several analyses were conducted for line managers on specific key employee groups. These analyses focused on eligibility for retirement data, as well as predictions regarding positions that would be vacant. Analysis of the population of likely feeder groups was then completed to identify the potential for filling these positions with existing internal resources, and/or to flag future gaps in supply versus demand.

3. The groundwork was laid to ensure that the organization had the necessary data and programs in place to meet the requirements of the federal employment equity legislation.

4. Analysis of the "hidden workforce" examined the use of personnel services contracts by different departments and discussed patterns regarding the implications of replacing these contracted resources with employee person-years.

5. Monthly snapshots of front-line employee population highlighted factors such as male/female ratios, anglophone/ francophone distributions, full-time/part-time ratios, as well as age distribution and eligibility for retirement. One object of these analyses was to monitor the progress of retrenchment activities underway at that time, and to provide feedback on the impact of redeployment on human resources (including staffing) policies and programs.

---

[5] Murray and Rampton (1986).

6. Population analyses were conducted on major functional groups (Operations and Marketing, Personnel and Labour Relations, Management Information Systems) with emphasis on factors to be considered in an accelerated attrition/downsizing program (e.g., differences in strength by division and by bargaining unit, ratio of male/female employees, eligibility for retirement and for accelerated attrition, and forecasts of the number likely to apply for accelerated attrition).

At the time those six (6) foundation activities were written, the organization was in the early stages of developing an HRMS-based human resources planning program. Most organizations in this situation will find, as this one did, that, of necessity, early analysis will tend to deal more with what is, rather than what will be.

Forecasting activities concentrated on predicting the eligibility for retirement and for accelerated attrition, estimating the numbers likely to apply for accelerated attrition, and extrapolating past natural attrition patterns into the future. This, of course, reflected the internal and external pressures on the organization at the time. The groundwork was, however, laid to use more sophisticated modeling/simulation techniques, among other things to prepare a proactive human resources plan.

In addition, while concepts such as Managerial Self-Service (MSS) have made it possible for line managers to access this type of data and to generate their own analysis and reports, it is still highly unlikely that they will do so. They will turn, and rightly so in most instances, to the specialists, HR, to provide the detailed analysis, focusing their own attentions on the decisions to be made.

8.7 — Measuring HRM Practices and Value

In order to plan effectively there also needs to be a feedback loop that allows the planner(s) to assess the accuracy and impact of the plans. Some degree of assessment of success is required, often at the individual, team, and organization levels.

Assessment of people and their organizations is most often both qualitative and quantitative.[6] Every activity, and the person/people performing that activity, can be measured using four (4) key attributes: Quality, Quantity, Cost (direct and indirect), and Time (both cycle and process time).

As mentioned throughout this book, and in particular in Chapter 3, there are many terms used for this activity, including, benchmarking (including best practices), cost/benefit analysis, metrics, balanced scorecard, utility analysis, and return on investment (ROI). On a personal level we have various performance appraisal

---

6 Belcourt and McBey, *Strategic Human Resources Planning*, 2nd ed. Nelson, 2004.

8.7 Human Resources Management Systems

options including the traditional supervisor/employee one-on-one, peer-to-peer and/or team review such as 360 degree feedback, etc.

The purpose in all cases is to assess the relative achievement and worth of an individual, a team, an organizational unit, or an entire organization. In the case of the HR Department the underlying question is, where is the value?

The role of a HRMS in these various measurement activities is to be the tool to collect, analyze and report on these measures. These measures can be applied to any functional area of human resources:

Training	Health & Safety
Organization Development — includes organization design, positions/jobs creation	Strategic & Tactical Planning
Compensation — includes base pay, performance management, variable pay, benefits, pension, payroll	Staffing — includes advertising/posting, managing applicants, internal employee movement
Worker records management	Employee/labour Relations

Measures are intended to make clear: what are we supposed to do? And How will we (and you) know when it is done, and how well?

Almost without exception, the HR (and payroll) systems available today allow for effective date management and data history so that any action is recorded by date (and often by time) as well as the individual making the entry, and the nature of the entry. These software functions, combined with Employee (ESS) and Managerial (MSS) self-service can be used to measure business processes.

Audit trails record every action and can be used (with the proper notice to workers) for monitoring levels and nature of activity. Individual processes can be tracked by type and then analyzed to determine effectiveness and efficiency at each step.

Figure 8.3 Staffing a Replacement Worker

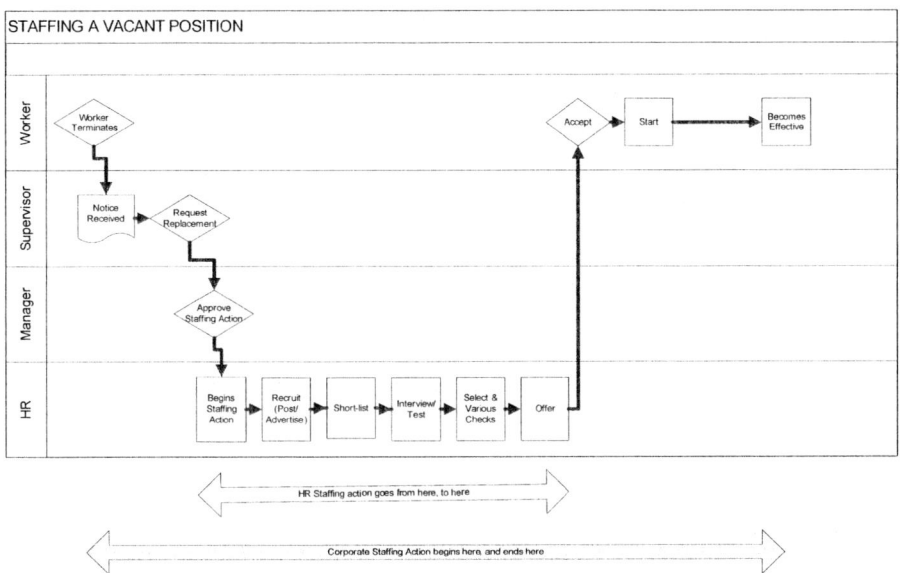

As you can see from the extremely simplified flow chart, above, there are TWO different timetables. One, the HR timetable, tracks from the date HR is notified until a person is hired. This is the metric that is most commonly captured. It is certainly useful to measure the Staffing Group, and/or a particular staffing officer's effectiveness.

BUT, the other charts the time that elapses from the moment notice is received until the date/time that the replacement employee becomes effective. THIS is much less frequently captured, and yet is far more useful in determining the real amount time (and therefore, the real cost) expended because of a worker's resignation.

Which measure is more important for Operations and Executive Management?

Similar illustrations to Figure 8.3 can be drawn for each functional area of HR. Measures can be specific to a unit, a department, the company, or a function such as HR. The more sophisticated the HRMS, the more possibilities exist in gathering and analyzing data on which to ground better decisions.

8.8 — Outsourcing

Outsourcing has become an extremely hot trend throughout business, and throughout HR, as both a strategic and tactical tool. Most organizations outsource some aspect of HR, namely benefits administration, and many other tasks have followed. Regardless of whether or not your organization outsources a task, or group of tasks, there are some fundamental rules that should be followed.

First it is important to realize that the responsibility still lies with the organization and not with the service provider.[7]

Second, every task that is outsourced needs to be clearly defined so that the organization and the outsourcer both understand what is being outsourced — i.e., the scope, and how the success of the outsourcing will be measured. Metrics are invaluable for this latter activity.

The Service Level Agreement (SLA) that is developed can contain specific metrics that allow both you and the outsourcer the opportunity to understand exactly how well they are performing, and to make service and or payment adjustments accordingly.

The use of a HRMS can help address any issue that is based in people and how they work. Occupational Health and Safety is becoming increasingly important as health costs rise and governments pass on more economic responsibility for health to employers.

8.9 — Case Study — Safety Statistics

A heavy manufacturer located in a Maritime province was experiencing extremely troubling safety issues. The four divisions had all experienced accidents on a frequent basis, there had been some serious accidents including one death, and the overall corporate safety record was barely seven days worked without a lost time accident.

The President was extremely concerned. He wanted to focus the attention of his management team, the supervisors, and the employees on prevention and mandated a new training program. He also wanted a tool that showed the entire work force that there was improvement, however slow it might be.

The solution was to enter accidents and injuries as they occurred by division, work centre, and various other factors. The data entered included all of the information generated by supervisors and health and safety staff from the time of the incident to the final resolution. Most of this information had been paper-based and was not easily analyzed or reported on. The HRMS implementation had included Managerial Self-Service (MSS) so line supervisors and health and safety staff could enter the information directly without the inefficiency of first documenting everything on paper.

Reports were designed to provide daily, weekly, and monthly statistics by work group, division and the organization as a whole.

---

[7] Ian Turnbull, The Outsourcing Challenge, Canadian Payroll Association, *Dialogue Magazine*, July 2005.

In addition to health and safety matters supervisors used MSS to enter/access various other pieces of information, including time entries and work assignments for their workers. To ensure that every supervisor focused on this problem the HRMS was set-up so that every supervisor was forced to go through four screens/panels:

- Screen/panel #1 – the welcome screen.

- Screen/panel #2 – an HRMS real-time generated chart showing corporate safety statistics for the last seven days, last month, and last year.

- Screen/panel #3 – the same information as Screen/panel #2 PLUS an overlay of the specific comparative statistics for the supervisor/manager's division.

- Screen/panel #4 – the same information as screen/panel #3 PLUS an overlay showing that individual supervisor's work team (direct reports) statistics.

The President was thrilled. Not only was the gathering of data more efficient, but every supervisor at every level would be seeing comparative statistics every time they logged on the system. He then required that divisional and corporate management meetings add those same safety statistics to their agendas. Not surprisingly the up-to-date information combined with the comparisons with the other work units and divisions had the desired effect; safety became a priority. Again, not surprisingly, the safety record improvements were far more dramatic than had been hoped.

NOTE: This case illustrates that the right tool (HRMS) can be used effectively for both HR purposes (health and safety records and reports) AND to directly support operational requirements. Although the specific example in this case is tactical, it achieves several important strategic goals:

- To make the workplace safer for workers;

- To make the organization a more desirable employer (since the bad safety record was well-known in the community);

- To improve profitability by achieving fewer lost days due to accidents, and by reducing the time (and expense) spent investigating and coping with accidents and injuries; and

- To reduce corporate exposure to damaging negative public relations and potential fines from government.

The preceding case also demonstrates that information can be generated and used in many different ways. "Reports", either standard or customized, can be generated and viewed without the necessity of printing hard copy. Want to see last month's information? Merely use the effective dating feature to re-create that month's view.

8.9 Human Resources Management Systems

Many vendors offer other display alternatives. If an organization uses an intranet (internal internet site), HR information generated by the HRMS can be placed on individual users' home pages or portal application.

Another reporting tool, known by various names, including "executive dashboard"[8] provides a series of visual — often colourful and graphical — views of data. Offered by HRMS vendors and third party software providers, dashboards are usually designed to display summary information that the user can then use to drill down to ever increasing amounts of information and data.

"Dashboards" displaying some type of analytics are driven by report tools and are limited only by the nature of the reporting and graphics packages of the HRMS. Some dashboards are numerical, some graphical, and most, both. The content and the look and feel vary as widely as the users of such tools.

In the example below (Figure 8.4) the organization's President specifically wanted statistics on health and safety issues, most particularly lost day accidents. He wanted these displays to be on every user's sign-on page so that the issue would be seen as important.

Figure 8.4 Lost Day Accident Data[9]

	Jan	Feb	Mar	Apr	May	June	Average
Unit 1	1	0	0	2	2	1	1.0
Unit 2	0	0	3	0	0	0	0.5
Unit 3	4	2	1	3	2	4	2.7
Unit 4	1	0	0	0	0	0	0.2
Unit 5	0	1	2	0	0	0	0.5
Unit 6	0	0	0	1	0	0	0.2
Units 1-6	6	3	6	6	4	5	5.0
Units 7-12	4	2	2	0	2	3	2.2
Units 13-17	1	3	2	2	4	4	2.7
Units 18-26	0	0	0	1	2	0	0.5
Division	11	8	10	9	12	12	10.3
Average Unit	0.423	0.308	0.385	0.346	0.462	0.462	0.397

---

[8] Gathered 06-07-10 from <http://www.visualmining.com/products/executive-dashboards.shtml?gclid=CJearKezj4YCFSFXPgodGQWW7w>.

[9] Actual case data from 2003. Organization identifiers removed. Courtesy Laird & Greer Management Consultants.

Human Resources Strategic & Tactical Planning 8.9

Figure 8.5 Executive Dashboard #1

The data above shows how the unit of the user (likely the supervisor of Unit 1) compares to the other units in her section (Units 1-6), and vs. the Division as a whole. It leads to a series of questions, such as:

- Why was January so high?
- Why was April so low for Units 1-6 and the Division while Unit 1 had an accident?
- Etc.

A second dashboard then followed the first providing even more comparative information:

Figure 8.5 Executive Dashboard #2

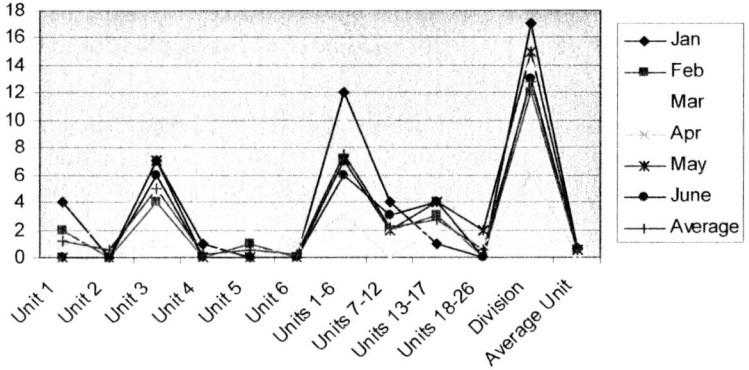

This figure highlights that Units 1-6 are high contributors to lost time accidents, and that Units 3, 1 and 5 are the worst offenders. It may be that there are perfectly acceptable explanations (although lost time accidents are rarely considered "acceptable").

There are other pieces of actionable management information that can be gathered from the data table in Figure 8.4, including the number of lost day accidents per month, and on average. In addition analysis could be provided to show the causes of lost time accidents, the number of lost days per accident, etc.

In the example above, the dashboard was available to the entire management group, but dashboards can be used to convey desired information to selected audiences as well. Some packages allow the user to define some or all of their own dashboard contents, while others have a core that can be supplemented by an individual user's choices.

These tools allow management much greater access to key operating information about the human resources under their control, thus improving their level of information and the timeliness of it. This, in turn, should mean a more nimble management group that can adjust to circumstances in order to meet their tactical and strategic objectives.

8.10 — Summary

Many organizations claim that their human resources are their most important asset. However, few actually devote the organizational priority and resources to fostering this asset to the extent that such a claim would seem to require.

There is some evidence that this is changing, as it becomes more and more evident to the leadership in progressive organizations that the key to future success in the quickly evolving business environment will be how they plan for and develop their workforce.

The volume and complexity of information required for effective human resources planning and development requires the support of an effective HRMS. Integrated data from all functions that is available to create actionable management information can be used to turn basic HR management into best-of-class human resource management. This chapter has discussed the use of an HRMS in this very important application.

KEY LEARNING POINTS

- HR is often not considered to be a strategic function.
- Tactical responsibilities have to be done well before strategic acceptance can occur.

- Strategic HR occurs when line management accepts the value of quality human resources and human resource management.
- The better the information on which a decision is based, the better the decision.
- HRMSs offer tool sets to capture data and to analyze and present quality information in a timely and actionable manner.
- Metrics (need to define) and other measurement tools are made possible by entering data into the HRMS and can be used to achieve tactical and strategic goals.
- The term "Reports" does not refer to hard copy paper alone. Increasingly a report is a temporary presentation of information that can be re-presented as required without the need to store anything more than the format.
- Visual tools such as executive dashboards provide a new level of information presentation in an effective and timely manner, facilitating the link between day-to-day management and strategic goals.

8.11 — References

Belcourt, M., A.W. Sherman, G.W. Bohlander, and S.A. Snell. 1996. *Managing Human Resources*, Canadian ed. Toronto: Nelson Canada.

Belcourt, M and McBey, K., 2004. *Strategic Human Resources Planning*, 2nd ed. Nelson Canada.

Cascio, W.F., and J.W. Thacker. 1994. *Managing Human Resources*. Toronto: McGraw-Hill Ryerson.

Christensen, R. 2006. *ROADMAP to Strategic HR*. New York, AMACOM.

Coates, J.F. 1990. *Change Requires Retraining: Success Depends on Workplace Skills*. Technical Report. Washington, D.C.: J.F. Coates Inc.

Director, S. 1985. *Strategic Planning for Human Resources*. Oxford: Pergamon.

Dyer, L., and G.W. Holder. 1988. "A Strategic Perspective of Human Resource Management." In L. Dyer, ed., *Human Resource Management: Evolving Roles and Responsibilities*. Washington, D.C.: Bureau of National Affairs.

Horsfield, D. 1991. "Human Resource Planning Applications." In A.L. Lederer, ed., *Handbook of Human Resource Information Systems*. New York: Warren, Gorham and Lamont.

Kazanas, H.C. 1988. *Strategic Human Resources Planning and Management*. Englewoods Cliffs, N.J.: Prentice-Hall.

Liker, J., and R.J. Thomas. 1991. "Prospects for Human Development in the Context of Technological Change: Lessons from a Major Technological Renovation." In D. Kocacglu, ed., *Handbook of Human Resource Information Systems*. New York: Warren, Gorham and Lamont.

Murray, L.A., and G.M. Rampton. 1986. *Human Resource Planning*. Ottawa: Directorate of Human Resources Planning and Development. Report, Canada Post Corporation.

Niehaus, R.J. 1987. *Strategic Human Resources Planning Applications*. New York: Plenum Press.

Rampton, G.M., and J.A. Doran. 1994. "A Practitioner's Guide for a New HRIS." Unpublished paper presented at the 9th annual CHRSP conference (October): 4-7.

Schneider, B., and A. Konz. 1989. "Strategic Job Analysis." *Human Resource Management* 28: 51-63.

Snell, S.A., P. Pedigo, and G.M. Krawiec. 1994. "Managing the Impact of Information Technology on Human Resources Management." In G.R. Ferris, S.D. Rosen, and D.T. Barnum, eds., *Handbook of Human Resources Management*. Oxford: Blackwell Publishers.

Snow, C.C. 1987. *Strategy, Organization Design, and Human Resources Management*. Greenwich, Conn.: Jai Press.

Soloman, C.M. "Managing the H. R. Career in the 90s." *Personnel Journal* 73, no. 6 (June): 62-76.

Stewman, S. 1986. "Demographic Models of Internal Labour Markets." *Administrative Science Quarterly* 31: 212-47.

Stright, J.F. 1993. "Strategic Goals Guide HRMS Development." *Personnel Journal* (September): 68-78.

Towers, Perrin. 1992. *Priorities for a Competitive Advantage, an IBM-Towers Perrin Study*. New York: Towers Perrin.

Urlich, D. 1986. "Human Resource Planning as a Competitive Edge." *Human Resource Planning* 9, no. 2: 41-50.

Wagel, W.H. 1990. "On the Horizon: HR in the 1990s." *Personnel* 67, no. 1: 11-16.

Walker, J.W. 1980. *Human Resources Planning*. Toronto: McGraw-Hill.

Chapter 9: Staffing

9.1 — Introduction

In helping to shape the organization's human resources, the staffing function plays an important role in maintaining the long-term health of the organization. Even in those organizations where HR staff (and possibly staffing specialists/ employment counselors) do not make direct selection decisions, but support line management in this role, the counselors still have great influence through file screening and specialized HR support provided to both line management and applicants.

The staffing function also has an important public relations role since employees' first impressions of an organization are often formed by contact with the staffing component of its HR function. Further, the organization's image and reputation may be significantly affected by the way that job openings are advertised and unsuccessful applicants are treated. An HRMS is an important support tool for staffing personnel to identify human resources needs and priorities, effectively and efficiently fill these needs now and in the future, and present a professional public image. This chapter discusses the use of an HRMS in support of the staffing function.

The computer and the Internet have become important tools for all of HR but nowhere more than in the staffing function.

9.2 — Staffing Model

In Figure 9.1, the human resources model is applied to staffing.

Staffing specialists often see their jobs as consisting solely of the functions outlined in the boxes at level 3. But, as we saw in Chapter 1, human resources personnel must adopt a broader perspective of their domain. Supported by an effective HRMS, the traditional human resources functions should be placed in the broader strategic context of the external environmental and business pressures impinging on the organization. These are then tied to traditional human resources programs through strategic planning and demand forecasting.

9.2 Human Resources Management Systems

Figure 9.1 Staffing

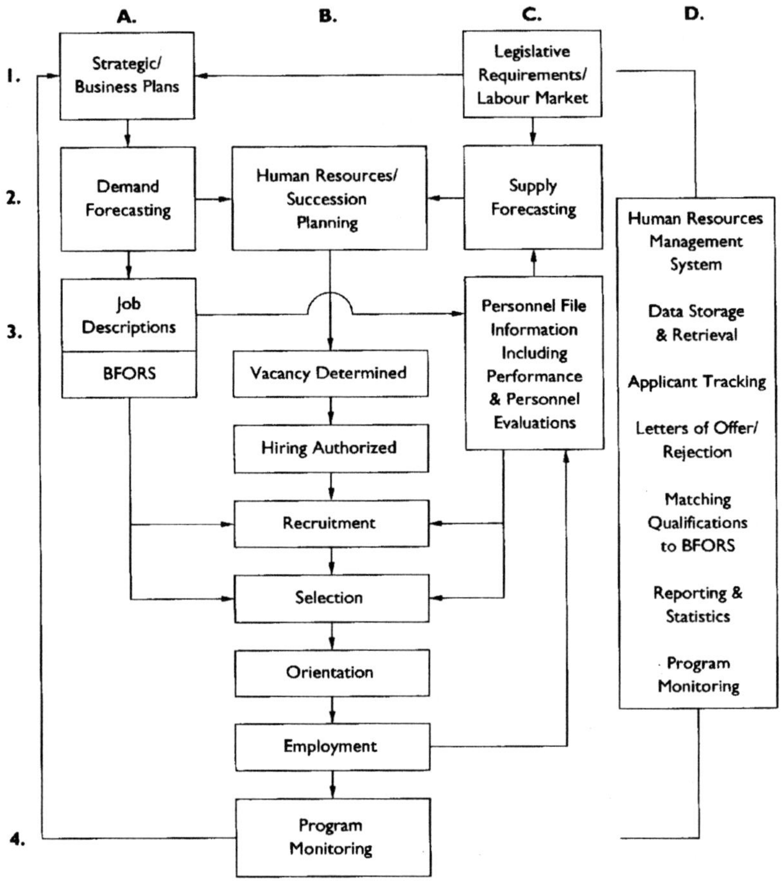

	A.	B.	C.	D.
1.	Strategic/Business Plans		Legislative Requirements/Labour Market	
2.	Demand Forecasting	Human Resources/Succession Planning	Supply Forecasting	Human Resources Management System
3.	Job Descriptions / BFORS	Vacancy Determined → Hiring Authorized → Recruitment → Selection → Orientation → Employment	Personnel File Information Including Performance & Personnel Evaluations	Data Storage & Retrieval / Applicant Tracking / Letters of Offer/Rejection / Matching Qualifications to BFORS / Reporting & Statistics / Program Monitoring
4.		Program Monitoring		

Most human resources programs are sufficiently complex that they cannot be changed overnight. The cost involved and the time required to implement change in these programs necessitates sound planning and lead time. To effectively support the organization's operations, human resources programs, including an HRMS, must be designed not only to meet current external and internal strategic requirements, but also to anticipate evolving requirements.

Thus, staffing specialists must understand the external labour market, as well as its socio-demographic context and evolving legal requirements. Only then can effective, efficient recruitment strategies be developed, in accordance with organizational needs and legislative requirements such as pay or employment equity.

An HRMS must be structured to contain information, perform analyses, and prepare reports that are useful in the organization's larger strategic planning processes. The nature and form of this support, information, analyses, and reports should depend on organizational requirements.

9.3 — Staffing Programs: An Overview

Block A-3 of the staffing model outlined in Figure 9.1 suggests that, at the individual level, the organization's human resources requirements should be reflected in job descriptions. In keeping with employment equity legislation, the minimal criteria (e.g., skill, experience, training/education and certification) required for each position are recorded on these job descriptions as "bona fide occupational requirements (BFORs)."[1] Essential job profile information on each position in the organization may be contained in the HRMS position module mentioned above. Information on employee skills, experience, qualifications, performance history, employment equity category, and biographical information will be contained in an HRMS employee module.

When a vacancy is determined and hiring is authorized, staffing specialists should check to ensure that up-to-date job descriptions/job requirements for the position are available. This information, along with documented bona fide occupational requirements, is then incorporated into a job posting. The advertising to be done will vary. In some cases it may be felt that the jobs should be advertised externally; some organizations, however, may prefer to fill a certain proportion of their vacancies through internal promotion. Such decisions may be made on the basis of information from succession planning, supported by documented performance and personnel evaluation information.

All recruiting and selection processes should be conducted objectively and fairly, based on BFORs, to ensure the most effective use of human resources, to fulfill employment equity requirements, and to ensure company morale and maintain confidence in the system. What is done must not only be fair and objective; it must be seen as fair and objective as well.

Once the individual is selected, he or she will normally pass through an orientation phase. A formal letter of offer will be accepted, and the new employee will be briefed about and signed on to benefits programs, entered on payroll, etc., prior to being employed on-the-job.

9.4 — Applications

Most mid-size and large organizations have found it necessary to develop effective HRMS tools to support their very complicated staffing and training functions.

Some large organizations such as the military, these organizations typically recruit most of their personnel at the beginning of their careers, and then provide them

---

1 BFORs, see Belcourt *et al.*, 1996; Cascio and Thacker, 1994.

9.4 Human Resources Management Systems

with the training and experience necessary to do their jobs. Many of these jobs are highly technical and demanding. Therefore, great care is taken in human resources planning, selection, training, and development, because errors cannot generally be corrected by terminating the employment of a trained serviceman and replacing that individual with an external applicant at the same level. These organizations are also very large, with recruiting being done from across the country, and training and deployment of personnel conducted not only across the parent country but in other parts of the world as well.

The processes involved in managing human resources functions such as human resources planning, staffing, induction, and training are complicated and interrelated, requiring extensive HRMS support. Large organizations commonly have separate headquarter directorates responsible for recruiting and selection, training, requirements control, manpower analysis, manpower utilization, career management, and second careers. All receive regular and ad hoc reports from central human resources files and/or systems on which they rely for data and analysis relevant to their particular needs.

On the position/structure side of the organization, other directorates exist for determining military occupational structures and performing on-site personpower reviews. Extensive survey/interview-based processes have traditionally been used for determining job requirements and organizational structures. The data thus gathered have generally been collected, stored, and analyzed using programs such as the Comprehensive Occupational Data Analysis Programs (CODAP). CODAP has been widely used by a number of Western military forces, as well as such civilian corporations as Ontario Hydro.

HRMSs are used to conduct human resources modeling to project the need for human resources in the various occupational classifications. The Canadian Government has established a set of National Occupation Codes (NOCs) and the U.S. has a similar process. There may also be industry specific code structures, one example being military occupational specialties (MOSs), as they are known in the American military forces.

Recruiting and selection quotas are then established and assigned to recruiting and selection units across the organization either by functional group and/or by geography. The timing of specific job openings is also coordinated, through the use of HRMS programs, with the availability of training slots for certain skills and/or knowledge courses. The scheduling of these training programs is based in large part on the human resources modeling made possible by an HRMS.

Information on individuals who are applicants for positions is often maintained on "applicant tracking files" That may be part of the HRMS or a add-on application. The more sophisticated applications allow the employer to track internal and external candidates for more than one staffing action/competition since applicants passed over in one competition may be a good match for another, with significant potential cost-savings.

Privacy laws usually apply to external applicants, and depending on the jurisdiction, to internal applicants as well. This is particularly true if the applicant comes from a recruiting firm of some kind since the personal information will be passed from that organization to the hiring organization.[2]

"Onboarding" — the process of bringing a new worker into the organization structure — occurs in every organization and is often triggered by the end of the staffing process. Onboarding includes orientation activities and also occurs when relevant information not previously collected in the Applicant Tracking module/application is collected and entered.

Some of the data normally not be collected at the Applicant stage could include (in Canada) an applicants date of birth, race, picture and Social Insurance Number.

Other additional data include biographical, selection (aptitude test scores, results of selection interviews), etc. The transition from being an "Applicant" to an "Employee", and therefore the start of the actual "employee file", occurs as of the effective date of the employment.

Staffing functionality is a key part of HRMS applications in most large and complex organizations. The same general concepts, however, apply in much smaller applications, although in these cases more informal techniques may be used in some areas.

For example, some years ago, similar procedures were implemented at the Pulp and Paper Research Institute of Canada (PAPRICAN), a research and education organization consisting of about 400 personnel, mainly scientists, engineers, and technicians. This prominent research centre plays an important role in keeping one of Canada's most important industries at the forefront of technology in its sector. Scientists and engineers are recruited from around the world. Human resources planning, staffing, and other human resources programs are very important to attracting and keeping the best possible personnel in research and research support roles. PAPRICAN's HRMS had virtually all of the capabilities discussed in the previous example. If anything, because of the nature of the personnel involved, more information was required on each individual in the primary HRMS modules, as well as in applicant tracking, although the numbers of individuals involved was many times less.

(a) — Shortages of Qualified Workers

As noted in Chapter 8, most developed countries, including Canada and the U.S.A., are facing shortages at all levels of the economy, most particularly shortages of "knowledge workers". As finding the right person at the right time becomes more difficult it will become increasingly important to use whatever

---

[2] Privacy in the Workplace — the Employment Perspective, The Canadian Privacy Institute, CCH 2004.

tools may exist to make your organization's staffing processes more efficient and effective.

Well-designed and effective HRMS, when integrated with the Internet and associated tools will give your staffing function that advantage.

(b) — Internet Job Sites

Job sites have largely replaced newspapers as the primary source of employment advertising, and they offer ancillary services as added incentive to employers and employees alike. For example, "My Monster" from Monster.com suggests, "We have changed more than our look. It is now easier to find great career advice, interesting articles and with the new My Monster we have made finding a new job even easier!"[3]

Benefits include reviewing open positions, getting the site to screen according to your criteria so that you only get advised of jobs that appear to be a fit with your criteria, track your applications, posting multiple versions of your résumé, etc.

Applying for jobs on-line can have positive and negative aspects. For the applicant it is usually simpler to send your résumé electronically. It avoids the cost and time required for postal service and is quicker and easier to use than a facsimile.

From the employers' perspective posting a job on the web is no more difficult than writing up a newspaper ad or internal posting, and the cost is normally less than the advertisement.

Many employers, especially those requiring computer skills, insist that applicants apply only by email or online. The theory is that this process provides some level of pre-screening.

But employers may have a different perspective as well. The ease of application means that many applicants can apply for a job with the investment of a couple of keystrokes. This has had the impact of significantly increasing the number of applications, and the number of poor-fit applications, considerably. Qualified applicants see this as a negative as well since the employer is now bogged down by a multitude of poor-fit applications and in the process of weeding those out some legitimate, qualified people may be screened out.

A significant pro, and con, of on-line posting is that it has no geographic boundaries. Advertise in a local paper and you are ensuring that the bulk, if not all, of the applicants will be local. Wider searches by traditional methods cost a lot more, but you can target specific areas. Want people in Vancouver? Then advertise there.

But post a job on the web and seconds later it can be read, and responded to, by people anywhere in the world. This is of particular concern for jobs where the

---

[3] Gathered 06/08/16 from <http://www.monster.ca/makeover/>.

employer has no interest in paying interviewing expenses, let alone paying for a household move. The increased volume of applications can significantly complicate the search competition process.

The speed of the electronic process — almost instantaneous receipt of applications, etc. — can contribute to another problem. In organizations that focus on efficiency rather than effectiveness recruiters may be evaluated on the speed that it takes to fill positions rather than ensuring that the most effective individuals are hired, which can be much more difficult to measure. Thus, focusing on getting someone in the door as quickly as possible may prevent getting the best and the brightest candidates.[4]

For many years western military forces have taken great pains to validate their staffing procedures against clear training and employment outcomes (see, for example, Wiscoff and Rampton, 1989).

Job Seekers Beware

Readers of this book, be they students, HRMS, HR, Payroll, I/T or general management are all, as individuals, job seekers. It is important to circulate a résumé when looking for work, but these days criminals and identity thieves are all too interested in finding and using résumés for all the wrong reasons. In the information economy, your résumé has a "street value." It's sad to say, but unfortunately your name, home address, telephone number, even your detailed work history can have value to identity thieves and fraudsters. It is also important to protect your résumé from people and businesses who want to use it primarily to make a profit instead of primarily to help you find employment.

To minimize risk while you look for a job, it is important to learn when and where to post a résumé. It's also important to know what kind of job offers to respond to and what ones are best to ignore. The key is to attract legitimate employers while avoiding the people and fraudulent businesses that can potentially harm you. Circulate your résumé by all means, but take care to avoid exposure to bad actors who don't have your best interests at heart.

#1: If you're going to post a résumé online, post your résumé "privately."

> Most job sites offer anonymous posting that lets you mask your contact information and e-mail address when you post a résumé. This résumé posting option allows you to decide who sees your real information,

---

[4] "Recruiting specialists share what works best, and what missteps to avoid. Don't let processes get in the way of a good hire, and other lessons" by Ann Macaulay, Canadian HR Reporter, June 6, 2005.

such as your home address. Masking this information is perhaps the single most important step job seekers who want to post a résumé online can take to protect themselves.

#2: Not everyone who has access to a résumé database should.

> It's not just employers that access your résumé on résumé databases. Criminals and fraudsters posing as recruiters can gain illicit access to résumé databases, among others.

#3: Not every job offer you see is for a real job — some jobs are just scams.

> After you post your résumé, you may hear from a person offering you a job that is a scam. Fake job scams have become a very serious problem in online job searching. If you are asked to send additional information or money, beware.

#4: The more general the e-mail "job" offer, the less valid it usually is.

> So you posted your résumé, and now you are getting responses. Be wise and discerning. Not every offer is worth your time. Some job offers are outright scams (see #3) and some job offers are just attempt to get you to post your résumé on a new job site. Other job offers are simply marketing emails to get you to spend money on "help" finding a job.

#5: Even the most careful, conscientious sites cannot control your résumé after someone has downloaded it.

> After you have posted your résumé, it can be downloaded and used in ways you may never have imagined, and may not like. Job sites do not have the ability to control how a recruiter or employer uses your résumé after it is has been downloaded. Most sites watch for problems such as rapid résumé downloads — and enforce terms of use agreements with employers and recruiters. But let the job seeker beware. When it comes to résumé databases, job sites place onus on the job seeker to understand the risks involved in posting a résumé online.

> The bottom line: after you have posted your résumé openly, you have almost no control over how it will be used, by whom, or for how long. You can ease this problem by posting your résumé privately, with your contact information hidden.

#6: Unless you are required to do so, never put an identifying number like a Social Insurance Number (SIN) on your résumé.

> You should only give your SIN to an employer after you have fully validated them as a legitimate employer. Beware of fake job offers, especially those for "work at home" offers.

#7: Using a disposable e-mail address and a P.O. Box can save you from many headaches later on.

> It is not a good idea to post a résumé openly online. But if you decide to post your résumé to a site that does not allow you to mask your identity, then mask it yourself. Use an e-mail address that you can cancel if you start getting spam, and don't give out your full name, phone number, or home address. Use a post office box, and do not give your street address to an employer until you have verified them fully.

#8: Things to omit from your résumés if you post it online . . . your references, for sure. Your school name, possibly.

> When you post a résumé online, there are some categories of information you need to think about leaving off. First, references. If you put your references' names and phone numbers on your résumé, you are giving their information away without their consent in what can be a very public forum. Omit this information, in particular when you put your résumé online in any fashion. As a courtesy to your references: leave them off of your online résumés.

> School information is tricky. Education is a necessary category on a résumé. The problem is that anyone can call up your school and get what is called "directory information" without your consent. This can include your name, date of birth, home address, and other vital information. Some people simply list their degree and date, and let the employer ask for the name of the college in the interview. But if you graduated from a prestigious institution of higher learning, you may want to brag about it, so, fine, but understand the risks and mitigate what you can.

#9: Some résumé databases are better than others.

> Before posting a résumé to any database, take the time to look for and read the privacy policy of that site and query the site owner with any privacy concerns. Be sure to look for specific privacy policy statements about résumés, registration information, and statements about how that information is used, stored, and shared. If the site does not have a privacy policy posted, that should be a signal that you should be especially cautious about posting a résumé there, if at all. And if you cannot delete your résumé, don't post it.

> One word about job sites: some job sites share résumés between themselves. Don't be surprised if after posting your résumé at one site, if it shows up at another.

#10: Delete does not always mean delete.

Make sure the job site or résumé site lets you delete your résumé whenever you want to. Also, look for information about how long a site says it will keep or store your résumé. This information can usually be found in the privacy policy or terms of use section.

Job and résumé sites should state that they promise to let you delete your résumé whenever you want to, and will only keep your résumé for a limited, specific amount of time, such as one to six months, after which the site will delete your résumé. Without specific, written statements about how long your résumé may be kept, your résumé can be archived for years, legally. Most job seekers do not want résumés circulating after they have gotten a job. Before you post a résumé, check to make sure you can delete your résumé after you have posted it

A note about résumé writing services:

If you plan on using a résumé writing service in your job search efforts, get an agreement in writing that the service will not sell or share your résumé with any third parties or partners. Unfortunately, this does happen at some résumé writing services.

Also, ask to see the privacy policy of any résumé writing services you may use and ask specifically about how the service handles and stores your résumé. This applies to traditional and online résumé writing services.

#11: Keeping good records is crucial for online job searching

Be sure to keep a record of where you have posted your résumé online. Sometimes, you will not have an e-mail record because you will have posted your résumé into a form on a Web site. Print all of these out when you post your résumé, and keep copies.

#12: Prevention is better than the cure.

If you believe your résumé or personal job search data, including your e-mail address or your name, has been shared or used in a way inconsistent with a job site's posted privacy policy, you have little ability if any to fix the problem after the fact. This is an unfortunate reality today. Perhaps this will change in the future, but for now, it is much better to prevent problems than to try and fix them afterward.[5]

---

5 Gathered 06/08/16 from <http://www.worldprivacyforum.org/resumedatabaseprivacy-tips.html>.

(c) — Managing Staffing

Many organizations have software that allows them to track applicants through the staffing process from first response to job offer (or to a pool of future candidates). Known by various names such as "applicant tracking", or "staffing" or "recruiting" this software has the capability of allowing an organization to quickly and efficiently manage the entire staffing process, starting with the vacancy and moving through hiring authorization, recruitment, selection, orientation and employment.

These processes may be accessed through a software application that may or may not be "web based." An organization may offer access through the web in one of three ways. Web pages that are used only internally are known as "intranet", while pages/functionality that are used internally and by selected external third parties is known as "extranet". The third access method is to use the Internet directly.

In some such applications managers/supervisors are able to directly initiate the hiring process, input their interview notes, and access the status of the staffing competition.

Similarly, if employee self-service has been initiated employees can see vacant job postings and apply for them on-line.

In order to understand the application of technology to the staffing function let us examine just some of the HR and Staffing activities that can be enhanced by technology:

- On-line Recruitment
- Referral
- Exit Interviews
- Accommodation

(i) Recruitment On-Line

A "Job Opportunities" page should be a prominent link on your organization's main home page and may be segmented into internal postings only, versus positions that are open to internal and external applicants alike.

Your Job Opportunities page/section should contain the following information and functionality. It should:

- Contain organization information that an external candidate should know about your company.
- Allow the job seekers to register in a structured way by asking them to check the skills, competencies and experiences they possess.

- Provide candidates with the opportunity to e-mail your organization and to have e-mail sent to them regarding their application and other potential openings.
- Offer an e-mail connection for the candidate to e-mail a résumé to your organization.
- Provide feedback to the candidate to confirm that their application, and/or résumé has been received.
- Advertise the fact that the "Job Opportunities" site is available.
- Link to colleges and universities that traditionally provide good candidates to your organization. Ask them to add your link to their student placement home page.

This functionality is offered to some extent by most HRMS as well as various specialty systems.

(ii) Referral Programs

Employee referral programs (often referred to as "ERPs", not to be confused with those other "ERP"s — Enterprise Resource Planning, see Chapter 5) are becoming a common tool for employers to find additional applicants.[6]

Why?

- First, an employee's recommendation about a qualified friend or former colleague is usually a strong lead, making it more cost efficient than other recruitment methods.
- Second, a 2000 study by Ohio State University shows that the retention rate for employees gained through referral is 25% better than for non-referred employees.
- Third, employers who have an ERP in place find that 40-60% of all new hires come this source.

These results combine with a workforce that is taking responsibility for growing their team of co-workers and in the process gain satisfaction and remuneration and/or recognition.

Many HR software solutions offer tools to receive referrals and to send them to the appropriate action point while also triggering whatever remuneration plan has been established for the referrer.

---

[6] Relying on Your Employee's Eye for Talent, Jacques Gaumond, Canadian HR Reporter, July 17, 2006.

(iii) Exit Interviews

Exit interviews are considered to be a key component of worker retention. SaskTel (Saskatchewan Telecom) used a web-based Lotus Notes survey to conduct its exit interviews for several years.[7]

The tool, a stand-alone application not connected to SaskTel's HRMS, worked well to collect data, but staff weren't using it to improve staffing or retention.

The problem was that the tool didn't lend itself to "slicing and dicing" the data to aid analysis. The solution was a new tool that offered strong reporting options that could be used for analysis and action.

This case demonstrates an extremely common problem in the use of all technology, including HRMS. It is not enough to gather and store data. You must analyze the data in order to learn from it and to form new plans of action. Software tools, stand-alone or integrated, offer considerable value-add to this requirement.

(iv) Accommodation

As noted in Chapter 12 – Occupational Health and Safety, the accommodation of injured and/or disabled workers has grown significantly in importance. Technology can play a huge role in assisting such workers to be productive. And worker shortages combined with aging baby boomers is already yielding a huge source of workers.

Training or retraining such workers has long been considered to be far more expensive than training those without a temporary or permanent disability, but in reality you may find that accommodating those workers can be a bargain. And using these (and other) available tools to assist workers who are on a limited return to work is usually a lot less expensive than training a replacement.[8]

Ergonomic and more specialized office furniture, from chairs to lower height desks and wheel-chair ramps are becoming commonplace. But technology is also stepping up to the challenge. In addition to the telephones with amplifiers that have long been available, today there are such tools as:

- alternative keyboards and mice with larger or modified keyboards and keypads (including some designed for one-handed use);
- voice recognition software which has become extremely sophisticated;
- Personal Digital Assistants (PDAs) that can scan text and then convert the text to speech;
- Optical Character Recognition (OCR) that facilitates enlarging text to a readable size, as does Screen Magnification Software;

---

7 Before You Go, Click Here, Shannon Klie, Canadian HR Reporter, July 17, 2006.
8 Technology Swings the Accommodation Door Wide Open, Laurie McArthur and Lynne Race-Head, Canadian HR Reporter, July 17, 2006

9.4 Human Resources Management Systems

- alert systems that notify the user of incoming phone, e-mail and even emergencies through enhanced visual, auditory and vibrating technology.

The pace of technological innovation ensures that these tools will be joined by many others, and increased demand will drive prices even lower making these solutions extremely competitive.

(v) No Staffing Software?

What if your organization does not have software staffing package? Well according to a 2005 survey by The Canadian HR Reporter "very few organizations are using software to help with recruitment. The vast majority (84 %) said they do not use recruitment software".[9]

Manager's Introduction to Recruitment Tools[10]

The Canadian Government works to create a HR framework that withstands scrutiny. In doing so it often generates leading edge approaches and processes that are well documented.

In this example, from 2003 to 2005 the Organizational Readiness Office (ORO) from Treasury Board Secretariat in collaboration with the Personnel Psychology (PPC) Centre developed and validated recruitment and assessment tools In the context of the development and implementation of competency profiles for "front line agents".

These consisted of: an experience screen, a candidate achievement record (CAR), a structured interview, and a structured reference check.

Let us examine one of those:

"Screening Tool — A screening tool that is valid, fair and efficient can have considerable added value for any assessment system. An effective screening tool typically focuses on a small number of critical qualifications can, with minimal commitment of resources, allow hiring authorities to quickly narrow their focus from a large number of applicants to a manageable number of candidates.

One of the challenges typically facing those engaged in large-scale recruitment exercises is the "paper burden" that is associated with sifting through résumés and cover letters to identify those candidates who meet basic requirements in areas such as education, certification and specific kinds of job experience. A structured, self-administered form, as a supplement to a

---

9 Recruitment isn't getting any easier, Todd Humber, CHRR, Report on Recruitment & Staffing, 05/05/23.
10 Gathered 02/08/06 from <http://www.solutions.gc.ca/oro-bgc/tool/recruitment/intro/introtb_e.asp>.

candidate's résumé can eliminate much of this burden by allowing those screening applications to focus on critical information and by making that information readily available. This kind of tool can be simple and short (1-3 pages, depending on the number and kind of qualifications being evaluated), and can help to reduce or eliminate "embellishment" of accomplishments. The objective of the tool is to focus the information presented on the most relevant areas to allow decision-makers to quickly make decisions with respect to key qualifications."[11]

You will note that while the key issue is identified as **paper burden**, the description of the recommended solution — a structured, self-administered form — does not deal with the question of how such a form could be administered: on-line, on a dedicated PC/terminal, or manually.

This is true of most functional challenges in HR. All can be accomplished manually. The question is, is automation worth it? What is the return on investment (ROI) for using software as the primary tool?

9.5 — Program Monitoring for Staffing

As noted above, many HR organizations are focusing more and more on measuring effort and results.

Staffing is a very dynamic area in many organizations, and although attempts are made to objectify it, many aspects, including those associated with applicant assessment and selection decisions, remain fundamentally subjective, based on the judgement of the person(s) responsible for the selection decisions.

It is a well-established principle that the quality of such decisions is improved when individuals have access to feedback concerning the consequences of their decisions, in this case, the performance in training or on the job of the employees that they assessed or selected. Other important aspects of the staffing process should also be monitored and correction or improvements made as the need arises.

As with other HR functions, the Staffing process can be measured across the organization, or only within Staffing. The blend of policies and procedures combined with your tools, such as a HRMS and/or specific staffing software, can be used to collect and analyse the activity and results.

Some possible measures for the staffing function include:[12]
- Add Rate – Both Internal and External Add Rates (i.e., the growth of the workforce from the two sources) can be used.

---
11 *Ibid.*
12 Metrics from Saratoga Institute Human Resource Financial Report, 1997.

- Replacement Rate – Both internal and external hires into existing positions.
- Accession Rate – Number of hires (internal or external); the Add Rate plus the Replacement Rate divided by the full-time and part-time headcount.
- Cost per Hire – Calculate advertising, travel, relocation referral bonuses and external and internal recruiter costs (Internal or External).
- Time to Fill – From the time the vacancy (or new position) is first known until a candidate accepts an offer. This is most often calculated for HR only but may be started with an employee
- Time to Start – From the time the vacancy is first known to the time the employee starts.

All of these measures can be calculated manually but automatic collection and calculation by a HRMS and/or a specialized staffing software package will provide comparative analysis for HR and/or managers.

In Chapter 3, the role of the HRMS in quality control of Canadian Forces recruiting and selection administrative procedures was used to demonstrate the return on investment that can result from implementing such a program. This is an important example of the HRMS-assisted program monitoring that can be done in the staffing domain.

Far more important, however, is monitoring the success rate of individuals actually making selection decisions, and feeding any trends back to them and to the individuals responsible for managing the recruiting and selection functions, so that appropriate adjustments can be made.

9.6 — Summary

This chapter has discussed information requirements in support of staffing, as well as the use of an HRMS in related applications. Staffing specialists have typically seen their role as administering recruiting and selection procedures on request from managers in other functions. In the future, these individuals will require an appreciation of how larger strategic and business requirements interrelate with and affect staffing. In support of this goal staffing specialists will also have to accept an HRMS as a fundamental staffing tool, and acquire a comprehensive working knowledge of those features of the HRMS that relate to the staffing function.

The use of self-service, both Managerial (MSS) and Employee (ESS), through technology reduces the workload on HR and staffing, improves the availability of data and information to Managers/Supervisors, and therefore centers the responsibility for staffing on those managers/supervisors, with the HR staff in a supportive role.

This chapter summarizes the impact of technology and in particular the Internet on how organizations have modified traditional recruiting, screening and selection processes to take advantages of the opportunities offered by that technology.

9.7 — References

Baker, G.B., and R.T. Ellis. 1989. "Computerized Vocational Guidance Systems." In M.F. Wiskoff and G.M. Rampton, eds., *Military Personnel Measurement: Testing, Assignment, Evaluation*. New York: Praeger.

Belcourt, M., A.W. Sherman, G.W. Bohlander, and S.A. Snell. 1996. *Managing Human Resources*, Canadian ed. Toronto: Nelson Canada.

Cascio, W.F., and J.W. Thacker. 1994. *Managing Human Resources*. Toronto: McGraw-Hill Ryerson.

Cascio, W.F., 1991. *Applied Psychology in Personnel Management*, 4th ed. Englewood Cliffs, N.J.: Prentice-Hall.

Ceriello, V.R. 1991. *Human Resource Management Systems: Strategy, Tactics, and Techniques*. Toronto: Maxwell Macmillan.

Kroeker, L.P. 1989. "Personnel Classification/Assignment Models." In M.F. Wiskoff and G.M. Rampton, eds., *Military Personnel Measurement: Testing, Assignment, Evaluation*. New York: Praeger.

McCallum, T. 1996. "Embracing the chip: State-of-the-art technology propels HR into strategy's front lines." *Human Resources Professional* (April): 13-16.

Miller, D.B. 1986. *Managing Professionals in Research and Development*. San Francisco, Cal.: Jossey-Bass.

Rampton, G.M. 1989. "Entrenching equity in employment practices." *The Equal Times: The Newsletter for Human Resource Professionals*. Toronto: Bedford House 2(3): 19–21.

_____. and J.A. Doran. 1994. *A practitioner's guide for a new HRIS*. Paper presented at the 9th Annual CHRSP Conference (October): 4–7.

_____. ed. 1980. *Proceedings of the 22nd annual conference of the Military Testing Association*. Toronto: Canadian Forces Personnel Applied Research Unit (October): 27–31.

Sankey, C.A. 1976. *PAPRICAN: The First Fifty Years*. Pointe Claire, Que.: Pulp and Paper Research Institute of Canada.

Schratz, M.K., and M.J. Ree. 1989. "Enlisted Selection and Classification: Advances in Testing." In M.F. Wiskoff and G.M. Rampton, eds., *Military Personnel Measurement: Testing, Assignment, Evaluation*. New York: Praeger.

Senge, P.M. 1990. *The Fifth Discipline*. New York: Doubleday.

Turnbull, I.J. Privacy in the Workplace – the Employment Perspective, the Canadian Privacy Institute, CCH 2004

Valaskakis, K., R. Coull, and R. Clermont. 1991. *Information technology and human resources: Prospects for the decade*. A report prepared for the Canadian Human Resources Scanning Association, Toronto, Ont. (April).

Wanous, J.P. 1992. *Organizational Entry: Recruitment, Selection, Orientation, and Socialization of Newcomers*, 2nd ed. Reading, Mass.: Addison-Wesley.

Webster, E.C. 1982. *The Employment Interview: A Social Judgement Process*. Schomberg, Ont.: S.I.P. Publications.

Wiesner, W.H., and S.F. Cronshaw. 1988. "A Meta-Analytic Investigation of the Impact of Interview Format and the Degree of Structure on the Validity of the Employment Interview." *Journal of Occupational Psychology* 61: 275-90.

Wiskoff, M.F., and G.M. Rampton. 1989. Military Personnel Measurement: Testing, Assignment, Evaluation. New York: Praeger.

CHAPTER 10: TRAINING AND DEVELOPMENT

10.1 — Introduction

It is rare to attract and hire someone with the exact knowledge and skills that your vacant job requires, so training becomes important. In addition, for many employees, knowledge and/or skills development and opportunities for self-improvement are important motivators.

As noted in other chapters, futurists, demographers and labour market specialists have been predicting skill shortages as the technological requirements of the information age become more pressing, and the "baby boomers" reach retirement.[1]

This "knowledge worker" shortage is clearly with us, especially in jobs with the highest knowledge components, such as I/T.[2]

Many organizations are responding by increasing the priority that they attach to employee training and development. This in turn has been reflected in more resources being applied to training and development, including the expertise required to determine the need for, develop, implement and manage the organization's training and development programs.

10.2 — Strategic Context

In Canada, the appreciation of the importance of training and development to corporate success has been a recent development. For example, a little more than two decades ago, the

> **What is a Knowledge Worker?**
>
> Defined by Peter Drucker, these individuals are "high level employees who apply theoretical and analytical knowledge, acquired through formal education, to develop new products or services".
>
> Knowledge workers are those who acquire, manipulate, interpret and apply information in order to perform multidisciplinary, complex and unpredictable work. They analyze information and apply expertise in a variety of areas to solve problems, generate ideas, or create new products and services.
>
> Examples of knowledge workers in-

---

1 Gathered 06-0-06 from Too Few People, Too Little Time: The Employer Challenge of an Aging Workforce Executive Action Report by R. Owen Parker July 2006, the Conference Board of Canada.
2 Gathered 06-09-06 from <http://www.itac.ca/Archive/ITACNewsRelease/NR-ITSkilled-LabourShortageReturningin2002.htm>.

secretary of the Treasury Board of Canada pointed out in an address to the Ottawa Branch of the North American Society for Corporate Planning (Manion, 1985):

> Canadians have not, traditionally, been good human resources planners and managers, either in the overall labour market, or in individual enterprises. We have tended to expect qualified people to be available when we need them, either from the domestic labour market or from the immigration flow. We have done far too little training and development for our own staff. We have tended to discard our workers when their skills became obsolete or redundant, rather than planning for their retraining, or redeployment.

clude professionals, scientists, educators and information system designers. Knowledge work is characterized by the use of information, by unique work situations, and by creativity and autonomy. Knowledge workers make decisions rather than physical items and work with ideas rather than with objects. Their work focuses on mental rather than muscle power and is characterized by non-repetitive tasks.

Knowledge workers use different methods and techniques to solve problems and have the authority to decide what work methods to use in order to complete their varying job tasks.[3]

By 1991, however, on the basis of a training survey, the Conference Board of Canada was able to report:

> The results of this survey indicate clearly that leading Canadian firms understand the strategic imperative of creating a competitive advantage through the training and development of their workforce. (Larson and Blue, 1991, p. 21)

This awareness has continued. In a June 2006 report the Conference Board of Canada stated that Alberta's projected massive shortfall of workers requires that a comprehensive strategy be introduced to dramatically increase the availability of qualified workers between now and 2025, including improved training and apprenticeship programs.[4]

10.3 — Training and Development Options

At the same time as we move towards a knowledge-based workforce we have begun to accept another important concept, "life-long learning" — the idea that we never stop learning.[5] Meanwhile improvements in technology have provided new tools.

---

[3] Gathered 06-09-06 from <http://www.referenceforbusiness.com/management/Int-Loc/Knowledge-Workers.html>.
[4] Gathered 09-06-06 from Alberta's Labour Shortage: Just the Tip of the Iceberg, Executive Action Report by Alicia Coughlin June 2006, Source: The Conference Board of Canada.
[5] E-Learning: Expanding the Training Classroom through Technology, IHRIM, p 7.

"eLearning," the current accepted catch-phrase, includes a number of aspects including:

- Distance Education – Originally known as "correspondence courses" where students can be physically apart from one-another and from the instructor. The first major technology leap was first made popular in Canada by Athabasca University in Alberta using the traditional correspondence mail service, the radio and the telephone to deliver education to other sites.

- Distributed Learning – A previous catch-all that was meant to include various approaches and tools, including "virtual learning", "internet-based learning" and "eLearning".

- Synchronous Learning – Students receive instruction at the same time but not necessarily in the same place. A "webinar" is a typical example of synchronous eLearning.

- Asynchronous Learning – Students learn independently and not necessarily or usually on the same schedule as other students.

- Non-Linear Instruction – Traditional classroom learning has a pace targeted just below average in an attempt to meet the most needs, the disadvantages of which have long been recognized. Non-linear instruction allows learning to be fully self-paced.

These are all supported by a host of technology-based tools: instant messaging (IM), e-mail, Internet based chat rooms and message boards, and audio and video streaming that combine to create "webinars".[6]

Many organizations are also looking to corporate content providers who merge content with technology.

One such example is eCornell (www.ecornell.com), integrating the knowledge and resources of Cornell University, a leading global research university, with the latest technology. In eCornell courses you interact with an expert instructor and a cohort of your peers to collectively develop knowledge, and to effectively apply that knowledge in your organization.

Authored and designed with one or more Cornell faculty members using the most current and relevant case studies, research and content, eCornell courses offer embedded "Ask the Expert" interviews with Cornell faculty, online access to library reference guides and additional professional and executive education opportunities at Cornell. The approach uses online case studies, interactive exercises and simulations based on authentic, relevant and "real-world" situations and results in Certificates from Cornell University, CEU credits and other industry-specific recertification credits.

---

6 E-Learning: Expanding the Training Classroom through Technology, IHRIM, pp. 9-12.

ECornell courses provide the convenience of structure and flexibility with new course sections starting every month, round-the-clock/round-the-world access to course materials, online and telephone customer support, and dedicated online instructors.

Canadians and others outside of the U.S.A. find that an Ivy League education provides a significant boost to their career, especially in this day and age of globalization.

10.4 — Training and Development: An HR Model

Figure 10.1 depicts the relationship among training and development processes, from strategic planning through human resources/succession planning and training development programs to program review and monitoring.

Bernard and Ingols (1988) outline a number of characteristics shared by effective training and development programs. Foremost among these is basing programs on a strategic vision related to the corporate goals and objectives of the organizations, including human resources philosophies and programs (block A1 of Figure 10.1).

Training specialists who understand the interrelationships between strategic planning and human resources training and development, and who can work comfortably in both domains, are gaining more influence and prominence in many progressive organizations. As in the case of staffing specialists, discussed in the previous chapter, training and development specialists must understand the business of the organization, including its strategic context and the implications that this has for human resources.

Thus, they must be experienced trainers, but much more as well. They must possess good analytic skills; understand the larger corporate perspective; have a clear vision of what human resources planning and development is, and should be, in their organization; and be able to explain this vision to others. Very importantly, training and development specialists must be change agents.

To be fully successful, training specialists will have to place increased emphasis on helping managers make the link between their organizational/operational plans, the skills that their staff will require to accomplish these plans, and how these skills can be developed. Training specialists should also have a sound understanding of the knowledge and skill individuals may be expected to bring to the organization, given specific levels of education and training from external sources. This external scanning component appears in block C1 of Figure 10.1.

Figure 10.1 Training and Development

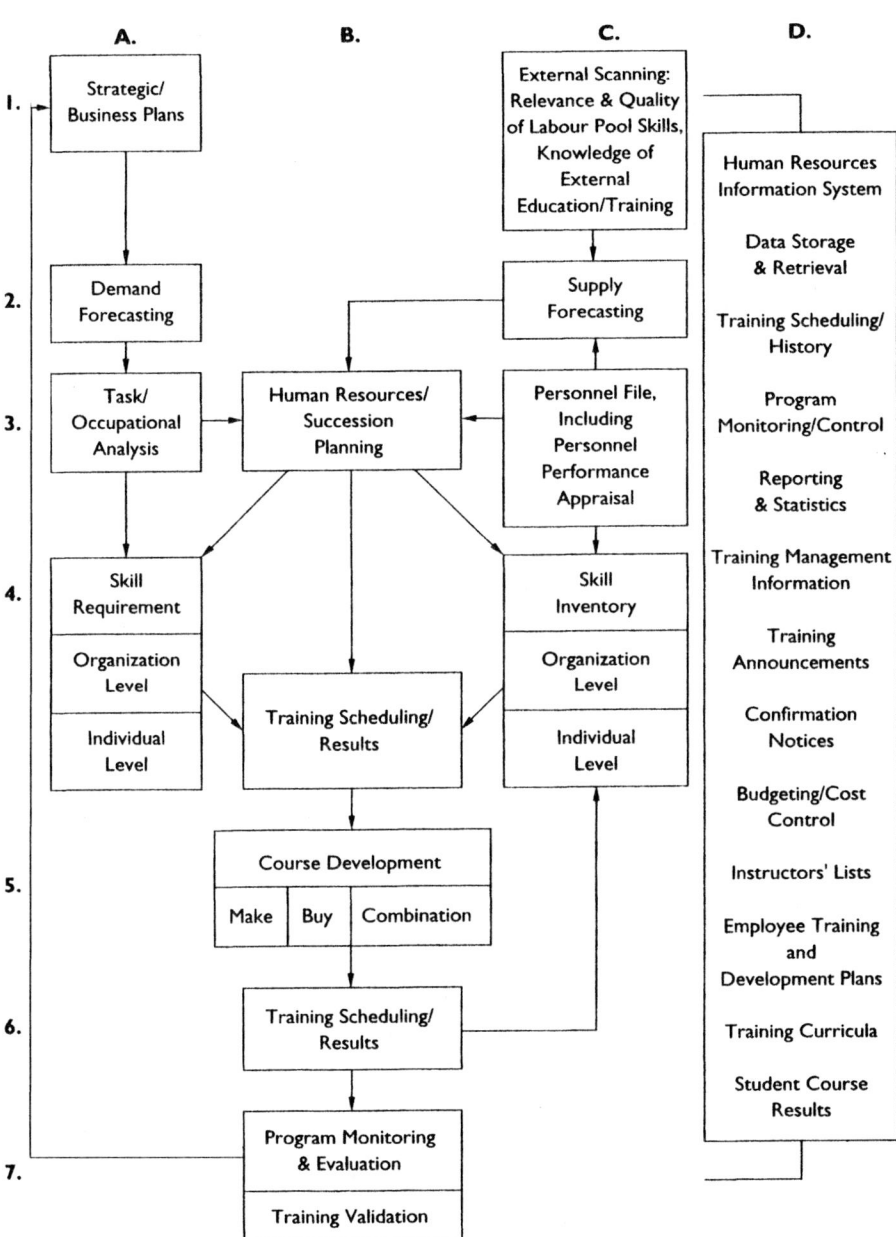

This awareness may be developed through membership in associations that focus on training and development, by attending relevant workshops, by being active

10.4 Human Resources Management Systems

in training and development associations, networking, and keeping up with the literature. By these means one may keep abreast of developments in the field as well as remain knowledgeable about available external resources and expertise that can be drawn on as required.

As noted in row two of the diagram, the strategic/business plans of the organization should translate into the need for training through demand forecasting. The internal and external availability of skilled personnel, resources, etc., on the right hand side of the model is reflected in supply forecasting; that is, what is expected to be available. The demand for skilled personnel should be translated into job requirements at the individual position level through task or occupational analyses.

The potential external labour supply, as well as its knowledge and skills, may be determined through external human resources scans (block C1). The internal supply of human resources, and the knowledge and skills inherent in it, should be available from the employee module of the HRMS (block D).

Human resources/succession planning (block B3) is used to determine how the need for human resources in the right numbers, with the right skills, doing the right things, will be met. Together with task/occupational analyses (block A3), it may be used to define the skills required for a position, or in aggregate, for a work unit (block A4). Coupled with personal/performance appraisal information, human resources/succession planning may also provide an inventory of skills that an individual possesses, or that exist across a work unit (block C4). Information about what skills exist or do not exist among employees may be used with training surveys of various kinds in training needs analysis to determine whether training and development is required (block B4).

Training needs analysis, in turn, may serve as the basis for decisions about what training and development might best meet the need (block B5). This may be formal courses provided in-house, external courses, or on-job training. Even with in-house courses, decisions must be made about whether to develop the training package in-house, to buy a ready-made package externally, or combine the two (e.g., buy a basic package and modify it to suit the specific needs of the organization).

Once training and development programs have been developed and implemented, procedures are required to schedule courses and attendees, to manage logistics issues, and to gather and store the results of training (block B6). A description of each course should be included, along with trainee results and evaluations of each course by trainees, instructors, and supervisors of the trainees.

The cost-effectiveness of training and development for the organization should be monitored continuously by program monitoring and evaluation procedures commonly referred to as "training validation" (block B7). Such program monitoring should include, but not be restricted to, the course reporting and evaluation procedures mentioned above.

10.5 — Training Management Information

The management of training and development in many organizations can be complex. As a consequence, training and development departments in some organizations develop independent training management systems. This situation may arise where training and development staff require automated assistance to help them manage their training and development information, but do not have access to an effective central HRMS; or want direct control of the collection and use of training information.

Training and development modules are included as integral parts of most comprehensive HRMSs. Nowadays, of course, seemingly independent training and development modules may be linked to other HRMS modules to form coordinated networks (see the discussion on HRMS modules in Chapter 5).

The data elements documented in Figures 10.2 to 10.4 are representative of data screens that currently exist in training modules of HRMSs operating in a number of organizations, across such diverse sectors as the government, post-secondary education, resource industries, business corporations, and the services sector.

The first of these screens, Figure 10.2, illustrates typical training and development information that may be gathered on each individual. The next, Figure 10.3, shows typical data gathered for course management purposes. The last screen, Figure 10.4, depicts useful data on each individual relative to courses taken by that individual.

In various combinations, data from the screens outlined above can be used for a broad range of training and development planning, management, and monitoring applications. An HRMS may be used to collect data and produce analyses and reports at many different levels in the training and development model depicted in Figure 10.1. It may be used, for example, for:

10.5 Human Resources Management Systems

Figure 10.2 Employee Training Request
(Screen/Panel From Hypothetical HRMS Training Module)

EMPLOYEE SCREEN

Employee Name	Joanne Smith
Employee Number	12345678
Position	Assistant Supervisor
Position Number	98764
Unit	Compensation
Department	HR
Training requested:	
• Course Type	Supervision skills
• Preferred Delivery Method	On-line or after work
• Suggested Course (if any)	Essential Skills for Managing People
• Suggested Supplier (if any)	eCornell
• Supplier Contact (if any)	www.earningthroughlearning.com
• Estimated Cost	$1150 Canadian
• Preferred start date	Earliest (understand course runs monthly)
Employee Comments	I want to take this course in order to meet my training objectives and to better perform my responsibilities as Assistant Supervisor. I have already completed Effective Interviewing and this course will help me get my Supervisory Certificate from Cornell.
Date of Request	October 17, 2006
Supervisor Name	Walker Shea
• Priority for this employee	1
• Comments	Joanne should take this program within the next 3-12 months to prepare her for her next promotion.
• Approval (enter your Employee ID)	XXXXX

Training and Development 10.5

Figure 10.3 Sample Course Detail
(Screen/Panel From Hypothetical HRMS Training Module)

TRAINING COURSE SCREEN

Course Name	Essential Skills for Managing People
Section Name	Overcoming Barriers to Successful Management
Section Name	Leading People to Higher Performance
Program	Management Essentials
Delivery Method	On-line
Course Duration	5-6 hours over 2 weeks for each section
Course Outline	Improve performance by shifting professional paradigms and improving employee performance and productivity.
Participants	All levels of managers, supervisors, and team leaders in any industry.
Certification/Degree?	Successful completion can be used for Cornell University Certificate in HR: Performance Management, Managing Essentials: Managing Performance, Managing Essentials: Managing Productivity, or Supervisory Skills
Course Start Date	Each section once a month
Course Time of Day	None; each participant sets own schedule
Course End Date	Each section once a month
Course Location	None; each participant works at own pace from location of choice.
Enrollment Deadline	Each section every month
Enrollment Minimum	None
Enrollment Maximum	None
Supplier	eCornell through Canadian HR Press, Canada's eCornell affiliate
Supplier Contact	Karen
Supplier Phone	1-866-607-0876
Supplier Address	14845-6 Yonge St, Ste. 165, Aurora Ontario L4G 6H8
Supplier eMail	info@earningthroughlearning.com
Supplier Web	www.earningthroughlearning.com
Course Tuition	$1,150 Canadian for 2 sections
Other Costs	None, no travel is required.
Prerequisites (if any)	None
Equipment Details	Internet connection
Instructor	Assigned Cornell faculty, plus individual participants will interact with a cohort of their peers.
Course Comment	We have a company contract with this supplier that provides us with volume discounts -- contact Training for details and status.

10.5 Human Resources Management Systems

Figure 10.4 Sample Course Enrolment Detail for Individual (Screen/Panel From Hypothetical HRMS Training Module)

TRAINING COURSE ENROLMENT SCREEN

Employee Name	Joanne Smith
Course Name	Essential Skills for Managing People
Section Name	Overcoming Barriers to Successful Management
Section Name	Leading People to Higher Performance
Program	Management Essentials
Delivery Method	On-line
Course Duration	5-6 hours over 2 weeks for each section
Course Start Date	Each section once a month
Course Time of Day	None; each participant sets own schedule
Course End Date	Each section once a month
Course Location	None; each participant works at own pace from location of choice.
Supplier	eCornell through Canadian HR Press, eCornell's Canadian affiliate
Supplier Contact	Karen
Supplier Phone	1-866-607-0876
Supplier Address	14845-6 Yonge St, Ste. 165, Aurora Ontario L4G 6H8
Supplier eMail	info@earningthroughlearning.com
Supplier Web	www.earningthroughlearning.com
Course Tuition	$1,125 Canadian for 2 sections
Billing	Contract with supplier so Company is billed directly against training credits.
Other Costs	None, no travel is required.
Prerequisites (if any)	None
Equipment Details	Internet connection
Instructor	Assigned Cornell faculty, plus individual participants can interact with a cohort of their peers.
Course Comment	Employee to provide evidence of successful completion and a course evaluation to her supervisor within 4 weeks of course completion.

Data Storage

- Lists of courses available by subject area
- Training curricula
- Employee training and development plans
- Student course results
- Results of training
- Training location
- Course evaluations
- Training history
- Lists of instructors
- Survey results (e.g., from training needs analyses, career and organization development, attitudes)

Training and Development 10.5

Training Management
- Creating class rosters
- Course scheduling
- Creating training announcements and confirmation notices

Reports
- Training costs, by student, per course, by organizational unit, etc.
- Numbers of employees trained by course, per year, by organizational unit, etc.
- Numbers of individuals requiring specific kinds of training and development
- Course evaluations by topic area or by instructor

There is one aspect in the gathering and storage of training information that deserves highlighting: the increasing need for organizations to be able to demonstrate that they have taken all reasonable precautions to safeguard the health and safety of the public, clients, and employees. This means that organizations must ensure that their employees are trained to recognize health and safety hazards, and to take corrective action. It also means that employees must be trained to respond appropriately when accidents happen.

For example, quick and appropriate action in medical resuscitation, in accident prevention, and in fire drills is critical in such health care and social services areas as nursing homes and residences for individuals with disabilities. Generally, serious medical incidents or accidents must be reported. Investigations are conducted to determine whether appropriate action has been taken by staff and others in the incident. The organization may be liable if it cannot demonstrate that it made all reasonable efforts to ensure that staff were qualified for the responsibilities that the organization was expecting them to perform. Similarly, all organizations in Canada must ensure that their employees are trained to carry out their responsibilities with respect to the Workplace Hazardous Materials Information Systems (WHMIS).

Again, not being able to demonstrate that the organization has conducted this training to a satisfactory level could render the organization liable to criminal and civil litigation.

Thus the organization is responsible for ensuring and demonstrating that it has taken all necessary health and safety precautions, including training, to ensure that employees understand their responsibilities and can carry them out. It is critical, therefore, that the HRMS be able to collect, store, and report health and safety training, as well as professional certification or other forms of qualifications, whether this follows formal training or not. These may take the form of

10.6 — Training Delivery

Training is now routinely delivered through various technical means. In the second edition of this book (1999) we referred to "computer-assisted training", that is training courses provided via personal computers often at a convenient time, place and learning speed.

In addition to computer-assisted training, be it on a PC or an employer's network, eLearning using the Internet has grown enormously in recent years.[7] In 2000, the Conference Board of Canada reported that:

- employers are increasing their use of learning technologies;
- seventy-five per cent of employers surveyed already use learning technologies, and they expect the proportion of skill development delivered to employees through learning technologies to increase;
- in 1999, employers used learning technologies to deliver, on average, 17 per cent of all skill development;
- the largest growth in learning technologies is in e-learning;
- while 47 per cent of employers have used the Internet for employee skill development, 82 per cent plan to do so in the future;
- Intranets, which are more secure from external sabotage and interference, are even more popular;
- 58 per cent of employers have used Intranets for skill development and 93 per cent plan to do so.[8]

Not only can such training programs be more cost effective than alternative methods, but the results of training can be monitored by and entered directly into the HRMS. In addition, learners can self-test using computer provided tools. Core course modules may be integrated with other modules to track and record progress, provide special tutoring for slower students, and provide proof of knowledge and skills learned for legal purposes.

Whatever the technology used, eLearning has proven to be flexible in that its use opens doors to a number of training options including integration with other training media for what has been termed as "multimedia presentations."

Keeping track of the above information, conducting and keeping track of survey results, and performing needs analysis by matching organizational requirements

---

7 Keen for the Screen, Canadian Employers Turn to E-Learning for Employee Skill Development, Debbie Murray, September 2000, the Conference Board of Canada.
8 *Ibid.*

to the resources available, both at the individual level and more broadly, require automation and integration with an effective HRMS.

10.7 — Application

No other sector of society spends as high a percentage of its budget on training and development, or coordinates these functions as closely with other human resources and operational functions, including strategic/operational planning, as do Western military forces. Demand requirements are translated into organizational or job requirements via formal occupational analyses. In the Canadian Forces this was done at a special directorate called the Directorate of Organizational Structures located in Canadian Forces headquarters in Ottawa. Occupational information was gathered in detailed survey form and analyzed by means of the software package, Comprehensive Occupational Data Analysis Programs (CODAP), mentioned in the previous chapter.

This information was then used to define the position/ organizational component of the Canadian Forces Personnel Management Information System (as its HRMS was known). The "employee module" of this system contained all performance appraisal and related information. Comparisons between job requirements and the kinds and amounts of skills of individuals at all levels led to planning for individual training and development. This information also led to the determination of the kinds of training and development courses required to meet these demands.

Western military forces provide a broad variety of occupational and training courses leading to full employability in such varying functions as the combat arms, electronics, high performance flying, and management courses. University courses at both the undergraduate and graduate level are offered internally in the military college setting and at external universities. Formal courses are only a part of the training and development involved. Career managers schedule these courses as well as orchestrate a planned series of career moves to enhance each individual's knowledge, experience, and value to the organization. The results of training and development are closely monitored, both at the individual level and across trainees, to ensure that the training provided is both validated and efficient.

Other large organizations attempt to recruit individuals who are capable of fitting into the organization at almost any level, on the basis of knowledge and skills previously obtained through public education or experience in other organizations. However, many of these organizations find that they cannot recruit all of the required knowledge and skills externally, and that they must develop and maintain extensive in-house training programs.

Some of these organizations have found it necessary to maintain an extensive array of training programs, involving a broad range of technical, management, and administrative courses. In addition to allowing the organization to plan for training on the basis of identified need (both at the individual and organizational level), training management systems assist trainers in course scheduling, course loading, data gathering, preparing course reports, and training validation.

10.8 — Attitude Surveys

There was a time when only the largest organizations, such as the Canadian Imperial Bank of Commerce, International Business Machines, Xerox, and General Electric placed a premium on employee training and development complemented their efforts by having their employees provide feedback on the perceived effectiveness of these programs along with other organizational issues. These organizations have found that upward communication can lead to reduced absenteeism and turnover, less waste and spoilage, improved safety records, increased productivity, and higher profits, if the result of such feedback is acted upon seriously and expeditiously.

As reported in Rampton and Innes (1985), for many years the Israeli Defence Forces (I.D.F.) have complemented their training programs with sociometric surveys to support the early identification of leadership and officer-like qualities. In addition, regularly administered paper and pencil surveys and interviews are held with personnel at all levels to provide feedback to commanders with respect to such issues as motivation and morale, perceived adequacy of training and equipment, confidence in leadership, and perceived operational readiness of the particular unit involved.

Today there are many sophisticated survey tools available on the Internet and designed to be used through Internet access.

Regardless of the tool(s) used, or the industry sector in question, the results of these surveys are considered to be an important indicator of operational effectiveness and a source of problem identification and resolution of command by the various levels.

Results are eagerly awaited by supervisors and employees alike. Conducting such surveys regularly and maintaining them in automated form allows management to can trace the results of any leadership or training initiatives that were taken.

10.9 — Summary

With the advent of the information society coinciding with a decreasing labour force as baby boomers retire, skill shortages in key areas are predicted. Many organizations have already experienced these pressures and are responding by increasing the priority attached to employee training and development. This in turn is reflected in more resources being applied to training and development. As organizations place an increased emphasis on training and development, they are finding it necessary to implement automated procedures to manage these programs and to document the results of training for each trainee. This chapter has discussed the implementation and use of an HRMS in support of these goals.

10.10 — References

Belcourt, M., A.W. Sherman, G.W. Bohlander, and S.A. Snell. 1996. *Managing Human Resources*, Canadian ed. Toronto: Nelson Canada.

Belcourt, M., and P. Wright. 1996. *Managing Performance Through Training and Development*. Toronto: Nelson Canada.

Bensu, J. 1991. "HRMS Training Applications." In A.L. Lederer, ed. *Handbook of Human Resource Information Systems*. New York: Warren, Gorham and Lamont.

Bernard, H.B., and C.A. Ingols. 1988. "Six Lessons for the Corporate Classroom." *Harvard Business Review* (Sept.-Oct.): 40-46.

Canadian Labour Market and Productivity Centre. 1990. *A Framework for a National Training Board: the Report of the Phase II Committee on the Labour Force Development Strategy*. Ottawa (July).

Cascio, W.F., and J.W. Thacker. 1994. *Managing Human Resources*. Toronto: McGraw-Hill Ryerson.

Ceriello, V.R. 1991. *Human Resource Management Systems: Strategy, Tactics, and Techniques*. Toronto: Maxwell Macmillan.

Coates, J.F. 1990. *Change Requires Retraining: Success Depends on Workplace Skills*. Technical Report. Washington, D.C.: J.F. Coates Inc.

DeSouza, J. 1995. "Training: The Key Human Resources Issue for the 1990s." In *Human Resources Management in Canada*. Scarborough, Ont.: Carswell.

Downey, J., and D. McCamus. 1990. *To Be our Best: Learning for the Future*. Montreal, Que.: Corporate Higher Education Forum.

Geis, G. 1991. *As Training Moves Toward the Next Decade: a Needs Analysis of Professional Development for Trainers*. Toronto: Ontario Training Corporation Report (May).

Human Resources Management in Canada. 1995. Scarborough, Ont.: Carswell.

Larson, P.E., and M.W. Blue. 1991. *Training and Development 1990: Expenditures and Policies* (Report 67-91). Ottawa: The Conference Board of Canada.

Manion, J. 1985. *The Integration of Human Resources and Corporate Planning*. Address to the Ottawa Branch of the North American Society for Corporate Planning Inc. Ottawa.

McIntyre, D. 1991. *Training and Development 1991* (Report 85-92). Ottawa: The Conference Board of Canada.

Mealy, Lynne and Loller, Bob, ed. 2000. E-Learning: Expanding the Training Classroom through Technology, IHRIM.

Rampton, G.M., and L. Innes. 1995. "The Role of the Behavioural Scientist in Support of Future Military Operations." In J. Hunt and J. Blair, eds., *Leadership on the Future Battlefield*. Willowdale, Ont.: Pergamon-Brasseys.

Senge, P.M. 1990. *The Fifth Discipline*. New York: Doubleday.

Smith, M.E., and D.C. Brandenburg. 1991. "Summative Evaluation." *Performance Improvement Quarterly* 4, no. 2: 35–38.

Chapter 11: Total Compensation — Salary, Benefits, Pension, Payroll and Time and Attendance

11.1 — Introduction

This chapter discusses the use of an HRMS in support of the total rewards/compensation functions of the organization.

Organizations accomplish organizational goals through their people. Workers provide services in exchange for a package of rewards with both financial and non-financial components. Total compensation flows from the total rewards program philosophy.

The concept of total rewards considers all aspects of the remuneration deal offered to workers, the sum of which is aimed at attracting, motivating, retaining and developing employees.

"Compensation" in the traditional use of the term has meant salary or pay. It included overtime and other direct financial payments but no more, not even Benefits. Readers interested in the evolution of such things can look back to the last edition of this book that was published in 1999 and see that "Benefits" and "Pension" were a separate chapter.

Today the term "compensation" still refers to that same economic or monetary part of the reward system,[1] but we recognize that "Total Compensation" includes direct and indirect financial rewards plus non-financial rewards, including: Salary, Benefits, Pension, Payroll and Time Management.

Whether all of the functionality defined by Total Compensation is held in one department, Compensation, or whether it is scattered across a number of departments — Compensation, Benefits and Payroll, for example — the essential concern should be to ensure that the administrative systems (preferably one HRMS) are capable of integrating the data for those various functions into one comprehensive set of analysis.

Remember that "all aspects of the employment situation — good, bad, or indifferent — have an impact on an employee's commitment to the employer. How individual compensation components are designed and delivered needs to be considered in the context of the whole picture, desired culture, and the impact of the components on each other".[2]

Today's work environment is extremely competitive for talent and is expected to become more so. The success of a total rewards program in relation to its goals

---

[1] *Strategic Compensation in Canada*, 2nd ed., 2002, Richard Long, p. 5.
[2] 2006 National Knowledge Exam (NKE) Study Guide, Canadian HR Press.

11.1 Human Resources Management Systems

will have a key influence on an organization's success in attracting and retaining the numbers and quality of workers desired. Total compensation flows from the total rewards program philosophy. There are direct and indirect components to the pay package.

Figure 11.1

Individual Performance + Team Performance + Department Results + Division Results + Company Results = Performance Pay

As can be seen in Figure 11.1, the financial side of today's total compensation can be quite complex. Add in such additional considerations such as:

- geographic adjustments (for certain countries or regions);
- hot job adjustments (temporary additional pay);
- performance pay (many annually, but some organizations make performance pay calculations quarterly);
- piecework (paying a worker for each piece processed);
- compa-ratio analysis (the relative percentage that the salary is of the job rate);
- job evaluation green (below the minimum of the job rate – thus "green" or good for increase) or red-circling (above the maximum of the job rate and thus on hold until the maximum surpasses the salary).

and you can see how complex all of these programs can be.

Is it possible to manage complex total compensation plans manually? Yes.

Should you? Not if you can help it. Not when judicious use of a spreadsheet, or better yet a specialty compensation software package or a HRMS can track changes, apply increases across groups, and provide graphical reports and analysis.

Total Compensation — Salary, Benefits, Pension, Payroll etc.   **11.1**

Figure 11.2 Total Compensation Model[3]

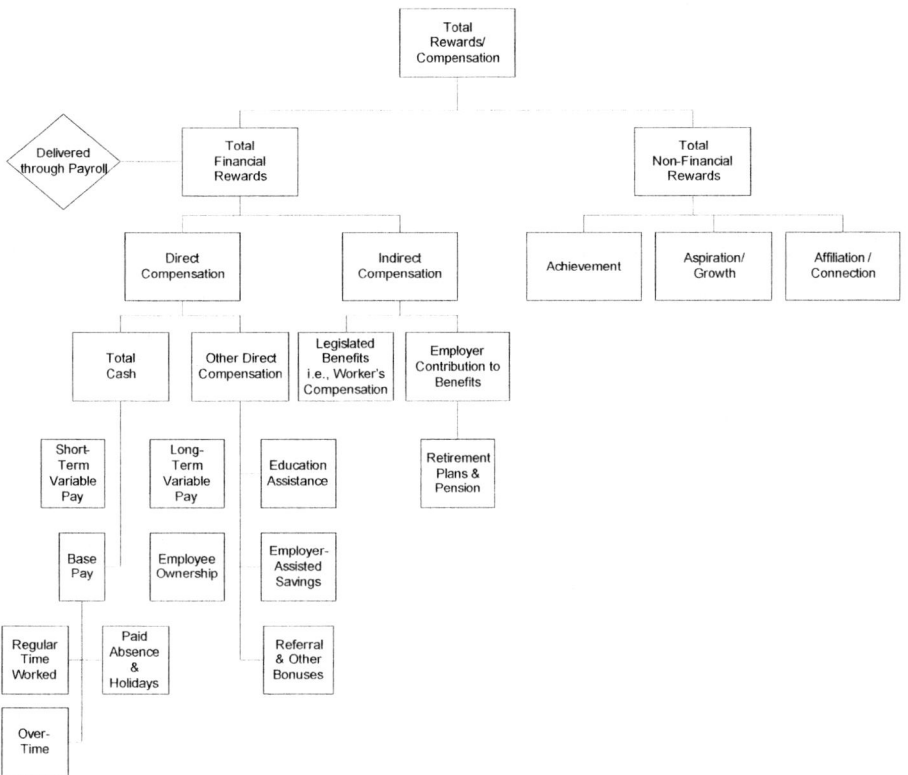

Fifteen or twenty years ago only the largest of organizations would have had such complex direct and indirect total compensation. But in the last several years it has become clear that size is no longer a predictor of complexity. In order to be competitive, and/or to operate successfully in a global marketplace, many organizations that would be defined as "medium" (1,000-5,000) or "small" (100-999) or very small (under 100) have the same competitive needs to compensate workers as do the largest firms.

In part, technology, and the Internet in particular, are to blame. Technology allows smaller organizations to compete more directly with larger organizations and on a more global basis. This, in turn, puts pressure on the total compensation plan requirements and results in the complexity being driven into smaller organizations.

---

3 Core diagram adapted from 2006 National Knowledge Exam (NKE) Study Guide, Canadian HR Press.

11.1 Human Resources Management Systems

(a) — Payroll

You will note the upper left hand diamond shape in the Total Compensation Model (Figure 11.2) labeled Payroll.

Historically, the need to handle large amounts of information accurately led to the early automation of payroll and related functions. Indeed, as pointed out in Chapter 1, many human resources management information systems evolved from adding a broader range of capabilities to what started out as payroll systems.

Although Payroll has traditionally been a function within Finance it now reports to HR at least half the time and that trend appears to be continuing.[4] The reason is two-fold.

First, it is clear that Payroll data and HR data are largely the same. In many organizations the data is duplicated and many resources are used to move the same data back and forth.

Second, traditional concerns about separation of responsibilities have been made largely moot by the sophistication of software security. At the same time however, readers should be aware of increasing government focus on separation of duties. This is due to various corporate financial scandals, the most notorious being ENRON, which in turn have spawned legislation such as Sarbanes-Oxley (SOX) in the U.S.

> SOX is a complex and demanding legal requirement. To comply you need to establish internal controls and procedures. Accurate reporting and record keeping are the 'best practices'. Manually collecting this critical configuration information is time consuming and relies on a human-based process. Organizations utilizing a human-based process invest enormous resources and allow tremendous room for human error.[5]

While SOX is American legislation, Canadian companies that operate in the U.S. and American companies operating in Canada are all subject to it. But regardless of whether or not SOX is legally applicable to your organization you will find that the principles regarding the establishment of internal controls will demand that data is collected and managed in an automated manner; it just won't be possible manually without a huge amount of effort. While the need for internal controls and the appropriate separation of duties apply to all systems that deal with and have discretion over significant aspects of the organizations resources, their application will not likely serve as a hurdle to payroll being assigned to human resources, since most of the scandals mentioned above, have had much more to do with financial systems.

---

4 Canadian Payroll Association, 1996.
5 Practical Guide to Sarbanes-Oxley IT Internal Controls Property of Ecora Software 19.

Total Compensation — Salary, Benefits, Pension, Payroll etc.   **11.1**

(b) — HR Model

Figure 11.3 applies the human resources model that we have been using throughout this book to the total compensation function.

Figure 11.3 Total Compensation

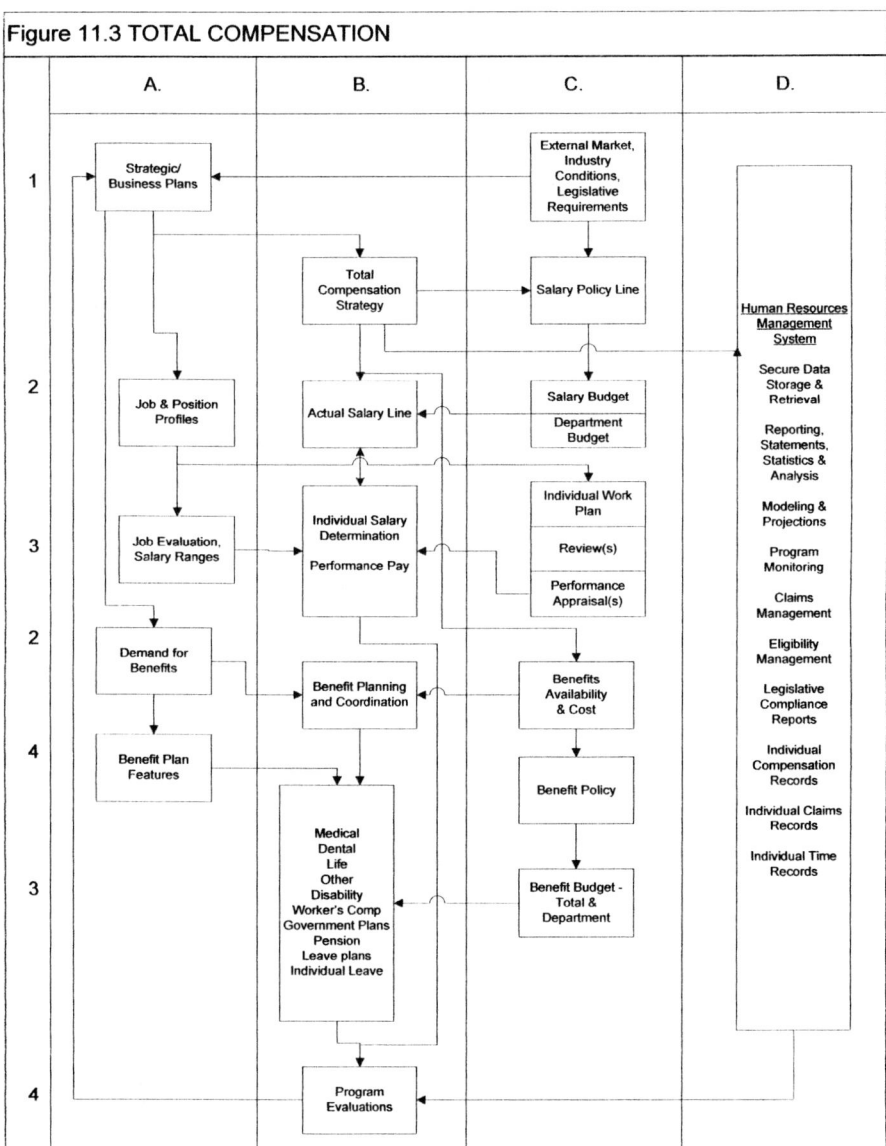

As in the previous applications, the upper level of the model refers to the global, strategic context. Level three refers to the practical, hands-on functions that we

11.1 Human Resources Management Systems

traditionally think of as human resources programs, for example: job evaluation, linking performance appraisal processes with pay-for-performance and individual salary determination.

Level two, between the strategic context and the hands-on programs, represents the planning and development programs that use information from the strategic context to shape and direct the form and operation of the human resources programs.

Level four, as in the other models, reflects the monitoring and auditing processes that ensure that compensation/payroll programs, in support of and in conjunction with other functions in the organization, are operating as they should.

At the global level, an organization's compensation strategy is generally influenced by:

1. The organization's financial situation: how much it can pay?
2. The salary market: how much other organizations are paying for similar jobs?
3. How much the organization wants to pay: some organizations want to be salary leaders (fourth or fifth quartile) and pay more than others in their sectors; others want merely to be competitive (mid-point & third quartile), and pay average salaries; while others prefer to pay less (2nd or even 1st quartile);

Figure 11.4 Salary Distribution Quartiles

1st Quartile	2nd Quartile	Average, or	3rd Quartile	4th Quartile	5th+ Quartile
0 - 25%	26% - 49%	Mid-Point 50 %	51 - 75%	76 - 100%	101 +

and

4. How the organization is going to pay its employees: that is, the payroll function and processes.

In considering the total compensation plan, and specifically where an organization targets its average salary, some organizations use non-compensatory factors to "sell" workers and prospective workers on their worth as an employer for non-financial reasons.

One such company is Google. Headquartered in California's Silicon Valley with small offices scattered around the globe, Google pays at or below midpoint but has no difficulty finding prospective workers. The reason? Google emphasizes that its workers are the best-of-the-best and recruits only graduates of the best schools. The net result is that having Google on your résumé as an employee is perceived to be worth a lot more than a few thousand more dollars in salary.

That kind of cultural-based strategy can also be reinforced by corporate communications using the corporate HRMS and/or portal structure.

(c) — Benefits

In most industrial countries organizations are expected to provide benefits and pension programs. These programs can be expensive, ranging from 12-15% and often moving up to as much as 35% or more of an organization's total compensation package.

Even a decade ago benefits tended to be applied only to full-time employees, but the competition for knowledgeable and/or skilled workers has led many organization to extend some or all of their benefits packages to part-time employees. This trend has been stimulated, at least in part, by the recognition that women and members of minority groups tend to be overrepresented in the part-time component of the labour pool. Extending benefits to this group has become an employment equity issue, and will have the effect of further increasing benefits costs.

An HRMS has a critical role in the cost-effective management of indirect compensation — benefits and pension programs (see examples in Chapter 3).

Figure 11.5 shows the human resources model considered from the perspective of benefits and pension applications. As with in the models presented in previous chapters, the top levels of the model reflect the global, strategic context in which the other benefits components exist.

The next level denotes planning processes designed to translate information from the global strategic/business context into the practical human resources programs reflected at the third level.

The bottom level in the diagram contains program evaluation processes designed to assess whether the programs are doing what they were designed to do, and to feed the findings of these analyses back into the system, so that continuous improvements may be made.

In deciding what benefit and pension programs to provide to employees, an organization will generally be interested in determining what it must provide (and can afford) to:

1. achieve the objectives of the organization;
2. remain competitive in terms of attracting and retaining employees;
3. satisfy employee requirements as defined, for example, through collective bargaining;
4. satisfy ever-changing government legislation (e.g., workers' compensation, maternity/paternity benefits, payroll taxes for health care);
5. fulfil its values/responsibilities as a good corporate citizen.

11.1 Human Resources Management Systems

Figure 11.5 Indirect Compensation (Benefits and Pension Model)

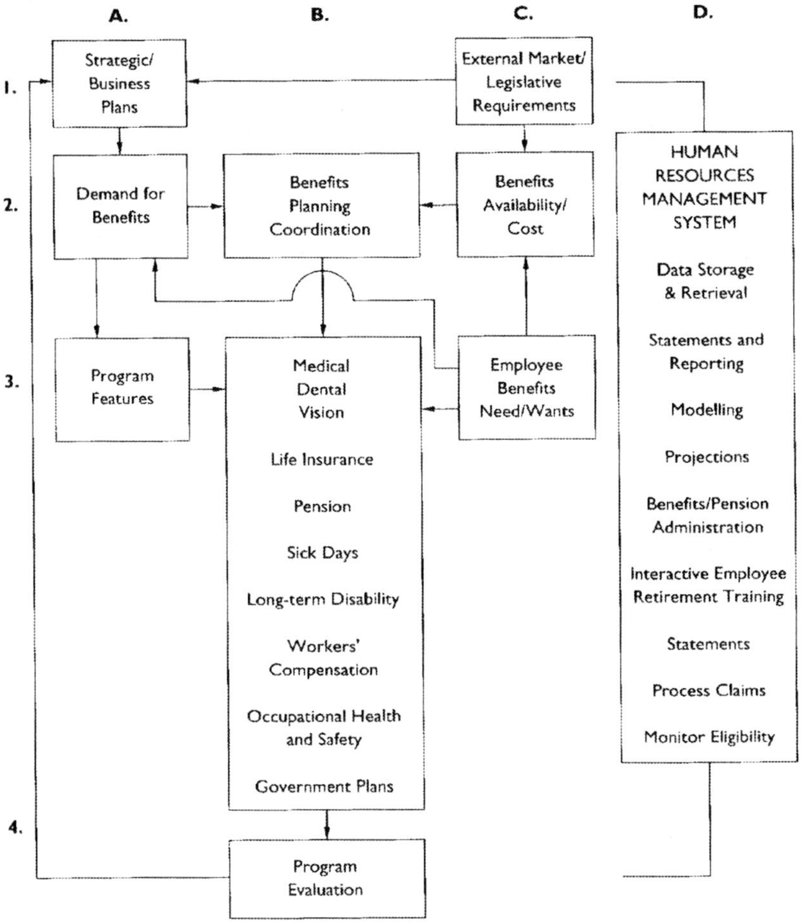

	A.	B.	C.	D.
1.	Strategic/Business Plans		External Market/Legislative Requirements	
2.	Demand for Benefits	Benefits Planning Coordination	Benefits Availability/Cost	HUMAN RESOURCES MANAGEMENT SYSTEM Data Storage & Retrieval Statements and Reporting
3.	Program Features	Medical Dental Vision Life Insurance Pension Sick Days Long-term Disability Workers' Compensation Occupational Health and Safety Government Plans	Employee Benefits Need/Wants	Modelling Projections Benefits/Pension Administration Interactive Employee Retirement Training Statements Process Claims Monitor Eligibility
4.		Program Evaluation		

Information related to the first point derives from the strategic plan of the organization together with what employees expect or want, while information related to the second may derive from market surveys of what other organizations are providing to their employees. Pressure to satisfy employee wants or needs may be reflected in labour negotiations. Benefits supply derives from benefits that are available from carriers, government, and other sources.

Benefits planning and coordination is used to determine how the demand for benefits is to be satisfied with the supply. The demand for benefits becomes translated into the specific features of the various benefits programs, while benefits availability and cost will have a bearing on the employee needs and wants.

Total Compensation — Salary, Benefits, Pension, Payroll etc. 11.1

Benefits programs per se will be determined by a combination of benefits planning, program features, vacation/holidays, sick leave/personal time off, and employee wants and needs. These programs may include: health-related plans like medical, dental, and vision programs; insured programs, such as life insurance, short- and long-term disability, and workers' compensation; safety programs, like occupational health and safety; and pension plans, whether defined benefits, money purchase, or mixed. Some organizations may also include such items as educational upgrading, top-up of maternity and paternity leave, stock options, financial counselling, employee assistance programs, day-care, and elder care.

As with the other models, the last, but very important function depicted is program evaluation, in which the performance and administration of benefits programs are evaluated so that continuous improvements may be made.

Those searching for a new, fully integrated HRMS are well advised to note the criteria set for the benefits module of the programs they are contemplating. To be effective across organizations, such modules must be complicated, since the nature and requirements of benefits programs vary widely. Growing legislative demands add to the complexity. It is difficult to create programs that can deal with these complexities effectively, while still being user friendly.

Some organizations have in fact found it more effective to develop their own benefits modules, or to buy separate ones that have been designed especially for benefits applications. The complication then becomes how the interface between such modules and the other module in the HRMS is handled.

Whether a benefits module integrated within the larger HRMS, or a "stand-alone" module is purchased, the following capabilities will be important.

To meet an organization's internal needs an HRMS must:

1. identify all employees, both active and inactive, who are eligible for the various benefits;
2. allow for efficient enrolment of new members, preferably as a normal part of the staffing process;
3. accurately monitor benefits eligibility, whether on enrolment or on change in employment status;
4. accurately track benefits coverage for each employee especially as changes occur during an individual's career;
5. facilitate the accurate collection and storage of both current and historical benefits and pension data;
6. be easily updated to reflect legislative, union contract, and policy changes affecting employee benefits;
7. allow automated monitoring of claims performance;

8. interface with the databases of other functions that may or may not have been integrated into the HRMS, such as payroll, occupational health and safety, workers' compensation, and medical records;
9. process claims payments; and
10. automatically effect payroll deductions through the payroll function.

An HRMS must also allow the ready but secure transfer of information to and from relevant external parties, such as reports and returns on pension and benefits information to government agencies; pension and benefits cost data to and from actuaries, auditors, and outside consultants on contract to the organization; rate and coverage information to and from insurance carriers; and information on money available for investment, investment strategy, and investment performance from investment managers and plan trustees.

11.2 — Modelling/Analyses

An HRMS must be able to:

1. provide information flexibly and quickly, in formats tailored to the requirements of the situation. This can include information for senior management decision making, strategic planning, or labour negotiations;
2. support modelling and analyses of benefits data so that problem areas may be identified, and the implications of usage, cost, and other trends explored; and
3. support cost control by automating benefits administration, and providing the means for monitoring excess use, abuse, and inefficiencies, as well as the means for taking corrective action.

11.3 — Trends

Several examples of the way in which automating benefits and pension programs can provide for the more cost-effective administration of these programs were provided in Chapter 3. One of these examples involved the purchase of a pension administration system. This system replaced a partially automated system that had served the pension and benefits staff well for many years, but because it was based on outdated technology, was becoming increasingly difficult to maintain and use.

Benefits and pension plans can be complicated, especially in large organizations. Further, the trend is to greater complexity. The increased use of "flexible benefits programs," leaves of absence, more and different categories of workers, special appointments, and other status changes can cause many variations in the status of compensation, benefits, and pension plans for any individual. All of these must be tracked and recorded if accurate estimates of pension status are to be provided to members on an annual basis, as required by law; and accurate pension calculations are to be prepared on retirement.

Prior to the implementation of a new pension administrative system, records in many pension programs must be cross-checked manually, with calculations reviewed at least once to ensure the accuracy of final pension calculations. This may take several hours for each individual. Organizations that have not automated these functions are well advised to consider doing so now or risk being at severe disadvantage as greater numbers of individuals retire with the aging of the baby boom generation.

(a) — Coordination of Benefits

With increasing numbers of "dual career families," both spouses may be in organizations that provide benefit programs. This may lead to "double coverage" in that each employer may cover both spouses. It is obvious that, in medical or dental programs, for example, this can lead to unnecessary expenses since coverage by just one of the plans is required. Premiums in the other can be saved through coordination across plans. When both spouses are employees of the same organization it should be a relatively simple matter to ensure that this coordination occurs. The HRMS must also be able to provide information to pension and benefits staff (or insurance carriers acting on their behalf) so that contact may be made with organizations or insurance carriers responsible for the benefits programs of each employee's spouse (where such exist) to coordinate benefits programs across organizations. As pointed out in Chapter 3, there can be a considerable pay-back to the organization when this coordination is done effectively.

(b) — Flexible Benefits

In an attempt to offer a greater range of benefits while controlling costs, some organizations are offering "flexible benefits" (also termed "cafeteria" programs) in which individuals are generally provided with a basic "core set of benefits" and then allowed to pick from a menu of additional benefits, until the cost of the benefits chosen equals a predetermined amount. This enables employees to tailor their benefits program to their needs, by selecting those components that are most useful to them, and not being compelled to pay for others that are not. It also places more demands on the benefits module of an HRMS, which must be able to keep track of and report on what are, essentially, unique benefits programs for each employee.

> **Example: Automating the Pension System**
>
> At one large Canadian university, the administrative work alone to process the retirements using the technology at hand was predicted to have required several additional staff at a time when the university was attempting to effect economies. Therefore, the decision was made to implement a new pension administration system that could provide:
>
> - Annual pension statements
> - Accurate reports for the plan's Pension projections to plan board of trustees members for planning Returns to meet government purposes
> - Accurate analysis of pension
> - Analysis/modeling capability to entitlements for retirees support potential plan changes
> - Accurate data to the for both active and retired university's actuary so that employees valuations may be done to determine the funding requirements of the plan
>
> This pension system represented a heavy up-front investment in getting it up and running and then loading it with accurate data, especially since it had to be implemented and run parallel to the older system for a few months. System implementation and debugging were stressful for the pension staff, but proved worthwhile in that the system is now operating well and more than living up to the original expectations held for it.

In a traditional "defined benefits" program, usage and cost are balanced out over all participants. In a flexible benefits program, individuals will select the components that they feel will be most valuable to them in terms of frequency of usage and cost. Those developing a flexible benefits program must take this into account and build safeguards into the system, or risk increased overall costs.

In the design and development of a flexible benefits program, an HRMS benefits module must be able to support research (including employee surveys), analyses, and modelling to help predict employee usage of each of the benefits components. After the program has been implemented, regular and ad hoc HRMS reports will be important to ensure that the program is managed effectively, including achieving its objectives, within cost limitations.

Thus, if used wisely, an HR home page with Benefits information can make it very easy to read and to understand essential benefit plan information. Information presentation is well thought out and can quickly and inexpensively be reorganized as required.

When new regulatory changes are implemented or when the company makes changes, the system can be updated quickly and inexpensively and then immediately communicated. If one wants everyone to know about the change, one can "broadcast", as appropriate, through the e-mail system.

Once employees can access their benefits information "on-line," one can move beyond allowing them just to "read" information to having them "input" information (whether this be selecting new benefits options, changing options already selected, or changing key biographical information). Of course, appropriate edits must be present to ensure that the employee doesn't make changes not allowed by the system, such as making changes to biographical information that is not possible (a date of birth of 1873, for example). All of this can happen without benefits' staff assistance and without paper!

In another kind of "on-line" benefits updating, Nolan (1995) reports that NorTel used an interactive voice response system to allow its more than 13,000 employees to select options from its flexible benefits program. This information was then transferred in automated form directly to the organization's HRMS, thus saving a considerable amount of benefits' staff time and effort.

(c) — Pension

Retirement plans, most commonly referred to as "pensions" are the single largest component of indirect compensation after mandatory benefits.[6]

Pensions have been shown to have a positive impact on worker productivity and a less-than-expected impact on cost. At the same time pensions impact continuance commitment and have been found to have a negative effect in unionized firms. Readers interested in reading more about these issues should refer to Richard Long's 2002 text for Nelson Canada entitled *Strategic Compensation in Canada*, 2nd ed.

Regardless of the relative merits of pension plans, or of a traditional pension plan versus such options as company-sponsored registered retirement savings (RRSPs), if your organization has one (or more) pension plans you will need a way to manage it (them).

Very few HRMS offer complete functionality around pension plans. Some will track contribution levels but it is more common to use specialty software.

11.4 — HRMS Requirements for Total Compensation

Organizing and maintaining all the current and historical information required to do salary determination, benefit management, total compensation calculations and pay equity analyses requires the assistance of a sophisticated HRMS.

Data on the HRMS is used in salary analysis and modeling exercises in preparation for such business processes as strategic planning, labour negotiations, and human resources planning.

---

6 *Strategic Compensation in Canada*, 2nd ed., 2002, Richard Long, p. 219.

11.4 Human Resources Management Systems

A comparison of today's offerings in the HRMS marketplace shows that every vendor has its own particular way of organizing the components needed to manage total compensation. Some have one module with all of the functionality that the vendor has determined to be necessary while other vendors provide a core module that can be combined with others.

In the end result what matters is that all of the components of total compensation exist within a structure that facilitates co-joined use and analysis.

To manage these functions effectively, an HRMS requires the capabilities described below:

AFFILIATION	An affiliation table is necessary to record the major affiliation(s) of each employee, whether this be employment function, professional affiliation, or union affiliation.
AUDIT TRAILS	Both the HR and Payroll components of the compensation need to be able to generate a complete record of all pay transactions, including employee, amount paid, pay type, cost centre, date paid. Analytical reports must be set up to do "real vs. planned" comparisons.
DATA ORGANIZATION	For cost effective updating and ease of data handling, all major data elements should be "table driven", that is, the possible values of each data element should be defined in tables that can easily be referred to in ongoing applications and amended as changes are required. Such changes may be necessary because of evolving organizational requirements or new legislation (e.g., new taxes or new employment equity reporting requirements).
DEDUCTIONS	The system must be able to deduct and track all standard deductions, such as Canada Pension Plan, unemployment insurance and tax.
EFFECTIVE DATE MANAGEMENT	Events that initiate compensation activity occur at throughout an operating cycle. Hirings, terminations, transfers, promotions, return-to-work, leaves, performance pay, benefits changes, etc., are constant happenings. In order to manage multiple worker events, and multiple events per worker, an effective system should allow for events to be future dated or dated retroactively. The actual sequencing of events may require time of day stamps and/or sequence of event listings in order to ensure that the correct relationships are captured and maintained.

Total Compensation — Salary, Benefits, Pension, Payroll etc.   **11.4**

EMPLOYEE/ POSITION HISTORY

The HRMS should track all individual appointments, showing all positions held. It should also track who is, and has been, in each position. The effective dating mentioned earlier is necessary for this to happen.

Some older HRMS and specialty systems may not keep history for each individual, and particularly for each position, and should be either updated or discarded..

EMPLOYMENT AND PAY EQUITY

The HRMS must identify the key data elements associated with employment and pay equity as related to the positions and employees, and be able to report this information in formats required by provincial and federal governments.

HEALTH TAX

In jurisdictions to which it applies, the payroll system must be able to calculate and remit payroll-related health tax. In the province of Ontario, for example, this was 1.95% of gross payroll for the year 2006.

HOURLY EMPLOYEES

The system must be capable of accurately calculating the pay for each hourly paid employee according to the rate of pay and hours worked. A complication in some organizations for both salaried and hourly employees is that individuals may work at multiple jobs at multiple rates of pay for different cost centres during a pay period. The system must also:

1. produce, on demand, time sheets for each employee and/or work unit;
2. track and analyze shift pay differentials;
3. store and report on a variety of salary related data including leave of absences, sick leave, workers' compensation, union duty and other union business including union education and vacation; and
4. have provision for extra fields for information that will be required in the future.

INCOME TAX STATEMENTS

The system must be able to produce accurate income tax statements at year-end. These will include statements of remuneration paid, as well as statements of pension, retirement, annuity and other income. In addition to the paper forms provided to each individual at year end, the system must also be able to produce electronic records of required income tax data for government purposes.

11.4 Human Resources Management Systems

INTERFACING WITH OTHER SYSTEMS

The HRMS containing the payroll system must be able to interface with accounting and other systems to ensure that the most effective use is made of the organization's corporate information resources. For example, most HRMS will now be able to interface with popular spreadsheets, such as Lotus 1-2-3 or Microsoft Excel, for downloading of pay information for analysis.

JOB INFORMATION

The HRMS should have a job class table to store salary information as well as NOC (national occupational code) and OC (occupational codes) used for coding jobs for various legislative and managerial purposes, not the least of which is employment equity (affirmative action for our American readers).

JOB/POSITION DEFINITION

The same processes that are used to define bona fide occupational requirements for staffing purposes are generally used to define job requirements for job valuation processes in salary determination.

As noted in Figure 11.3, job requirements derive from organizational requirements as reflected in strategic/business plans. Traditionally, job requirements were documented in formatted job descriptions. Increasingly, however, job surveys are being used to gather this information. Well prepared job surveys can have the advantages of being more objective, requiring less time and effort to complete, and being more easily automated.

However gathered, job requirements information must be evaluated to determine the relative value of jobs, and thus, relative salary ranges. This is generally done by job evaluation committees according to established evaluation guidelines. Job surveys can produce automated information in weighted form that could be used directly to determine salary ranges; however, evaluation committees are most often used to evaluate the information derived from this source. Such committees can compensate for employees and supervisors who might tend to under-or over-represent the job described.

Most HRMS products offer some degree of job evaluation functionality but the most robust applications to manage job evaluation are specialty products, most of which are distributed by consulting firms (Hay and Mercer, to name two).

Total Compensation — Salary, Benefits, Pension, Payroll etc.   **11.4**

LEAVES OF ABSENCE	The system must be able to track periods of leave of absence (LOA), with and without pay, maternity leave and unpaid sick leave.
MASS CHANGES	The payroll system must be capable of making mass changes of data, such as when pay increases are processed. Major data entities, such as organizations and jobs, must be table driven. A name change to an organization unit in a table will result in a name change of the organization of all employees linked to that organization.
ON-LINE COMMUNICATIONS AND ADMINISTRATION OF BENEFITS PROGRAMS	Brochures and pamphlets have traditionally been used to inform employees about what benefits are available, and how to access them. Unfortunately these brochures and pamphlets are sometimes hard to follow and quickly become out-of-date.

In the past, benefits personnel have found it difficult to keep up-to-date written documentation available. This has often led to confusion among employees about their benefits, and the need for benefits personnel to spend a great deal of time in one-on-one information and counseling sessions.

Organizations are increasingly providing their employees with direct on-line computer access to selected HRMS information (see Chapter 13). This raises the possibility of allowing employees to access their benefits and pension information in forms that are designed to communicate what benefits the individual has, as well as what options are available.

This may be done directly via screens that the individual calls up on a computer (with, of course, appropriate security safeguards under "password" protection), which may or may not be supplemented with "help menus," or automated tutorials.

Some progressive organizations have been making benefits information available "on-line" by putting their benefits information on a web site where it can be maintained and updated electronically.

11.4 Human Resources Management Systems

ORGANIZATION

An organization is best defined as a number of positions that have been created and linked to bring people together to work in some structured way. It is typically defined by one or more tables that link approved (active) positions and assign them to the appropriate cost centre.

Organizations are often displayed visually through "organization charts" that are created and displayed by the HRMS and display positions. Sometimes the position titles and the name of the incumbent, if any, is included.

In actual fact most HRMS products do not achieve this directly but rather utilize available third-party software for the display aspects of an Organization Chart. Various products can achieve this including Microsoft products such as Visio and PowerPoint, but most dedicated users tend to use products designed for organization charting and nothing more.

Figure 11.6 Typical Organization Chart

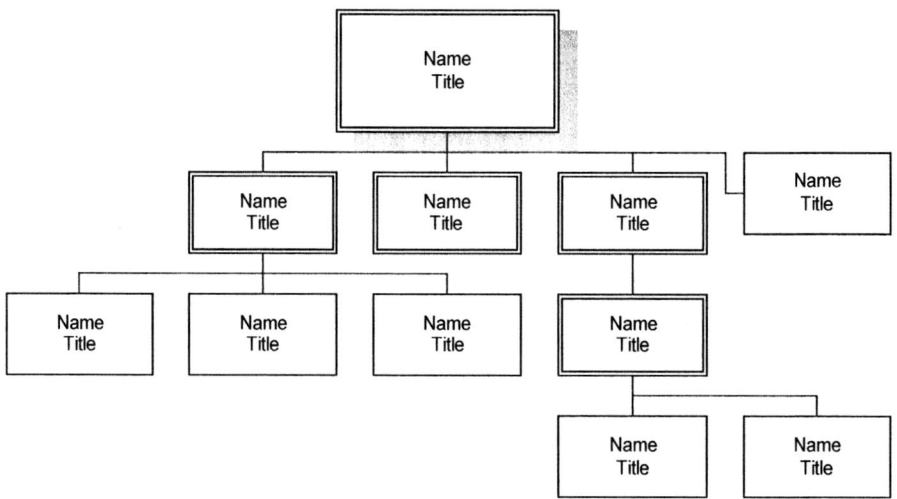

Total Compensation — Salary, Benefits, Pension, Payroll etc. **11.4**

PAY EQUITY

Where pay equity legislation applies, a salary policy line may be determined by the pay rates of male-dominated jobs. In Ontario's pay equity process for example, a comparator is defined to be the lowest paid male-dominated job class of equal value. When suitable comparators do not exist, then extrapolation across points in the salary line is possible. When too few male comparators exist even to do this (for instance, in highly female-dominated worksites such as day-care settings), proxy comparators may be chosen from other settings to serve as points on the salary policy line. The salary adjustments required to bring the salaries of individuals in female-dominated job classes to the salary policy line represents the pay equity adjustments.

Obviously, one would prefer a smooth ascending curve when dollars (Y-axis) are plotted against job evaluation level (X-axis). A major problem with the job class to job class comparison method for determining pay equity in Ontario is that it is possible to get inversions in the curve when a highly paid male-dominated class has to be used as a comparator at one level, while a lower paid, but more highly evaluated male-dominated job is the comparator at a higher level. For example, the coaches of most professional hockey teams make less than their team captains, although the job of coach would probably rank higher than the job of team captain in most evaluation schemes. Therefore, if the jobs of coach and team captain were identified as two male comparator job classes, an inversion of the type mentioned would occur.

To establish internal equity within an organization, any such anomalies are usually resolved by smoothing out the salary policy line even when this means raising the line overall to compensate for these anomalies. Adjustments required to raise salaries to the policy line are made across all jobs at a given evaluation level, whether or not the job falls into a female, male, or neutral job class.

PAYROLL VARIABLES

A data element for each of the key variables linked to calculating pay for salaried and hourly employees. Note: it is useful to develop a data dictionary encompassing each of these essential data elements, so that the definition of each element is readily available for users.

11.4 Human Resources Management Systems

PENSION REPORTS — The system should be able to track and report all pension deductions.

PERFORMANCE EVALUATION — The HRMS should provide for the tracking of goals and objectives, performance intervals, and evaluation.

HR has been forever mired in a "chicken and egg" type argument regarding performance assessment and whether or not it should like to salary. Many organizations think that the linkage between performance assessment and financial compensation should exist. Others argue the reverse.

For example, a major world-wide component manufacturer[7] has an extremely complex performance management process that is heavily tied to direct compensation:

Q1 – assessment #1 – based on selected factors and paid in Q2

Q2 – assessment #2 – based on selected factors and paid in Q3

Q3 – assessment #3 – based on selected factors and paid in Q4

Q4 – assessment #4 – based on selected factors and paid in Q1 of following year

Annual Summary – Q1+Q2+Q3+Q4 – assessment #5 - a summary of #1-4 **plus** a final overall rating and paid in Q1 of the following year (together with the payment for Q4).

As you can imagine, the interplay between the performance management processes and system and the variable compensation processes and system are very closely managed. Using two (or more) different systems would be possible but would make ongoing management a nightmare.

POSITION MANAGEMENT — There is an ongoing debate about whether or not a HRMS needs to be position driven.

Proponents (which we declare ourselves to be) suggest that to be truly effective a HRMS needs to capture data for both the organization structure and for the people who inhabit it. As illustrated in Figure 11.7 both the organization and the people who inhabit it are separate, but linked.

---

7 Identity withheld by request.

Total Compensation — Salary, Benefits, Pension, Payroll etc. **11.4**

Jobs and Positions (filled or vacant) exist apart from the people. They can be counted (as in, the number of approved positions, the number of filled/occupied positions, the number of vacant positions, etc.).

The attributes of a job accrue to a position and include:
- Cost centre paying for the position
- Level (as per job evaluation)
- Salary and benefit package (as per "Level")

In order for a person to be recorded by the system as "employed" they must be attached to a position that, in turn, has certain attributes which accrue to the position and the person assigned/hired to it, i.e., salary scale, benefits package and so on.

Those who oppose the concept of position management do so because they feel that it imposes a level of bureaucracy that is unnecessary and nonproductive. Certainly there are many organizations that have struggled with the process, and several HRMS do not handle the process well.

As noted above, we believe that the positives heavily outweigh the negatives. The setup tasks can be time-consuming, but once completed the ongoing maintenance should be relatively easy and worthwhile. If you are considering the acquisition of a new HRMS this is clearly one of the areas that you should focus on.

RECORD OF EMPLOYMENT	The system must be able to produce accurate records of employment as required. The calculation of these records of employment for each individual must be based on actual history.
RETROACTIVE PAY	The system must track all pay events and facilitate the calculation of retroactive pay.
SALARIED EMPLOYEES	The payroll system must be capable of accurately calculating the pay for each salaried employee. Salary must be calculated according to the number of days (entitled to be paid) if the employee starts/stops work during a pay period. The HRMS must calculate additional pay if additional pay is earned. Adjustments must be able to be made accordingly.

11.4 Human Resources Management Systems

Figure 11.7 Organization and People Relationships

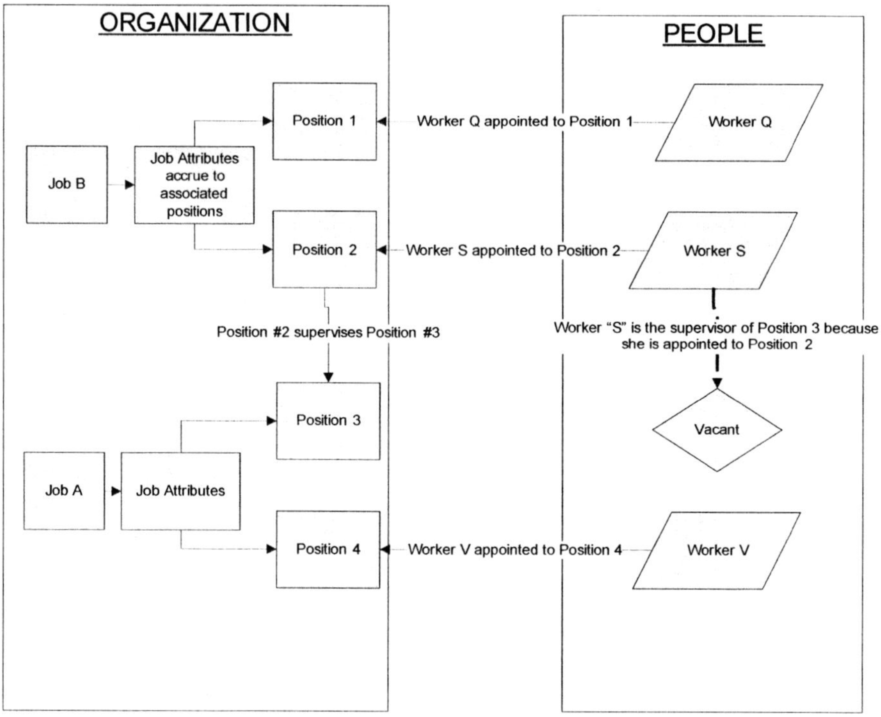

```
ORGANIZATION                                          PEOPLE

                    ┌─► Position 1 ◄── Worker Q appointed to Position 1 ── Worker Q
         Job Attributes
         accrue to
Job B ──►associated
         positions
                    └─► Position 2 ◄── Worker S appointed to Position 2 ── Worker S
                                                                              │
           Position #2 supervises Position #3    Worker "S" is the supervisor of Position 3 because
                                                 she is appointed to Position 2
                                                                              │
                    ┌─► Position 3                              Vacant
Job A ──► Job Attributes
                    └─► Position 4 ◄── Worker V appointed to Position 4 ── Worker V
```

SALARY MARKET SURVEYING

Many organizations keep track of the salary rates paid by others in and outside of their industrial sectors by participating in and subscribing to published salary surveys. Other organizations prefer to conduct their own surveys. The information gathered may be entered into the HRMS and used as a context against which to conduct analyses to determine a salary policy line. A salary policy line outlines the salary that the organization wishes to pay at each job evaluation level.

The difference between the actual salary line (what the organization is actually paying at each job evaluation level) and the salary policy line represents the salary adjustments required to align actual salaries with the established salary policy line (see Figure 11.8).

Figure 11.8 Relation Between a Salary Policy Line and Actual Salary Line

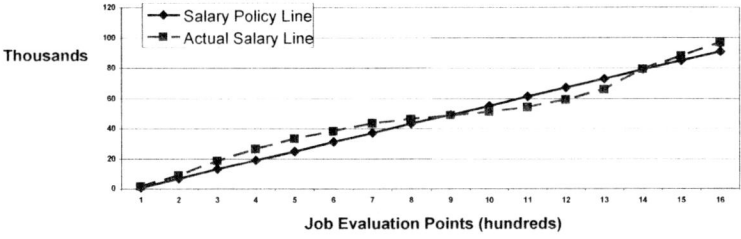

SALARY POLICY LINES	Salary policy lines may be established in different ways, for different purposes. Traditionally, however, they have been established by senior management, based on the organization's compensation strategy and knowledge of external salary conditions.
	The organization's compensation strategy should be rooted in its strategic/ business plans, since the salaries paid by the organization will reflect the quality and availability of human resources. As a consequence, strategically, some organizations decide that they want to pay above average salaries for their sector, while others choose to pay average salaries. Economic and business conditions for some organizations may mean that they have to pay less than average salaries for their sector.
SENIORITY	The HRMS should provide a field that can be updated manually to reflect seniority date. Many organizations can have multiple seniority dates, and we have seen as many as five separate dates for one employee in one organization. Seniority is one place where effective date and time can be an issue and we have known organizations that tie effective time of day to Greenwich Mean Time so that all employees world-wide can be shown as "hired" on an absolute world-wide basis.
SHORT- AND LONG-TERM DISABILITY	If applicable, the system must continue to pay the employee on short-term disability (STD) if the employee has sick leave accumulated. The system must be able to track and administer long-term disability (LTD) where this is required.

11.4 Human Resources Management Systems

TIME - IN LIEU — Where it applies, the system must be able to track time off in lieu of overtime. This must link to attendance management.

TIME - ACTUAL — Actual time worked represents either the recorded time or the assumed time worked by an employee. Compared to scheduled time, actual time will produce variance reports showing employee utilization and liability for overtime. Actual time can be captured in many ways including several automated methods.

McCallum (1996), for example, reports that employees at Niagara Paints in Hamilton, Ontario, use an electro-magnetic card to record hours of work and breaks. Entries from this card are automatically analyzed by the HRMS time and attendance/payroll modules. These can be entered into an HRMS for payroll, human resources, operational and other purposes. Actual time is often broken into the following three components, particularly in heavy and resource industries:

(a) Direct labour generally reflects employee time spent at work in productive activity. It is often recorded against volume of output produced, machine utilization and other such components. It often includes activities that are directly related to productivity such as set-up and wash-up times. It is used by line management and finance groups to assign production costs and measure production efficiency and is not normally a concern of Human Resources.

(b) Indirect labour involves employee time spent at work, but not in directly productive activities. Examples include training, union business and time spent on performance appraisal or discipline. This time is separated from direct labour in order to provide a more accurate estimate of the cost of production. Operations and Finance are concerned with indirect labour, particularly in reducing it, but most indirect labour activities are also of concern to Human Resources.

TIME - AVAILABLE — This is the amount of time available to be worked by each type of employee. It is derived from union employment contracts, applicable legislation and organization policies and practices and includes regular time and overtime.

Total Compensation — Salary, Benefits, Pension, Payroll etc.   **11.4**

TIME - MANAGEMENT REPORTING

There are many different ways of handling the capture and reporting of time worked. Traditionally, the most common has been the use of time cards on which an individual employee's actual time at work (direct and indirect) is recorded. This card is then passed to production accounting where the values are entered for production purposes, and then passed to payroll for pay processing. Time cards can be manual or automated by use of mechanical time clocks, scanners, or direct computer entry.

It is desirable to collect all data as close to the source as possible, to minimize manual data entry and to maximize access to the data. Many organizations collect employee time data for all actual time, but some organizations are making a strategic decision to move away from that level of detail to "exception reporting."

The use of exception reporting of employee time assumes that an employee works as scheduled unless otherwise reported. Exceptions, such as scheduled direct labour being attributed to indirect labour or daily sick leave, are still reported, but the volume of time information that must be collected and entered is significantly reduced. Exception reporting has been used for some time, but has normally been restricted to salaried, non- unionized employees.

New technological options for reporting time are also easing this task. Interactive voice response (IVR) systems utilizing touch-tone phones for entering into computer systems from remote sites are now being marketed. Using such equipment, the employee or supervisor can call the system from home, car, or office and use the phone keypad to enter the exception information. The IVR system is interfaced with the main HRMS so that the data is automatically transferred

TIME - NOT AT WORK

"Time not at work" may be for legitimate reasons (e.g., leaves of absence (LOAs)) or not (e.g., absence without permission to pursue personal interests). LOAs may be with or without pay depending on the nature and duration of the leave. It includes sick leave, short-and long-term disability, vacation, education leaves and time off on personal business (bereavement, jury duty, voting, etc.). Line management is often responsible for monitoring and dealing with poor attendance, usually expressed as a percentage of available hours, although Human Resources is

11.4 Human Resources Management Systems

sometimes responsible for managing an overall organizational absenteeism or attendance program, when one exists.

Payroll concerns itself with the payment or nonpayment of time not at work, pursuant to input from operations and interpretation of employment contracts and legislation. Human Resources usually has a significant role in the management of LOAs and associated benefits administration, to ensure adherence and consistency of application with organization policies and collective agreements.

TIME - OVERTIME
This refers to time worked in excess of standard hours for which an additional payment is provided (most often 1.5 times the regular hourly payment). In some jurisdictions a provision for building up or banking time may provide time off in lieu of payment. Where this banking of time is permitted, the time off is normally calculated at a ratio of 1:1, overtime to time off, rather than at 1.5:1. Overtime is normally authorized by line management within guidelines set by organization policy and union agreements (which dictate seniority and other factors used to assign overtime).

TIME - REGULAR OR STANDARD
This refers to the number of hours/shifts an employee is normally expected to be at work in a given period. It will include direct and possibly indirect labour as well. Legislation varies widely by jurisdiction, but normally sets maximum allowable hours an employee is allowed to work regardless of overtime, and often specifies minimum hours of work for which an employee must be paid if called in to work. The payroll group is usually charged with the responsibility of auditing actuals against legislative, contract and organization limits.

TIME - SCHEDULED
This refers to the times an individual employee is scheduled to work within the parameters of available time. Schedules may include overtime. Individuals are sometimes scheduled as part of a crew or work group. This is most often expressed in hours, days, or shifts. This could be 37.5 hours per week, or 1980 hours per year. Shift workers often work cycles of shifts which, when averaged, produce an average number of hours per week.

Total Compensation — Salary, Benefits, Pension, Payroll etc.   **11.4**

Most scheduling of employee time is done by line management with no direct reference to either Payroll or Human Resources, except of course, for staff working in those functions.

TIME AND ATTENDANCE

The management of time and attendance is a neglected and misunderstood management activity in many organizations. It often takes far too much supervisory time, including such activities as:

- Forecasting
- Scheduling
- Labor Distribution and resultant analysis of productive/ non-productive time
- Additional workers to meet additional workload

- Absence reporting
- Replacement workers for absences
- Time Capture
  - Positive or exception
  - Elapsed & punched

Most of these issues are significant in most industries, and some are significant in every industry. Manufacturing, retail, health care, education, services — each industry has its own set of time management challenges.

As noted above, each payroll system must have the capability to accurately capture, analyze and report attendance on the job, as well as the time worked in the various categories for which an individual is eligible. Because of the complexity of "time and attendance," many HRMSs have special modules for this purpose.

Figure 11.9 provides a graphic illustration of one such module and shows how the various types of employee time feed to the HRMS and the G/L.

Many software offerings are found wanting with regard to some aspect of time and attendance management. Organizations that bought software found (and often continue to find) that human resources systems and integrated HRMSs lacked key capabilities required by either Operations or Payroll. The function of scheduling of time, for example, is often ignored by HRMSs, with the time cycle being picked up at the reporting of actuals.

11.4 Human Resources Management Systems

Figure 11.9 Time and Attendance Management Model[8]

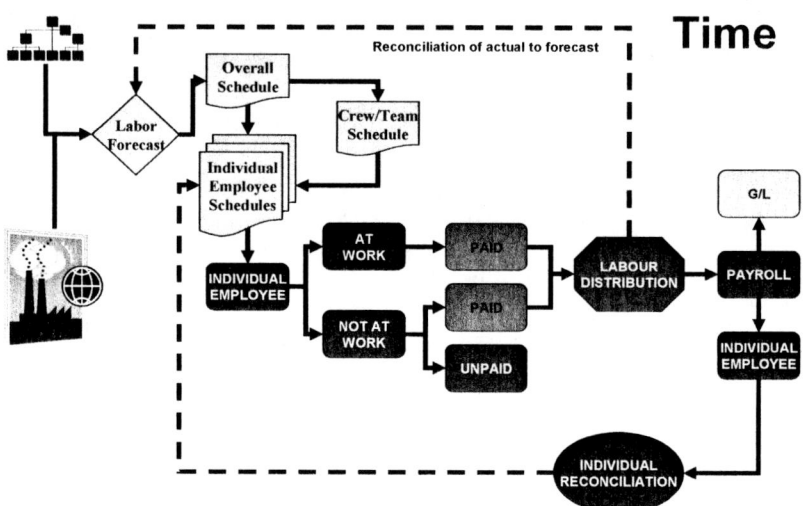

The unsophisticated security that most of these systems contained meant that users could not be restricted to their particular area of interest; in this case, line management and Payroll could access confidential compensation and other human resources information on employees in their own or other areas for which they had no need or authority to access. Fortunately, with improved techniques for managing security, it is no longer a barrier to integrated systems.

The existence of multiple systems holding related information also led to duplicate data capture and entry. The time records of one employee could be captured by as many as four separate systems; the foreperson's paper record, production labour reports, Payroll and Human Resources. In addition, in some instances the same supervisor would enter essentially the same data all four times.

The trend toward coordination of information systems holding time and attendance and payroll information has forced those responsible for the design of work processes to consider how those processes might better be designed to be more integrated and reduce duplication.

---

8 Courtesy of Laird & Greer Management Consultants, 2007.

Total Compensation — Salary, Benefits, Pension, Payroll etc.   **11.5**

	The HRMS should provide sufficient fields and capacity to record all absences by type, date, paid/unpaid, etc., AND time spent by project or other measure of work.
WORK PLANNING AND REVIEW	The requirements of the job provide the context or mandate against which individual work goals may be developed. At the end of the performance period, performance may be measured against these goals and the assessment used to determine merit pay, in those organizations that use merit as a determinate of pay increases.
YEAR-TO-DATE INFORMATION	The system must be able to accumulate earnings and deductions, and to display year-to-date information.

11.5 — Program Evaluation/Metrics

As noted in previous chapters many HR organizations are focusing more and more on measuring effort and results. It is important that the effectiveness of the processes outlined above be monitored and upgraded continuously.

As with other HR functions, the Total Compensation process can be measured across the organization, only within the Compensation function, or within the specific sub-units: Compensation, Benefits, Pension and Payroll. The blend of policies and procedures combined with your tools, such as a HRMS and/or specific staffing software, can be used to collect and analyse the activity and results.

Some possible measures for the Total Compensation function include:[9]

- *Total Compensation Revenue Factor* – calculates total compensation as a percent of organization income generated.

- *Total Compensation Expense Factor* – measures the extent to which total compensation expense is a percentage of total operating expense. The ratio tends to vary widely by industry, from a low of 16.9% in Utilities to 43.2% in Healthcare.[10]

- *Executive Compensation Percent* – calculates the executive compensation as a percentage of total compensation.

- *Comparatio* – this measure is specific to one individual worker's compensation in relation to the grid in which their job has been placed.

- *Benefit Revenue Factor* – dividing benefit costs by revenue, this measures the percentage of revenue spent by the benefits program.

- *Benefit Expense Factor* – dividing benefit costs by total operating ex-

---

[9] Metrics from Saratoga Institute Human Resource Financial Report, 1997.
[10] Specific metrics from Saratoga Institute Human Resource Financial Report, 1997.

penses, this measures the percentage of revenue spent by the benefits program.

- *Benefit Compensation Factor* – provides the cost of benefits as a percentage of total financial compensation.
- *Payroll Manual Cheque Ratio* – calculates the effectiveness of payroll with regard to the requirement for manual cheques.[11]
- *Payroll Head Count* – measures the number of payroll staff required.
- *Payroll Cheque Cost Ratio* – measures the cost per pay cheque generated.
- *Payroll Expense Percent* – measures the cost of payroll.
- *Controllable Absenteeism* – measures the rate of casual sick and absence due to minor injury.
- *Uncontrollable Absenteeism* – measures the rate of absenteeism from uncontrollable factors such as accidents, heart attacks, family illness, etc.

All of these measures can be calculated manually, but automatic collection and calculation by a HRMS and/or a specialized compensation software package will significantly ease the burden and provide comparative analysis for HR and/or managers.

You will note that some of these measures require data from a source outside of the HRMS. Calculation of the Total Compensation Revenue Factor, for example, requires organization income, pre-tax sales and service revenue, that will derive from the Finance system.

HR people often complain that HR is not given its due as a contributor to overall organization results. One of the outcomes from using measures that factor in organization financial results is that human resource data can be directly linked to those overall organization results.

Another aspect of the metrics that can be generated from a HRMS is that a metric in one area, Compensation Expense Factor, for example, will be reflected in others, in this example, turnover and staffing costs. These relationships underline the usefulness of a single integrated HRMS that can draw on data from all functional parts of the system to produce meaningful, actionable analysis.

Gathering, and then presenting these measures may put HR in a different light, including emphasizing the need by others in the organization to consider HR more strategically, as noted in Chapter 8.

---

11 Payroll metrics courtesy of Laird & Greer Management Consultants 04/04/14, Metrics Workshop held at 2004 IHRIM Conference Presentation.

11.6 — Summary

This chapter has discussed the use of an HRMS in support of the Total Compensation and payroll functions of the organization. The interrelationship between these and other human resources functions, including an HRMS, were demonstrated with the assistance of a human resources model. Emphasis was placed on contemporary issues such as evolving strategic/business trends and pay equity.

Complexity tends to be greater in large organizations but has been a general evolution toward greater complexity over time for all organizations, as employee expectations have increased and legislation has imposed further demands. Even relatively small organizations are consequently finding it necessary to use an HRMS to store and manipulate the information required to manage benefits and pension programs. This includes doing costing and other analyses required to reconcile the demand for benefits from various sources with what can be done within available cost constraints.

The capture of employee time as an important data component for several functional areas was also discussed. These areas have traditionally kept their data separately, but new strategic thinking and technology have combined to make it possible to collect and enter the data once and treat it as an organization-wide resource. Integration of these multiple data streams into one set of data within the HRMS provides an excellent example of the organization-wide applications of the HRMS. Such integration also provides concrete savings.

Providing employees with the capability of direct "on-line" access to, and updating of, their benefits information — known as Employee Self-Service (ESS) — is leading to reduced costs for benefits administration, and more informed and satisfied employees.

11.7 — References

Agarwal, N.C. 1986. "Wage and Salary Administration", in *Human Resources Management in Canada*. Scarborough, Ont.: Carswell, 1995.

Belcher, D., and T.J. Achtison. 1987. Compensation Administration. Englewoods Cliffs, N.J.: Prentice-Hall.

Belcourt, M., A.W. Sherman, G.W. Bohlander, and S.A. Snell. 1996. *Managing Human Resources*, Canadian ed. Toronto: Nelson Canada.

"Benefits Communication: Linking costs and commitment." 1992. *Canadian HR Reporter* (February): 13.

Canadian Payroll Association. 1994. Student Guide for Introduction to Payroll, Level I, 3rd ed. Toronto.

Cascio, W.F., and J.W. Thacker. 1994. *Managing Human Resources.* Toronto: McGraw-Hill Ryerson.

Ceriello, V.R. Human Resource Management Systems: Strategy, Tactics, and Techniques. Toronto: Maxwell Macmillan.

Coward, L.E. 1991. *Mercer Handbook of Canadian Pension and Benefit Plans.* Don Mills, Ont.: CCH Canadian Ltd.

Delaney, R. and Turnbull, I.J. 2006. National Knowledge Exam Study Guide. Aurora, Ont.: Canadian HR Press.

Doran J.A., and G.M. Rampton. 1994. "Making a Business Case for a New Human Resources Management Information System." Canadian Human Resources Systems Professionals Resource Magazine (June): 4-8.

Freedman, S.M., J.R. Montanari and R.T. Keller. 1982. "The Compensation Program: Balancing Organizational and Employee Needs." Compensation Review (2nd quarter): 47-54.

Kavanagh, M.J., H.G. Gueutal, and S.I. Tannenbaum. 1990. Human Resource Information Systems: Development and Application. Boston, Mass.: PWS-Kent.

Kelly, J.G. 1991. "Benefits Applications." In A.L. Lederer, ed., *Handbook of Human Resource Information Systems.* New York: Warren, Gorham and Lamont.

Lederer, A.L. 1991. Handbook of Human Resource Information Systems. Boston, Mass.: Warren, Gorham and Lamont.

Long, R.J. 2002. *Strategic Compensation in Canada*, 2nd ed., Toronto, Nelson.

MacPherson, D.L., and J.T. Wallace. 1992. "Employee Benefits Plans." In *Human Resources Management in Canada.* Scarborough, Ont.: Carswell.

McCaffrey, R.M. 1988. *Employee Benefits Programs: A Total Compensation Perspective.* Boston, Mass.: PWS-Kent.

McCallum, T. 1996. "Embracing the Chip: State-of-the-Art Technology Propels HR into Strategy's Front Lines." Human Resources Professional (April): 13-16.

Milkovich, G.T., and J.M. Newman. 1990. Compensation. Homewood, Ill.: Richard D. Irwin.

Nolan, C. 1995. "Plugged In: Delivering the Benefits Message Goes Interactive." *Benefits Canada* (June): 34-35.

_____. 1989. "Organizational Performance and the Strategic Allocation of Indirect Compensation." *Human Resources Planning* 12, no. 3, 229-38.

Rampton, G.M., and J.A. Doran. 1994. "A Practitioner's Guide for a New HRIS." Unpublished paper presented at the 9th Annual CHRSP Conference (October): 4-7.

Total Compensation — Salary, Benefits, Pension, Payroll etc.   **11.7**

Schuler, R.S. 1984. *Personnel and Human Resources Management*, 2nd ed. New York: West Publishing.

Stelluto, G.L., and D.P. Klein. 1990. "Compensation Trends into the 21st Century." *Monthly Labour Review* 113, no. 2: 38-45.

Stonebraker, P.W. 1995. "Flexible and Incentive Benefits: A Guide to Program Development." *Compensation Review* 17, no. 2: 40-53.

Theriault, R. 1994. "Mercer Compensation Manual: Theory and Practice." Unpublished paper presented at the 9th Annual CHRSP Conference (October): 4-7.

CHAPTER 12: OCCUPATIONAL HEALTH AND SAFETY

12.1 — Introduction

Occupational health and safety (OH&S) is receiving increased workplace emphasis, fueled by government legislation, pressures from organized labour, and increased awareness on behalf of many progressive organizations that healthy, safe working environments are cost-effective. As noted in Robertson (1992), OH&S legislation has three major aims:

1. *Prevention.* Setting minimum standards in the workplace, together with the means of enforcing these standards.

2. *Employment security/Compensation.* Ensuring that injured workers receive appropriate Workers' Compensation, medical attention, rehabilitation support, a suitable job to return to once they are able to work, or extended financial support if they are not.

3. *Employer liability.* Ensuring that the employer meets the established OH&S standards, and is accountable when the standards are not met.

This chapter discusses the use of an HRMS in support of occupational health and safety.

12.2 — Occupational Health and Safety Model

Figure 12.1 applies the human resources model to occupational health and safety.

Occupational health and safety can be described as the identification, evaluation, and control of hazards associated with the work environment and for the purposes of this text includes industrial hygiene (environmental monitoring of air and water quality and noise levels), as well as ergonomics.

12.2 Human Resources Management Systems

Figure 12.1 Occupational Health and Safety

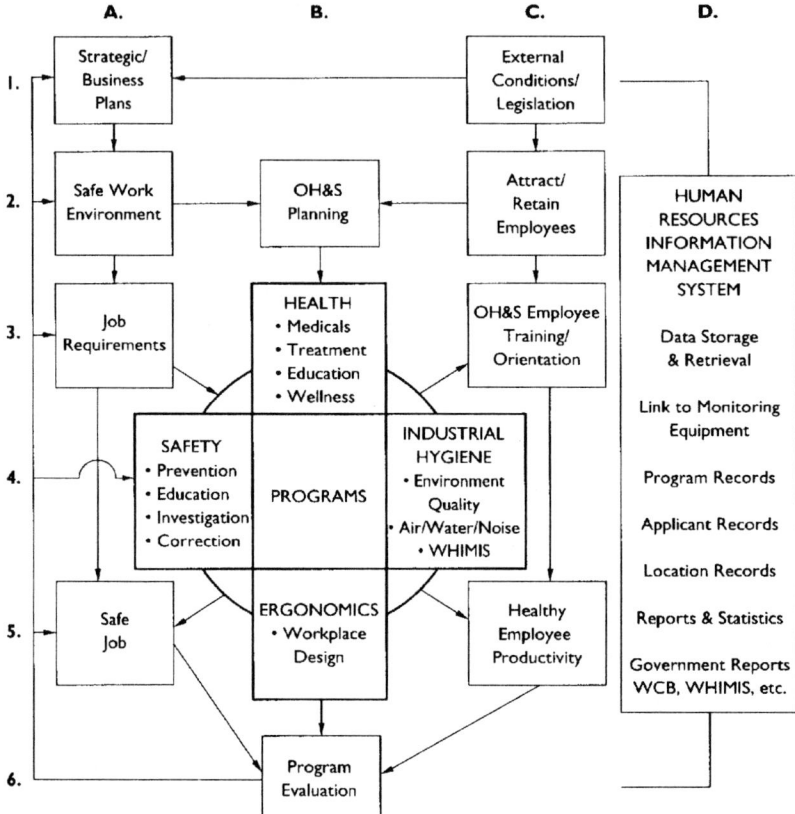

Other general activities covered under the heading of OH&S include medical testing, medicals (pre-employment, during employment, post-employment), medical treatment, first aid, preventative measures (e.g., flu and travel shots), accident prevention and education, accident investigation, recommendations for correction of procedures, equipment, union and management committees, and workers' compensation boards.

Traditionally, hazards have included *physical hazards* such as falling objects, dangerous tools or machinery, footing, noise, light, temperature, radiation and vibration; *chemical hazards*, including carcinogens; and *biological hazards* such as bacteria, viruses and allergens. More recently, ergonomic issues — appropriateness of work environment, tools, etc. — and workplace stress have gained prominence.

Of particular interest today is the question of pandemics and the challenge to keep business going if an avian influenza virus, bird flu, or other problem arises.

Technology is already part of drug distribution infrastructure, with computer models as standard tools for studying pandemic preparedness and most eyes peeled for warning signs are looking at computer screens.[1] From an HR perspective the challenge will be how to let more people work from home, staying productive without getting exposed to or spreading the virus. For HR staff, for managers/supervisors, and indeed all workers in a self-service environment, a HRMS would have to be accessible by Internet to meet the challenge.

12.3 — Legislation

In Canada, OH&S is a provincial responsibility, except in federally regulated settings like the federal public service, Crown corporations, broadcasting and transportation companies, banks, grain elevators and the Canadian Forces. Whereas in the United States, OH&S is regulated by the federal Occupational Safety and Health Act, separate legislation exists in each of the 10 Canadian provinces and there is federal legislation as well. In specific areas, such as the Workplace Hazardous Materials Information System (WHMIS), the federal government and the provinces have cooperated to establish common standards.

Legislation and jurisprudence in most western countries require that organizations exercise "due diligence" in protecting clients, workers and others on the organization's property, using the organization's property, or acting on the organization's behalf. This means that all reasonable precautions have to be taken to ensure that the workplace and property are safe and that workers are trained and skilled in doing their jobs safely.

The following are among criteria that are likely to be used to determine "due diligence" in the case of an investigation of an accident or unsafe working conditions:

1. Whether appropriate OH&S policies and procedures exist, based in substantial part on applicable OH&S legislation, but also on the genuine will of the organization to maintain a healthy and safe workplace.

2. Whether legislation, policies, and procedures are translated into effective OH&S programs, including written infor- mation, training for management and staff at all levels (including orientation training for new employees), joint health and safety committees (which meet regularly, and are qualified and empowered to conduct accident investigations and workplace health and safety inspections), and clear evidence of the commitment of the organization's board of directors and executive to OH&S, including the commitment of necessary resources.

3. Whether OH&S legislation, policies, procedures, and pro- grams are un-

---

1 Gathered 06-09-06 from <http://www.eweek.com/article2/0,1895,1957931,00.asp> Facing Off a Flu Pandemic with IT, M.L. Baker, Ziff Davis, May 4, 2006.

derstood, applied, and monitored throughout the organization, and whether appropriate follow-up action, including discipline, when appropriate, is taken for non-compliance.

12.4 — Application

The Pulp and Paper Research Institute of Canada (Paprican), with a number of sites across Canada, conducts research using a large number of potentially hazardous equipment and chemicals. Occupational health and safety must be a priority for employees at all levels of the various laboratories and research sites included in this research. A copy of the preface of the Pulp and Paper Research Institute of Canada's OH&S Manual (1996) is provided below to illustrate how an organization can demonstrate its commitment to health and safety:

> Safe working conditions and a healthy workplace environment are important for all of us. These conditions do not just occur automatically — they require thoughtful, conscientious effort to ensure that safety is a routine part of our work. To assist employees, Paprican has developed this Occupational Health and Safety Manual. It provides guidelines and procedures aimed at helping us to work safely. I urge all employees to read this manual carefully and to become familiar with the sections that apply to their work area.
>
> Despite these precautions, we are all aware that many of our research activities are not routine in nature. Therefore, we must also rely on common sense and a spirit of cooperation to help prevent potentially hazardous situations. All employees, whether they be officers, research management, supervisors, researchers, technical or support staff, must work together to identify potential hazards by appropriately analyzing operations, planning experiments, and installing equipment with safety in mind.
>
> Inspections by the Safety Committee and investigations of incidents and accidents are also important milestones in our ongoing commitment to safety. Clear, direct communication and a willingness to share information openly and to discuss issues frankly and objectively are essential.
>
> Compliance with our safety guidelines and regulations, whether contained within this document or otherwise communicated, is not optional, it is a condition of employment. Failure to respect safety procedures could endanger not only your life but the lives of your fellow workers. It should be understood that willful infractions will result in disciplinary action.
>
> All employees should feel free to discuss any aspect of safety with their supervisor or safety representative. Health and safety are the right and responsibility of each employee. (p. i)

An organization's HRMS has a key role to play in collecting, storing, and reporting of information to assist personnel at all levels of the organization carry out their OH&S responsibilities. An HRMS can be used, for example, to:

1. keep a roster of safety inspections, maintain the results of such inspections,

and conduct analyses to identify either particularly good (to be rewarded) or problem areas (for corrective action);

2. maintain the results of accident investigations, as well as identify and report on trends;
3. maintain a roster of employees that have received OH&S training and/or certification (see Chapter 10) or have otherwise passed or met specific knowledge targets, as well as individuals who are qualified to provide OH&S training; and
4. collect information and provide regular reports on injuries, medical time-off, and workers' compensation statistics so that the organization can identify trends; compare and manage costs (see Chapter 3); identify priority areas for joint safety committee attention; allow comparisons with other organizations in the same sector; and provide reports and returns both for the government and for internal use, quickly and efficiently.

Information for the reports and returns mentioned in points 1 to 4, above, should be available from the results of formal health and safety inspections, accident and hazard investigations, workers' compensation reports, and other HRMS modules, such as training or benefits, discussed in previous chapters.

12.5 — Relationships Between OH&S and HRM Data

The following list shows some of the areas that either share information with OH&S, or share closely related information.

1. *Staffing*
   - Pre-employment health declaration
   - Pre-employment medical
2. *Benefits*
   - Medical and drug requirements
3. *Attendance Management*
   - Medical/health reasons for absence
   - Accident investigation
   - First aid
4. *Wellness Programs*
   - Preventative measures
   - Periodic medical testing
   - Education
   - Safety inspections
   - Industrial hygiene programs
   - Employee Assistance Program (EAP)
5. *Employee Relations*
   - OH&S union or management committees

- Incident report

Selected HRMS data may be required in specific OH&S programs. For example, administration of an employee assistance program (EAP) could require the following HRM data elements for each worker, his or her significant other, and immediate family:

- Name
- Address
- Phone
- Date of birth
- Social Insurance Number
- Emergency contact(s)
- Work location
- Job title
- Level of benefits
- Medical history
- Job performance records

12.6 — Occupational Health and Safety Inspections

These inspections are often the responsibility of joint (union/ management) occupational health and safety committees. Inspections should be conducted systematically, according to an established checklist. The following items will generally be covered in such a checklist:

1. Safe use and maintenance of machinery, tools and equipment.

2. Environmental factors such as noise, atmosphere and temperature.

3. State of storage areas and facilities, especially as pertaining to hazardous materials.

4. Storage and use of hazardous materials. (Do material safety data sheets exist, and are the materials concerned being stored and used properly? Has training been completed in accordance with WHMIS?)

5. Existence and quality of personal protective equipment.

6. State of working and walking surfaces.

7. Adherence to safe working practices.

8. State and quality of emergency facilities and equipment.

In each of the above areas the HRMS should be able to document and report on the following:

1. Department inspected, date, time.
2. Name of inspectors.
3. Hazards observed.
4. Recommended action, date action taken.
5. Result of follow-up review by safety committee, date of follow-up.
6. Safety committee sign-off.

12.7 — Accident Reporting

An HRMS health and safety module should contain accident report information such as the following:

1. Description of accident, location, date, time.
2. Machinery, tools, equipment involved.
3. Any mitigating environmental conditions (lighting, atmo- sphere, chemicals, working surfaces).
4. Name of person(s) involved.
5. Description of injury.
6. Job being performed.
7. Analysis of causes.
8. Recommendations.
9. Name and signature of investigator, date.
10. Follow-up action taken, date.

Figure 12.2 illustrates common steps that occur after an accident at work, and the way in which an HRMS may be used to capture, analyze, and report significant data about these steps.

12.7   Human Resources Management Systems

The effect of these steps on human resources tasks is described below:

Figure 12.2 Accident/Injury Process Flow

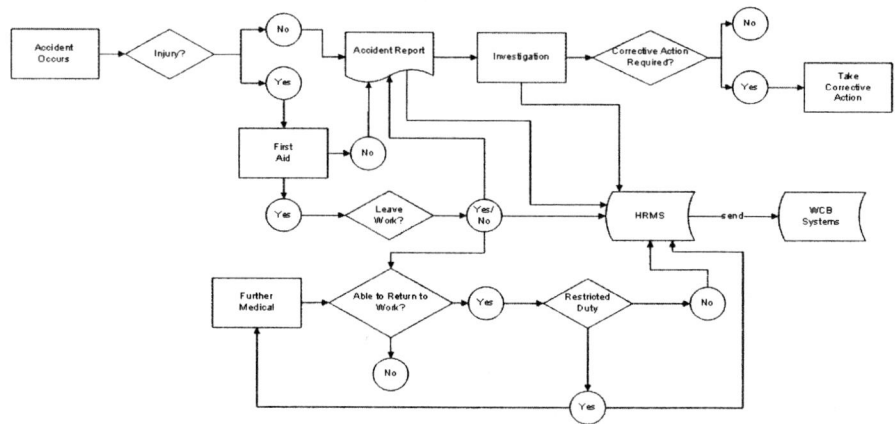

1. Time lost from work due to an accident often triggers the requirement for either a replacement worker or overtime. In unionized settings, seniority usually governs who is to be engaged as a replacement or to be given overtime. Seniority is generally calculated and maintained on the HRMS by Human Resources.

2. An injured employee's progression through sick leave, short-term disability, long-term disability, workers' compensation, restricted return to work and unrestricted return to work, must be tracked, preferably with the HRMS.

3. External agencies (i.e., Workers' Compensation Boards) and contractors (such as health case workers) both require and generate data. Most of this information should come from and/or be entered into an HRMS.

4. Depending on the nature and cause of an accident, labour relations issues may arise, up to and including strike action. Information regarding other accidents in the same location, or of the same nature or cause, would normally be required by all parties to such a dispute.

5. Additional benefits or levels of benefits may be triggered for an injured employee and, depending on the nature of the employer's coverage, there could be increased costs for the employer and/or employee. Overall benefit plan costs are normally based on the prior period experience so that close monitoring and control of accidents and workers' compensation benefits can result in significantly reduced costs to the organization.

Other occupational health and safety programs have much in common with Human Resources' domain. As noted in Chapter 10, programs such as employer wellness programs, designed to prevent health problems and accidents through education, should be monitored to determine their direct and indirect effects and cost-effectiveness.

Many organizations work on creating a more positive OH&S culture through programs such as monitoring the amount of time a facility/plant/department has operated without a lost time accident, and some link compensation or reward programs to positive results in this area.

12.8 — Increased Awareness of OH&S Issues

Several factors are raising the awareness of managers about the importance of occupational health, safety and industrial hygiene. Some of these include:

1. *Workers' Compensation Board (WCB) Costs.* Workers' compensation board costs have risen dramatically over the last few years. Since these costs are traditionally charged back to employers, there has been a direct bottom-line impact.

2. *Safety legislation.* Governments are enforcing safety violations much more strongly than in the past. Nevertheless, Canadian fines remain low compared to those in the United States.

3. *Increasing health care costs.* In Canada, health care has been paid for by provincial governments under the umbrella of a national plan. In the U.S., health plans are provided by employers. In either case, in North America and elsewhere in the world, increasing health care costs, and burgeoning debt at all government levels have combined to produce a different payment strategy. In Canada, several provinces have enacted employer health tax legislation which shifts an increasing amount of the burden to employers.

4. *Trends in health care responsibility.* As costs rise and are shifted to employers, the future offers little hope of relief. Frantisak (1993) predicts that an illness will more often be determined to be caused by an individual's prior exposures at work (i.e., exposure to asbestos prior to the 1980s when precautions began to be taken). The implications are significant. It appears likely that prudent employers will increase the amount of health data they collect about workers (before, during, and after employment) and their environment, and retain that data for a lifetime.

5. *Technology.* Advances in technology have made telecommuting — working from home, or a remote location, and only rarely, if ever, appearing "at the office" — a reality, and has raised an interesting question. Is an employer responsible for worker safety in the home? In some jurisdictions, such as Manitoba and Nova Scotia, employers may be faced with responsibility for independent contractors as well as home-based employees. How they are expected to manage this responsibility, track this potentially

new and different data, and what the impact on an HRMS or other systems will be, are questions that have not yet been fully answered. Beginning in 1992, Canadian government conducted a three-year study named "Telework" (Currie, 1995). Home OH&S concerns were carefully addressed, as were ergonomics, the validity of home insurance, and even potential zoning issues. The study concluded that while telework was increasing rapidly, the administrative framework in which these workers function (including health & safety) has not kept pace. The questions it raises about employer liability for health or safety issues within the home while the employee is teleworking, have yet to be fully explored and resolved.

An examination of various models of human resources management (HRM) reveals that the HR community is split as to whether OH&S is or is not part of that community. The Canadian Council of Human Resources Associations (CCHRA), however, includes OH&S in its model of HRM.

There are both clear differences and connections between OH&S and the rest of the HRM community. Most HRM professionals rarely have specialized training or experience with occupational health, safety, or industrial hygiene. OH&S professionals include medical (occupational health nurses, doctors, including specialists in occupational medicine, registered occupational hygienists), safety professionals and other specialists. There appears to be little cross-over from these professions or avocations to HRM and so the two functions have often remained separate, even when a common reporting relationship exists. Safety professionals, for example, represent several disciplines, including engineering, psychology, preventative medicine and industrial hygiene. However, many OH&S activities serve as the starting point for HRM data, or provide parts of the record. For example, HRMS subsystems such as time and attendance and employee benefits are closely tied to OH&S related events, such as employee accident, first aid, medical treatment, workers' compensation and restricted work duty.

Reviews of various HRMS offerings reveal that OH&S modules are not generally well handled by commercial HRMS packages. Many HRMSs offer no or limited OH&S capability; very few offer a complete OH&S module. This is probably because of a perception that occupational health, safety and industrial hygiene are Human Resources responsibilities.

Take, for example, the case of a mine and process operation located in the Canadian Maritime provinces. The organization chart of this operation reflects not only the separation of various occupational health and safety activities and responsibilities from human resources, but also the disjointed manner in which this organization (and many others) deals with this functional area.

The organizational structure illustrated in Figure 12.2 should not be judged as wrong or inadequate as long as it works to meet the organization's needs. However, because it is fragmented, duplication of roles and responsibilities seems highly likely. Here we have further proof that traditional human resources functions need to be placed in a broader strategic context, and evidence of the need for an organizational structure that draws together disparate tasks into one functional group.

Figure 12.3 Organization Chart of Occupational Health

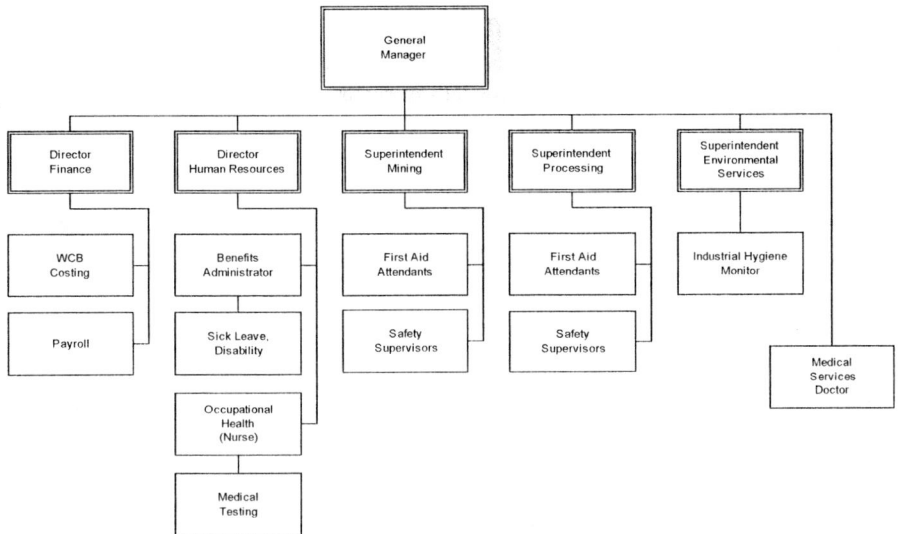

12.9 — Security and Privacy

Organizations that designed their own functional "stand-alone" systems may have done so because OH&S was not seen as a part of Human Resources, while those that bought HRMS software found (and continue to find) that HRMSs did not have all of the capabilities required by OH&S professionals. Functional separation may also have been due to the fact that access to the organization's separate information systems could not be restricted to a particular area of interest, and both OH&S and HR personnel were concerned about (and perhaps jealous of) the confidentiality and security of information, which each regarded as sensitive.

Maintaining the confidentiality of health records is a problem. At the heart of this problem is the fact that, while paid by employers, occupational health staff believe that their primary client is the individual worker, and that workers who have no assurance of privacy will not use their services. Health professionals can be under pressure from safety or HRM staff, or an employee's supervisor to provide employee health-related information. Cann (1994) reports on a survey of occupational nurses in the province of Manitoba, which revealed that:

1. 62.7% of those surveyed reported receiving requests for health information from a worker's direct supervisor within the last six months;

2. 49.3% reported receiving requests from a manager other than the employee's direct supervisor;
3. 45.3% received requests from the employer's worker compensation specialist;
4. 48% reported that 75% of all requests for information were not supported by written authorization.

It would not be surprising if these health professionals resisted using general HRMSs unless they had assurance that health data could and would be held in confidence.

Fortunately, improved techniques for managing security means that this is no longer a barrier to integrating a broad range of organizational functions into one system, or developing a coordinated network of subsystems that can act as an integrated system.

Legislation providing for the privacy and security of personal data, including health-related data, has been inadequate and poorly coordinated between the federal government and the provinces.

While the federal Canadian legislation, the PIPEDA, provides for the protection of "personal health information" (physical and mental) it also permits the provinces to create similar legislation. In the case of Ontario and others, that corresponding provincial legislation can cause confusion and little protection to the individual.[2]

12.10 — Health and Employability

Employers have long been known to discriminate against people with various disabilities and/or health issues. The criteria for determining employability have changed over the last decades.

Police and fire services, for example, used to have set height and weight criteria for prospective employees. Today the test is ability to perform tasks that are considered to be representative of the job. HRMS used by such organizations have to document the results of such testing as part of the hiring process.

But the bar keeps changing. In the last few years various employers have required that their employees not be smokers, or not be too overweight.

Why? Employers argue that the cost of employing people with certain medical conditions, such as being overweight, is recognizable and that they, the employers, should not have to pay.

---

[2] Privacy in the Workplace – the Employment Perspective, the Canadian Privacy Institute, 2004, CCH Canada.

A 2005 study has concluded that overweight employees cost more annually. Obese employees each cost an additional $460 to $2,500 annually in medical expenditures and work absences compared with normal-weight workers, according to a new report published in the September/October issue of the *American Journal of Health Promotion,* USA Today reports. The study found that normal-weight men miss an average of three work days annually, compared with five for men who are 60 or more pounds overweight, and that normal-weight women miss an average of 3.4 work days annually, compared with 5.2 days for women who are 30 to 60 pounds overweight. Women who are 100 or more pounds overweight miss an average of 8.2 work days annually, the study found.[3]

Meanwhile you may not have to actually be seen smoking that cigarette or be observed to be overweight. In 2005, IBM's CEO Sam Palmisano stated that, "IBM promises it will not use genetic information in its employment decisions." Says Palmisano, "During our lifetimes, the practice of medicine and society's approach to healthcare have changed in fundamental ways. But what lies ahead — perhaps in the next decade alone — seems likely to eclipse that progress dramatically." While work in genetics is "enormously promising," it "raises very significant issues, especially in the areas of privacy and security."

The company said consideration of the policy change started long before IBM began working with National Geographic on the Genographic Project and is unrelated. The Genographic Project is a five-year effort to collect and analyze DNA from hundreds of thousands of people in order to map how humans populated the planet. The results already constitute one of the largest genetic databases ever.[4]

Can employers track employee weight or smoking habits? What about an employee's family history that shows a trend toward heart disease or some other condition? Some employers are certain to use their systems, including HRMS to enter this hazy world.

12.11 — Summary

Recent significant increases in health care and benefit costs and the trend to shift the funding of health care to employers have served to intensify the focus on occupational health and safety issues. This, in turn, has created an increased need for reliable, available data on which to make decisions.

A general lack of sophistication and integration of occupational health and safety records with HRMS and other information systems is seen as preventing this data from being readily available, and management is looking for alternatives. One

---

3 Gathered 06-09-06 from <http://www.californiahealthline.org/index.cfm?Action=dspItem&itemID=114615> Overweight Employees Cost More Annually, Study Finds, September 12, 2005.

4 Gathered 05/10/20 from <http://www.ibm.com/news/us/en/2005/10/2005_10_11.html>.

solution being explored is to integrate occupational health and safety processes and information systems with those in Human Resources.

In Chapter 8 we used an example of Lost Day Accidents to show how Executive Dashboards are used. Health and Safety practitioners should be aware of the usefulness of a HRMS to highlight and present health and safety issues in a meaningful way.

This chapter has discussed some of these process links and the potential benefits the use of an HRMS could offer.

12.12 — References

Belcourt, M., A.W. Sherman, G.W. Bohlander, and S.A. Snell, 1996. *Managing Human Resources,* Canadian ed. Toronto: Nelson Canada.

Biggs, F. 1991. *Guide to Health and Safety Management.* Don Mills, Ont.: Southam Business Publications.

Canadian Privacy Institute, I. Turnbull, Editor - Privacy In The Workplace – The Employment Perspective , 2004 CCH Canada

Cann, B.J. 1994. "Maintaining Confidentiality." *Occupational Health and Safety Canada* (September/October): 90-92.

Currie, M.B. 1995. "There's No Place like Home." *Occupational Health and Safety Canada* (March/April): 30-31.

Firenze, W.J. 1978. *The Process of Hazard Control.* Dubuque, Iowa: Kendall/Hunt.

Frantisak, F. 1993. "The Future of Occupational Health and Safety." Presentation to Noranda Minerals: Montreal.

Heinen, J.C. 1994. "Automating the Process for HRIS Selection." *Employment Relations Today* 21, no. 4 (Winter): 371-80.

Hunt, S. 1995. "Twenty Cost-Cutting Tips." *Occupational Health and Safety Canada* (July/August): 44-50.

Laing, P. 1992. *Accident Prevention Manual for Business and Industry: Administration and Programs,* 10th ed. Washington, D.C.: National Safety Council.

Montgomery, J. 1996. *Occupational Health and Safety.* Toronto: Nelson Canada.

Moser, C. 1995. "Our Changing Workplaces." *Occupational Health and Safety Canada* (July/August): 26-31.

Paton, T. 1995. *The HR Matrix.* Mississauga, Ont.: HRMS Directions, Inc.

——— . 1999. *The IT Matrix.* Mississauga, Ont.: HRMS Directions, Inc.

Plog, B. 1988. *Fundamentals of Industrial Hygiene,* 3rd ed. Chicago, Ill.: National Safety Council.

Pulp and Paper Research Institute of Canada. 1996. *Occupational Health and Safety Manual.* Pointe Claire, Que.

Robertson, D. 1992. "Occupational Health and Safety." In *Human Resources Management in Canada.* 1995. Toronto: Carswell.

CHAPTER 13: TRENDS IN HRMS

13.1 — Introduction

There is a new reality in business today, one that has grown out of a number of social and economic trends and that overlies the business community worldwide. Organizations are still trying to adjust to this reality, with mixed results.

Some of the parameters of the ever-increasing pace of change facing society in general and organizations in particular, were documented in Chapter 1. This chapter discusses the implications of these changes on information systems technology, as well as how such technology may be used in human resources management and the organizational functions which it, in turn, supports.

13.2 — The New Economy

Beck (1992) suggests that key driving forces in organizational processes may be defined as having passed through the following three phases over the past 150 years. In historical order, there are:

- Commodity-driven processes
- Manufacturing-driven processes
- Technology-driven processes

Beck (1992) states:

> Every era has its engines — a handful of strategic industries that drive the entire economy and typically have risen rapidly out of humble origins . . . The high-growth strategic businesses — the engines — (today) fall into four categories:
>
> - computers and semi-conductors (including software and information services)
> - health and medical care (including drugs, biomedicine)
> - communications and telecommunications
> - instrumentation
>
> Industries like cars, steel, petroleum and housing, which were once the driving force of the economy, still dominate the headlines with their continuing troubles, but they are simply no longer as important as they once were. (p. 20)

Some of the features of this new economy are:

- Globalization
- Outsourcing

13.3   Human Resources Management Systems

- Restructuring work
- Technological advances
- Access to information
- Information management
- Human Resources management
- E-commerce

Each of these is discussed in more detail below.

13.3 — Globlization

High speed communications and transportation networks mean that a competitor may be just down the block or on the other side of the world. Businesses have discovered that operating in third-world countries offers the competitive advantage of low pay rates, which translates directly into lower product prices. This has created pressure on North American business to be more competitive. With labour laws blocking reduced pay, many organizations have responded by reducing human resources costs in other ways, first through downsizing and more recently by rethinking the fundamental concepts of what makes an organization.

13.4 — Outsourcing/Contracting Out

Increases in the number of competent but unemployed professionals, along with organizations' need to reduce the number of full-time employees, has led to an increased use of contract employees and consultants who are available for specific projects or for a set duration of time but remain off the permanent payroll. Rivard (1995) lists the advantages of using such a temporary "external workforce" as reducing employee turnover, easing legislative compliance, reducing health care benefit costs and Workers' Compensation Board (WCB) costs and, most importantly, moving these HRM services from unvalued overhead to measurable expenses that add value.

Outsourcing human resources is just one option. Another is to outsource technology resources, a trend that grew from 63% in 1992 to 72% in 1993. Almost all technology resources that now exist in-house can be outsourced, whether these resources are applied to system development, system operation, or system maintenance. Mainframes, or servers on which the systems operate, can also be leased from agencies operating across town, or across the country. Communications networks can be leased, as can other hardware. Sookman (1994) cautions that this option is not without risks (e.g., being locked into pricing arrangements, unexpected licensing and leasing costs, loss of control) that must be carefully weighed before a decision to outsource human resources or technical services is made.

13.5 — Restructuring Work

Various techniques, such as business process engineering/ re-engineering (see Chapter 4), are and will continue to be used to restructure or eliminate work processes and to establish new, more cost-effective ways of doing things. The net effect will usually involve the use of fewer people, combined with new or better use of technology.

13.6 — Technological Advances

Beck (1992) has defined our era as the technological era. Harry Copperman (1996), vice-president, Digital Systems' Business unit, recently used an analogy to illustrate the degree of technological change: "If air travel had changed as dramatically as information systems in the last ten years, a trip from San Francisco to New York would take four minutes and the plane would be only three inches long." The impact of today's technology and its rate of change may be more dramatic than anything since the invention of the printing press or of gunpowder.

History is full of examples of people who ignored change with devastating results; sword makers who thought firearms were not a competitive threat, buggy whip makers who thought automobiles were a passing fad.

Burrus (1993) states:

> First, in a broad and general way, it is necessary to understand the nature of the profound technological changes that are under way. There's never been anything comparable in all of human history! Second, just as our ancestors and we in turn, learned to use basic tools like hammers and crowbars, it is time to understand that no matter how complex the specific technology may appear to be, it too is a tool that must be mastered. And third, with new tools come new rules that determine how institutions and individuals function effectively. (p. xii)

Many people are overwhelmed by the perceived complexity of information technology, when they should be concentrating on its functional applications. It is not necessary to know how a telephone or telephone networks are designed in order to make a telephone call, nor does the lack of knowledge about the inner workings of television seem to dampen its use. The same is true of modern computer-based information technology.

Burrus (1993) suggests that:

> The status quo has been shattered by technological change. As a result, success or failure hang in the balance for the remainder of the 1990s and the twenty-first century. Ignoring this reality would be tantamount to having shrugged off the development of water and steam power and the invention of the steam engine. Many of those who did were left behind by the modern age, marooned in pockets of poverty and despair,

deprived of the sustenance of the past and denied the promise of the future. Those who repeat the same mistake in our era are doomed to a similar fate. (p. xii)

While many people are afraid of technology and its implications, there are also dangers in embracing change too quickly. Hardware and software suppliers sell the concept of "the leading edge," to describe the latest and greatest innovation. To this has been added the concept of "the bleeding edge," which graphically describes the experience of using untried or under-tested technology.

13.7 — Flexibility

Ten years ago most software was designed to operate on one type of computer. But, as the Arthur D. Little Forecast on Information Technology and Productivity predicted, users demanded the ability to share data and programs, regardless of what kind of computer they possessed. Today the concept of "open systems" means that software can (or should be able to) operate on many different makes of computers, databases and communications networks.

The need for software programs that can run on many different types of computers has led to much more competition in computer hardware. As the performance of various makers' products keep pace, the costs, reliability and service that software suppliers are able to offer becomes more important than the make of the equipment per se in many customers' choice of computers and ancillary equipment. The job of software developers has become more complicated, as they struggle to ensure that their programs are operational on the many types of equipment that are available. User demand for flexibility of this sort is unlikely to abate.

13.8 — Other Technical Issues

Other notable trends that are affecting the development and use of HRMSs are described below:

CLIENT-SERVER (C/S): The concept of client-server is that one computer, or server (sometimes also referred to as a host), can work with many other computers, often referred to as clients (see Figure 13.1). The data resides in the server which can be any computer, from a laptop to a mainframe, as does a portion of the application software. The client holds the rest of the application software and has its own processing power. Colour capabilities and graphical user interfaces (GUIs) are used to make the system as user friendly and efficient as possible.

This distribution shares the processing power between the client and the server, utilizing each to maximum advantage and (hopefully) reducing costs, while increasing speed.

The concept of client-server is currently very popular in software design. Bartholomew (1995) states that client-server accounting systems account for almost 50% of today's multibillion-dollar worldwide financial services market.

INTERACTIVE VOICE RESPONSE (IVR): IVR is the use of touch-tone telephones to access and provide information verbally/orally. Although no longer considered new technology, IVR offers considerable untapped potential and is likely to gain in prominence in the future.

IMAGING: Scanning technology or imaging acts much like a photocopier, except that the result, instead of a piece of paper, is an image represented by bits and bytes in a computer. Documents or pictures can be scanned and then stored electronically, reducing paper and paper-filing systems, while also being available to be added to other documents or transmitted via e-mail or Internet. Over the past several years the process has become cheaper and faster, with colour scanners now available. At the same time, quality, measured in dots-per-inch (DPI), has improved. These trends should all continue, making the movement of data from paper into electronic form easier and cheaper.

Figure 13.1 Client Server

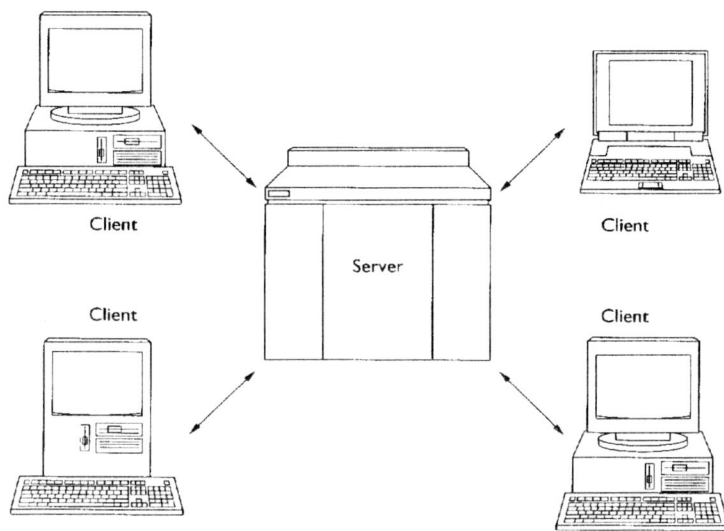

13.9 — Impact of the Internet and Related Innovations

We are frequently told that we live in the information age. Certainly the volume and variety of information available to everyone has mushroomed and this trend should continue. It is perhaps best characterized by the Internet.

From a network that was started by the American military under the acronym of ARDANET and for a number of years was little known outside of higher education and some government agencies, the Internet, "Cyberspace," or the "Information Highway" has grown dramatically: from 30,000 connected computers in 1987, to 1.3 million in 170 countries in 1993, to more than 20 million users by the end

13.9 Human Resources Management Systems

of 1996 and a projected 100 million by the turn of the century. Figure 13.2 provides a graphical representation of this growth.

Figure 13.2 Internet Users

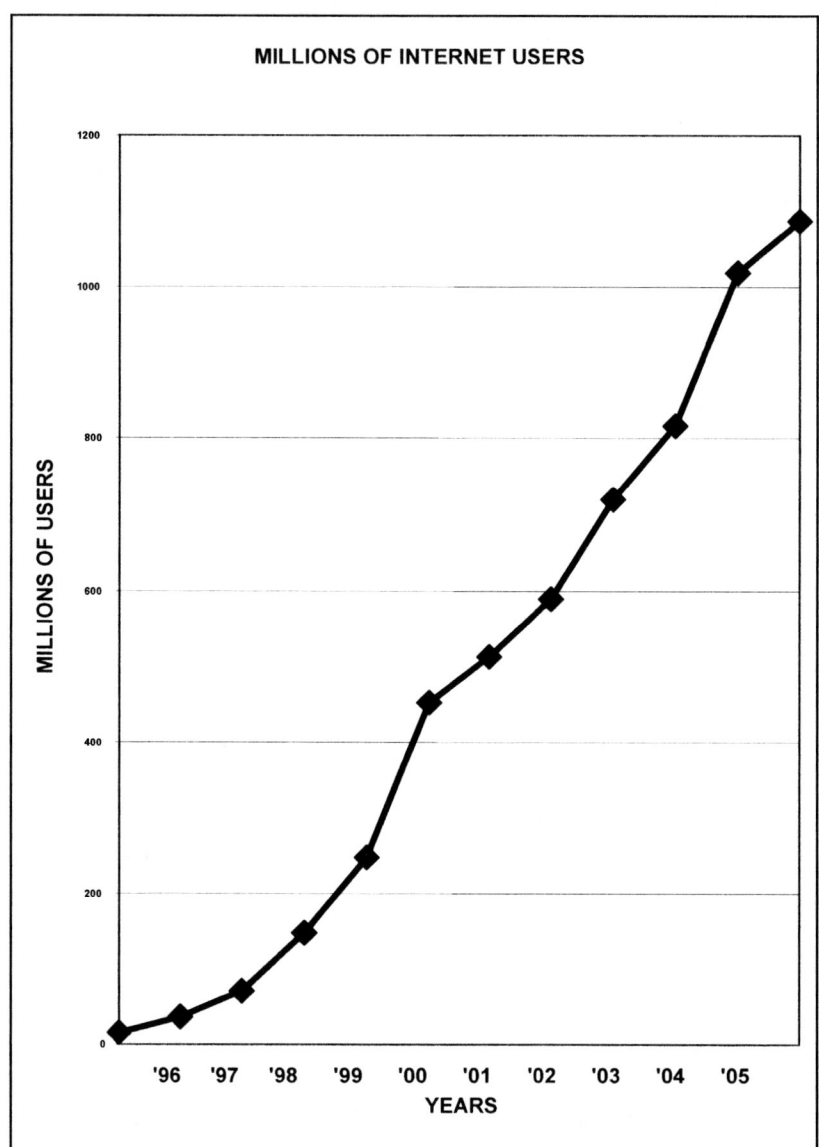

Gathered 06-11-13 from <http://www.internetworldstats.com/emarketing.htm>.

The Internet gives users access to a system of electronic mail (e-mail) around the world, often within seconds, with no long distance or special charges. It also gives access to the World Wide Web (WWW); literally a web of information sites where anyone can access libraries anywhere from their computer: at the office, at home, in the car, or on a mountain-top.

Several human resources information management systems today recognize the power and potential of the "Net" by offering easy ways to receive and send information from an HRMS via the Internet. One good example of the use of this tool is advertising job openings. Many jobs are now advertised on the Internet and many firms allow or encourage applications and résumés to be sent via the Internet instead of by fax or regular mail. Once in the organization's own electronic network these résumés can be saved electronically, searched for, e-mailed from desk to desk, annotated and, if necessary, translated into hard-copy via a printer.

The now familiar fax machine was in limited use in the mid-1970s, gained prominence in business in the mid-1980s and now occupies a place in many homes. Children fax each other homework assignments and many children's television shows offer fax numbers more often than voice telephone numbers or regular mail service addresses. But faxes cost money to send by long distance telephone, while Internet e-mail messages do not and many feel that the Internet is easier to use.

Improvements in computer supported technology include:

1. Computers are becoming more powerful and that power grows cheaper daily.
2. Components are getting smaller, encouraging a move away from "desktop computers," to "laptops," "notebooks," "subnotebooks," "palmtops," and "Personal Digital Assistants" (PDAs).
3. Batteries are lasting longer and getting lighter, both boons to the portable computer user.
4. Other than batteries, power can come from many sources including a car cigarette lighter, or solar power.
5. Linkage between computers can still be "hard-wired," but it can also be accomplished via infrared, cellular phone, or satellite.

13.10 — Internet/Intranet

The many uses of the Internet for applications within an organization have led to the concept of "Intranet," or use of the Internet within the walls of one organization for employee communications. Benefit plans, job openings, organization policy manuals and new energized versions of the company bulletin board all appear in this new environment.

In accessing the World Wide Web (WWW) through a URL (Universal Resource Locator), one becomes linked to information in a specific web server, someplace in the world. For example, by clicking on the URL http://www.ihrim.org/ one links to the website of the International Association for Human Resource Information Management. This site physically is in Chicago but could be anyplace in the world. This is an example of the use of the "Internet"

Intranets are like Internets except that linkages are made within a company, association of companies, or some other definable network, whether large or small. Most often there are also linkages from the Intranet to the Internet, so that an individual having access to such an Intranet, also has access to the Internet.

Thus, Intranets are being set up in different ways, the most common being:

1. *A dedicated internal web server that is accessible only for internal use.* The internal web server has no connection out to the WWW so that someone outside of the company, even if they had the URL, could not access the site; there is simply no physical connection. Only those people connected physically through wiring within the company can connect to the server. This is called controlling the security through a physical firewall. The company may add on an additional level of security if it wanted to limit access to only certain employees. This would be via a software firewall that would ask each "visitor" to the URL to sign in with a User Id and Password or PIN (personal identification number).

2. *The web server hosting the Intranet has a physical connection to the outside world via the WWW.* This would mean that anyone with the URL could get to the home page of the company, but would be denied entry "at the front door", where they would be asked for a User Id and Password or PIN. This is called controlling the security through a software firewall.

3. *Many Intranets are being developed using a combination of the two types of systems mentioned above.* In systems with both internal and external web servers, the most sensitive corporate information is managed internally on the internal server and less sensitive information is passed to the external server for more public access.

The key value of an Intranet is the ability to collect, communicate and share information with employees. This can be done economically using readily available tools such as a Web Browser. One of the most valuable benefits of an Intranet is empowering employees to update their own information. Making changes to the corporate HRMS related to address changes, emergency contact, benefit changes, course registration, etc. can be time consuming when it's paper driven and routed through various levels of management and HR. Given adequate edits, each employee can update his or her own information. Other applications that are made possible by use of corporate Intranets include:

- Communicating:

Trends in HRMS   13.10

- communicating corporate HR Policies
- publishing company news bulletins "on-line"
- downloading company forms
- communicating through e-mail
- Recruiting and staffing for job openings:
  - applying for job openings
  - providing feedback on applications
  - pre-screening applicants
- Updating personal data:
  - home address
  - emergency contact
  - dependant information
  - benefit coverage
  - vacation schedule
  - training schedule (course selection/self registration)
  - submit expense claims
- Providing direct on-line feedback to employees regarding file information:
  - claims status
  - job application status
  - total value of compensation package
  - earnings
  - pay information on-line
  - benefit coverage
  - retirement planning - options

13.10 Human Resources Management Systems

Figure 13.3

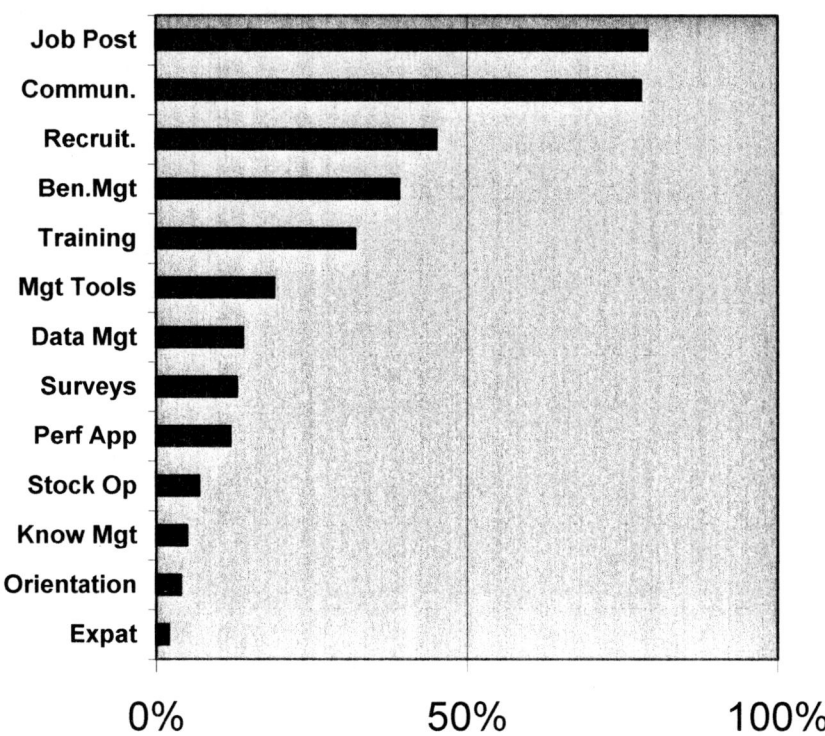

Source: IOMA 1999 HRMS Survey (published by IOMA)

One of the most important benefits of an Intranet system is the way it can be used to simplify the delivery of complex information. For example, HR policies can be very detailed; by using the HTML (Hyper Text Markup Language) or some other web authoring software, many policies can be presented more graphically for easier understanding. Employees can use simple "search forms" to locate information on topics. Employees can "jump" from one topic to another using the links provided.

Some of the characteristics and advantages of Intranet applications are as follows:

- Information can be highly personalized
- Information can be provided to employees quickly and efficiently in a common format
- The communications channel used to provide information is changed from one in which information is distributed to employees, to one in which employees access information wholly or selectively as dictated by need

- Information may be provided in a timely fashion and may be updated as required
- Costs of data entry, training and documentation may be reduced
- Significant cost savings on paper, printing may be realized
- Customer service may be improved.
- Information for modelling and calculating cost/benefits should be more readily available
- Errors may be reduced by giving employees the responsibility for entering and maintaining some of their own file information

13.11 — E-Commerce

Electronic commerce (most often written "e-commerce") — the use of the Internet to buy and sell goods — is a phenomenon rising from the astounding acceptance of the Internet as a business tool. The growth of e-commerce is so rapid as to totally defeat the efforts of any published text such as this to keep pace. Nevertheless we feel obliged to make an attempt.

As noted earlier, the Internet gives every user, no matter how remote, access to unimagined volumes of data world-wide. "Yet at the heart of E-business growth is an interesting paradox." E-business has been built on technology, but it's not about technology. It's about the same old thing that solid business growth has always been about: the satisfaction of individual customers' needs." (pp. vii-viii, Thomas M. Siebel and Pat House, *Cyber Rules*, Doubleday 1999).

Figure 13.4

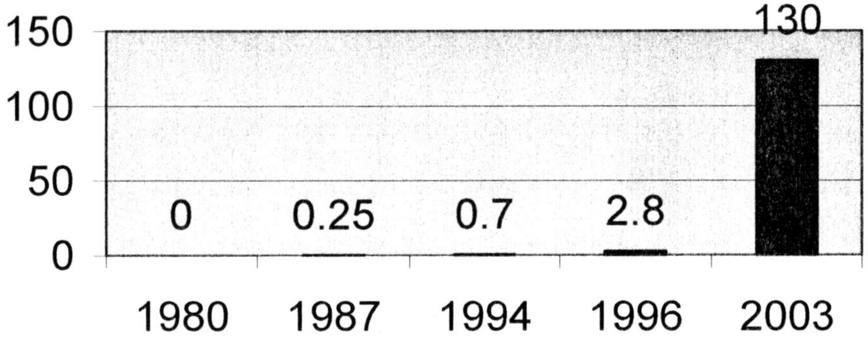

Year	Value
1980	0
1987	0.25
1994	0.7
1996	2.8
2003	130

At the same time, e-commerce is not just about buying traditional products from traditional vendors and just substituting the Internet for either a telephone or mail order.

Sellers can display their wares (and the specifications thereof) in on-line catalogues extremely quickly — a matter of hours instead of months for the more

13.11 Human Resources Management Systems

traditional mail order catalogue. Buyers can hop from seller to seller in a virtual shopping mall and many websites can be found which compare like products for the buyer.

In addition, whole new "metamarkets" are emerging. A metamarket is a market defined by consumers' processes and not the way business defines itself. For example, traditional real estate agents dealers sell houses, condominiums and apartments. They normally do not sell appraisals, home inspections, mortgages, home insurance, landscaping and so on.

But on the Internet all of these services can be linked. Buyers can wander around Real Estate agent websites looking at various homes, viewing 360 degree pictures in and out and so on. The difference is, they can also access each of those other services from that same website. And the providers of the appraisal, inspection, mortgage, insurance, landscaping, etc., know exactly who they have to thank — the site provides the relevant link back to the Real Estate site.

How fast is the internet growing? In 2007 it is estimated that world-wide Internet usage has reached 28.8%. Geographically it ranges from just 3.5% in Africa to 10.5% in Asia and 38.6% in Europe. North America, with 8.5% of world population has just 8.1% of world Internet users. The penetration of the Internet in North America is 69.4%.

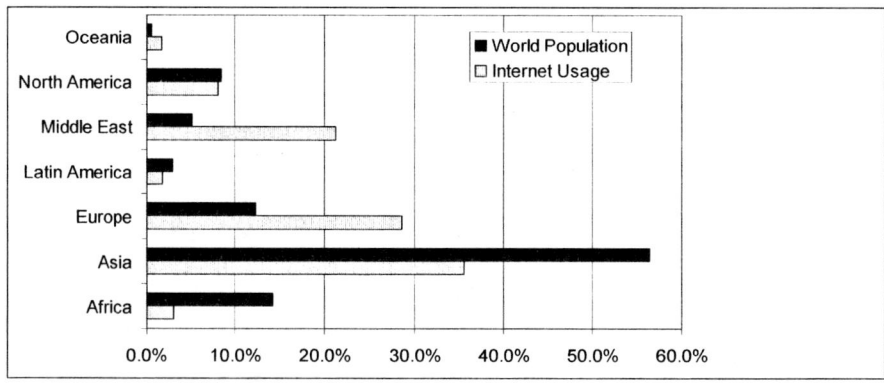

(www.internetworldstats.com. Copyright © 2007, Miniwatts Marketing Group. All rights reserved worldwide.)

The chart below counts only the first language of Internet users (many are bi- or multi-lingual). Although English is the most common language, it is only used by 30% of global Internet users. It is double the next most common, Chinese, that is at 14.1%.

What are the implications for global marketing, or for self-service?

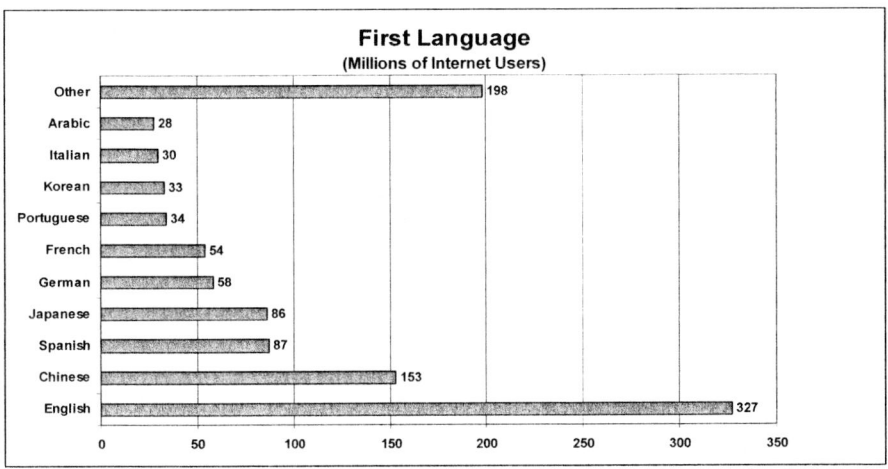

(www.internetworldstats.com. Copyright © 2007, Miniwatts Marketing Group. All rights reserved worldwide.)

Organizations considering global self-service, with large employee populations outside of North America, should conduct some research to determine user accessibility (availability and speed).

One interesting element of the growth of the Internet and e-commerce is that some "rules" of business seem to be completely reversed. The industrial age axiom was that value flowed from scarcity (think back to "supply/demand" lectures we all have sat through). Today the reverse is true. Siebel & House:

> In the emerging networked economy, Kelly writes (author note: quoting Kevin Kelly of Wired Magazine), every increase in connectivity creates an increase in value. According to "the law of plentitude", the value of every individual fax machine goes up each time another fax machine is plugged in, because of the greater information flow.
>
> Quoting Eric Schmidt, chairman and CEO of Novell:
>
> Moore's Law says that computing capacity, as measured by the speed of microprocessors, doubles on average every 18 months. That's a startling enough estimate when you compare the eighteen month estimate to, say, the doubling times for technology in heavy manufacturing. But as Eric points out, an even more dramatic "law" is the one that was named for the founder of 3Com, Robert Metcalfe:
>
>> Metcalf's Law, which is a modern version of the old law of increasing returns, says that the value of a network increases in direct proportion to the square of the number of machines that are on it. Is that a statistically verifiable law? No. But it's a good way of articulating an important message, the message of what we usually call the network effect. (p. 6-7, *Cyber Rules*)

Readers may be asking themselves what e-commerce and Moore's and Metcalf's Laws have to do with the practice of human resources or human resources information management. We can only speculate, but we would be poor prognosticators if we could not see the impact of these trends within organizations as well as without.

Anything that affects how people work or interact with each other impacts Human Resources, human resource management and the systems that support them. Readers of Best Practices: Building Your Business with Customer-Focused Solutions (Hiebeler, Kelly and Ketteman of Arthur Andersen, Simon & Schuster, 1998) will gain an appreciation for Arthur Andersen's *Global Best Practices*. More importantly (from our point of view) is that most best practices illustrated here rely to a greater or lesser extent on technology and on sharing information.

The growth of the learning organization and the knowledge organization is based in more effective and efficient information flow and yes, HR should pay attention: "In the information age, knowledge workers will clearly replace manual laborers as the dominent workforce in developed economies." (p. x, *The Distributed Mind*, Kimball Fisher and Mareen Duncan Fisher, AMACOM, 1997).

Meanwhile, the profile of Generation X (Gen Xers — those born in the 1960s and 1970s) is enough to create an enormous pain in the neck of most traditional employers:

> They want to come and go as they please, wear what they like, work the hours that suit them — and not too many, thank you — because they value a balanced life more than piling up possessions. They want to work in small groups and be a part of every decision. Direct orders set their teeth on edge. You must explain why you want them to do something, or, better, show them by example. You earn their respect by doing what they do. (David Berreby pp. 52-53, The Hunter-Gatherers of the Knowledge Economy, *Strategy & Business*, Issue 16, Third Quarter 1999)

The challenges brought to HR therefore, are enormous. As organizations' specialists who help create the environment in which people function, HR must not only understand and use technology within its own business processes, it must also understand the implications of these technological trends for work and workers as a whole.

13.12 — Networking

In addition to its use as a research tool and its increasing Intranet application within organizations, the use of the Internet as an important professional networking tool is quickly gaining importance. Professional associations such as the International Association for Human Resources Information Management (IHRIM) provide the opportunity to network, through its chapter meetings, annual conferences, training events, membership directory, magazine and the Association web page http://www.ihrim.org/. Meetings and conferences enable members to meet in person and other vehicles enable them to locate vendors, colleagues, experts, etc., through the telephone, fax and the Internet.

There are a number of different ways that professionals are using the Internet to network and share information. Because of the growing importance of these applications to human resources professionals in general and human resources management systems specialists in particular, the more important of these applications are discussed in some detail below.

Electronic discussion groups represent a new way of accessing and sharing professional information. Examples of three such electronic discussion groups that may be accessed at no cost are:

- HRIM: Human Resources Information Management
- HESIG: Higher Education Special Interest Group
- GSIG: Global Special Interest Group.

It is quite simple to subscribe to a list. One sends a command to the server hosting the lists, e.g.:

- HRIM-request@ls.ihrim.org for HRIM
- HESIG-request@ls.ihrim.org for HESIG
- GSIG-request@ls.ihrim.org for GSIG
- JOBS-request@ls.ihrim.org for Jobs
- WAR-request@ls.ihrim.org for Work Analysis & Reporting

For the first of the lists mentioned above, for example, the command to send to the host is: "subscribe HRIM."

The same goes for the other discussion groups (or lists); one sends the same command to name@ls.ihrim.org, with only the command changing to reflect the name of the list you want to join. The server (name@ls.ihrim.org) will respond to your request, usually within minutes, welcoming you to the list and recommending you save the message you receive as it contains the instructions on how to unsubscribe should the day come you wish to remove your name or change your Internet address. Once you have received your welcome message, you will be able to send messages to everyone on the list.

Most e-mail discussion groups are managed using packaged software called Majordomo, ListServ, or ListProc. There are subtle differences between some of the commands but for the most part, subscribers seldom know, or need to know the difference. name@ls.ihrim.org is the computer server that looks after all the commands for the IHRIM website.

Unless you have an urgent, burning issue, the recommended course of action is to wait and see the kinds of posts that come to you via the list. This is known as "lurking" and is much like listening in on a party-line telephone conversation, without saying a word. But when you are ready, to either post a question of your

13.12   Human Resources Management Systems

own, or to reply to another subscriber's post, go for it; this is a discussion group, share your thoughts, concerns and questions.

A tip on replying to a post that someone else has made: before and after you have typed in your reply to the note, say to yourself "Do I want everyone on the list to see this, or just the person who made the original post?" If the note is only of interest to the originator, send it just to them. If your note will have value to many of the others on the list, then by all means send it to HRIM@ihrim.org (the list).

If you have a question for everyone on the list, you may wish to write out your question just like one would in a business letter. People who post to human resource discussions groups (lists) have found that the number and quality of the replies often depend on how you present yourself in writing. It is generally useful to identify yourself, your position, your company and your city. This lets members of the list put your question into perspective. Respondents often formulate their replies depending on who they are dealing with. Also, respondents tend to react very quickly to questions that are short and to the point, but delay responding to a full page of questions.

There are many lists for Human Resources, with over 65,000 e-mail discussion groups. The following website provides examples of lists of various sorts: LISZT — Directory of e-mail Discussion Groups — <http://www.liszt.com/>.

One can find more general information on websites at Yahoo: <http://www.yahoo.com/Computers_and_Internet/Internet/Mailing_Lists/>.

There are several places where one can find a full or partial list of Human Resource discussion groups including <http://www. pmihrm.com/p5a.html>.

One of the oldest and largest HR lists around is HRIS-L. This HRMS/HRIM/HRIS discussion group was created in 1989 with about only 50 subscribers. Today it has over 900 HRMS professionals subscribed, worldwide. Topics range from, "Who are the vendors selling HRMS software to the small company?" to "Do you have a dress code in your IT shop?" Postings to HRIS-L tend to average less than three a day so don't be too worried about having a ton of mail filling your mail box.

Commands go in the body of your e-mail note; do not use a topic in the Subject block; and turn off your signature.

If one joins a discussion group and then finds that there is too much mail coming in, one can usually set one's subscription to "Digest". This means one gets a single long post a day, (everything that was posted), including a list of the topics at the top of the post. If one just wants the topics, one can sometimes set one's subscription to "Index", where once a day one will get a list of the topics discussed and will have to go to the Server to retrieve the full post. One can use one's e-mail reader to filter out topics one is not interested in, or one can do a quick browse and selectively delete the topics. One can then quickly reply to either the original person making the post or to the whole list.

When signing on to a new list some people may wish to monitor incoming traffic for awhile using the digest option if it's available.

In spite of the great interest in the Internet and the World Wide Web and even with all the great browsers like Netscape, Explorer, Mosaic, etc., many people have found that e-mail discussion groups have a lot more to offer, as you are dealing one-to-one and one-to-many with real people and you can actually "discuss" topics in great detail. It is also amazing just how cooperative members of a list are in sharing their knowledge with fellow subscribers.

Other popular HR Discussions Lists and how to join them are as follows:

- HRIS-L (HRMS/HRIS/HRIM List)
  majordomo@hr.trends.ca
  subscribe hris-l (your internet address)

- HRD-L (Human Resources Planning and Development List)
  majordomo@hr.trends.ca
  subscribe hrd-l (your internet address)

- HRNET (Important HRM-Network)
  listserv@cornell.edu
  subscribe HRNET (your name)

- TRDEV-L (Training and Development)
  listserv@psuvm.psu.edu
  subscribe TRDEV-L (your name)

- HRIM (IHRIM HRMS/HRIS List)
  majordomo@ihrim.org
  subscribe HRIM (your internet address)

Forums. As anyone who has joined some of the human resource ListServers has found out, these ListServers can result in a large volume of e-mail traffic in one's e-mail reader. However, this can be controlled to some degree by setting one's subscription format to "digest" so that one only gets one big message a day, with all the day's posts in it. One can also make effective use of some of the newer e-mail readers like Pegasus or Eudora by directing traffic from specific sources like a ListServer to file folders using "Filters".

A filter can be set to direct all mail from a specific source to a file that you can read later. However, no matter which way one chooses to receive or store e-mail messages from ListServers, eventually one either has to read it or delete it. Quite often one subscribes to a list like HRNET to obtain information on a specific topic, such as Performance Management, so one does not really care about other topics discussed. Unfortunately, to find out what each post is about and if it has anything related to performance management, one at least has to scroll through all the subject areas of the incoming traffic.

13.12 Human Resources Management Systems

Human Resource Forums are becoming very popular with those who do not have the time or the patience to deal with the volume of traffic in their e-mail reader. A Forum uses the same or very similar format that we are accustomed to seeing on lists but the content does not come to our e-mail reader, it goes to a website where one can look it up at one's convenience.

This methodology of sharing and discussing HR issues has an additional benefit, in that there is no danger of accidentally erasing an important post; the information will remain up on the website, sometimes almost indefinitely. However, one does have to go looking for the information; it is not going to come to you. This can, however, be simplified by bookmarking all the important HR forums of interest and developing a routine of checking the forums according to a schedule.

There are several formats for HR forums but since they are easy to read it's not important here to go into the technical details of how they work. It is worth mentioning, however, that there are subtle differences between HR forums, such as the ability to post to them on the web. For example, a popular ListServer for HRMS/HRIS issues is HRIS-L and two sites "mirror" the posts to that list. The posts one sees at HR On-Line, HRIM Mall and ESCRIBE are just there to view; one cannot reply to members of the list, nor can one post a note to their website. But one can find the address of someone that made a post of interest and send him or her a personal note. Both of these sites also offer a host of other HR resources in addition to access to HR ListServer archives. For HRIS-L archives see <http://www.escribe.com/business/hris/> and for HRD-L archives see <http://www.escribe.com/business/hrd/>.

Other websites provide the opportunity to reply to existing posts or to post a new question. One should keep in mind that once one has posted a question or a response on a Forum, there is a "netiquette" responsibility to come back on a regular basis and see if anyone has replied. Some Forums have the option of sending a personal e-mail to a person you are replying to while others only provide the website as the communications vehicle. So, if one finds a Forum one likes, one can add a bookmark to one's browser and pay return visits on a regular basis.

The rules or "netiquette" for a Forum are similar to those of a ListServer, with rule #1 being "think carefully about what you want to say" before posting it. It is important to remember that what one writes may sit on this site for public viewing for months or even years to come.

Most HR Associations are developing HR Forums on their websites to serve their members and to attract new members. The International Association for Human Resources Information Management (IHRIM) and the Society for Human Resource Management (SHRM) are two sites worth investigating.

As more HR associations, consultants, vendors and magazines/newspapers add HR forums to their websites, the number of options available to seek useful information and to network with other human resources professionals, grows rapidly.

In the future, more and more of these websites will offer "search capabilities" to make their use more "user-friendly." They also will be offering "push technology" to send you articles on topics in which you are interested via e-mail.

13.13 — Information Management

Directly flowing from the increased access to information is the need to better manage information, otherwise, "information overload" becomes a significant problem. Users can drown in facts that are not always relevant.

Organizations are finding that there is a strategic advantage in being able to access the right information at the right time and to share it properly within an organization's own Human Resources. Many things will combine to make this possible.

"Groupware" is one key. Groupware is software that permits groups of people to share data and applications. Caldwell (1995) states that:

> Major consulting firms and systems integrators are focusing their information technology efforts on groupware and, increasingly, the Internet. The strategies enable them to share as much information as possible with their customers. Groupware is a near-universal effort in the industry, helping professional firms identify the human resources needed for client services. At the same time firms are boosting their mobile computing abilities, providing staff with remote access to database and electronic-mail servers so that they can work at customer sites and still have needed resources at hand. Mobile computing helps keep overhead costs low by reducing the need for office space. (p. 57)

"Telecommuting", linking to work via telecommunications devices which range from pagers to laptops and videoconferencing, is seen as contributing to the growing trend toward more people working at home and is applauded for reducing air pollution, corporate office space and the need to hire key talent.

The general business and technological trends outlined above have an enormous impact on the way organizations of every size manage their human resources. In theory, the transition of the HR function from recordkeeper to strategic manager was accomplished some years ago but the reality may still be tantalizingly out of reach for many human resources professionals.

One basic change has been the definition of human resources. Once defined as "employee," perhaps including part-time as well as full-time employees, an organization's human resources today can include retirees, contract employees, consultants, the families of these groups and customers. Payment of those non-employee human resources and ad hoc payments to employees, such as expenses, can be made through payroll, relieving the burden on accounts payable. Advancing technology such as relational databases has made it possible for an HRMS to accommodate this broadening to human resources.

Traditionally, human resources has been driven by the need to conduct such functions as hiring, firing and salary changes. Today business goals and the value

13.13 Human Resources Management Systems

that HR adds to those goals are becoming more important. So too is a new recognition of the importance of line management taking a more direct role in managing human resources and accessing the HRMS to do so, thus, assuming some of the functions that were previously performed by human resources personnel. Traditional HR systems do not allow line mangers to perform these functions, because direct access to critical human resources information is often only available to human resources staff.

Recent technological advances, however, are leading to the following changes:

- Much-improved security in relational database structures allows users to access only their own "need-to-know" data. Client-server systems make an HRMS much more usable by casual users such as line managers.

- Operational supervisors are no longer tied to an office. Laptops and clipboard style computers give supervisors the freedom to travel within the warehouse, mine, factory and forest and still be able to access and modify records.

- Cellular phones and modems allow almost worldwide access to an HRMS.

- Workflow automates more of the business process, thus, directly engaging line management in an automated process and allowing them to interact more closely with an HRMS.

- Scanning/imaging makes it possible to integrate paper records into one electronic file, making central files more complete and removing that administrative burden from line management.

- Interactive voice response (IVR) can give line managers access to employee absenteeism (and other) records from their phone or in the car.

The relatively new profession of human resources information specialists combines technical and human resources management skills and knowledge. It represents a departure from the norm of having two distinct groups — information technology specialists and human resources practitioners — with distinct skill sets. Also, it represents a bridge to future organizational structures required by organizations operating in today's new economy.

As we pointed out in Chapter 1, the need to respond to quickly changing organizational requirements means new ways of doing business. The argument has also been made that now, as never before, the human resources function, supported by effective HRMSs, can have a critical strategic role in supporting the adaptation of new and more effective organizational structures and processes.

More than a decade ago Davis (1987) wrote:

> It wasn't until the 1920s that Sloan developed at General Motors what was to become the basic model for industrial organization — a decentralized operating system com-

bined with centralized policy and financial control. This was more than one hundred and sixty years after the industrial revolution began in England and sixty years after it had transformed America from an agrarian to an industrial economy. It was not introduced, in other words, until the twilight of the epoch, just twenty years before the industrial period drew to a close. Now, thirty or forty years into a new, post-industrial economy, we find that Sloan's industrial model is still the major one used for organizing corporate America.

We have industrially modelled organizations running post-industrial businesses. It is no wonder that we manage our way to economic decline. Our managerial models, the "context" in which we manage, don't suit the "content" of today's business. (pp. 5-6)

The above quotation was written before the rapid spread of personal computers in the home and before the Internet became more than the almost exclusive reserve of government employees and academics. Today we are just beginning to see organizations responding to the demands of post-industrialism.

13.14 — Non-Traditional HRM Approaches

Huva (1995) points out that systems to help understand and use human resources more effectively are becoming increasingly important and that we must look beyond the traditional approaches because we have new work methods and organization patterns. Three non-traditional HRM concepts that are gaining acceptance are Competencies, Work Flow and Teams.

(a) Competencies

Spencer and Spencer (1993) report that the job-competency approach emphasizes validated criteria that cause and predict superior performance. "Competencies are underlying characteristics of people" (p. 9) and include motives, traits, self-concept, knowledge and skill. Thus the traditional HRM activities of staffing and job design may translate to finding people with specific competencies, to fill positions with required competencies.

The demands on the HRMS will be to provide appropriate data elements and comparative tools to facilitate and document this process in much more detail than is now usually the case. One example of technology supporting the competency approach is computer-based training (CBT). Belcourt and Wright (1995) point out several advantages of CBT over traditional training, including greater mastery, reduced learning time, scheduling flexibility (self-paced learning available 24 hours per day) and tests that can provide proof of competency where required by law.

(b) Workflow

Dunivan (1996) defines workflow as automation of information flow, typically without imbedded business rules:

> The distribution of memos represents a traditional workflow, one that we now take for granted in the form of electronic mail. It automates the physical tasks of carrying a document to a photocopier, making a copy and delivering it. (p. 11)

The concept of a flow of work has taken on new perspectives with the growth and use of technology. Business process re-engineering (BPR) has supported the implementation of technology and technology is beginning to return the favour with the development of computerized tools to help sequence processes into workflow.

Dunivan (1996) suggests that both of the concepts of BPR and workflow are immature, but today's new modeling tools and techniques will help to integrate the two. Workflow technology has much in common with the Groupware mentioned earlier in this chapter and the flow chart tools mentioned in Chapter 5 and it supports the new focus on work teams.

(c) Teams

People have always worked together, but HRM practices over the last decades have focused on the individual. Compensation, performance standards, measurement or appraisal, training and development have all dealt with people as single entities, but:

> To review the performance of an employee assigned to multiple teams working on various projects overlapping several divisions, one needs to go beyond a traditional single-manager, single-profile evaluation model. (Bryant, 1996, p. 17)

The current trend is to focus on teamwork in an attempt to increase organizational flexibility (including the ability to respond quickly to change), employee effectiveness, productivity and accountability and to decrease administrative overhead. It is thus becoming *avant garde* to have "multi-skilled workers" employed in "self-directed" work teams, in "flat, flexible" organizational structures.

As with other management concepts that have become prominent over the past few decades, some of these will undoubtedly have a lasting beneficial impact, although their effects are unlikely to be as significant as their advocates predict. In the meantime, they are certainly influencing the way in which organizations are structured and operate and thus will influence the development, implementation and operation of HRMSs, at least in the short term. It is important, therefore, that HR staff generally and those responsible for the HRMS specifically, understand these concepts and their implications.

(d) Downsizing

The need to maintain profits in a highly competitive, increasingly global business environment has led organizations to restructure their operations to try and maintain the productivity and quality of what they produce with fewer employees. This is often referred to as downsizing or rightsizing, and has been greatly aided by efficiencies offered by computer automation.

However, Tomasko (1993) reports that downsizing is not the answer to the many challenges facing organizations today. In a survey of over 1,000 American firms that had downsized, the report of achievements vs. goals was bleak. This study found, for example, that:

1. Almost 90% wanted to reduce expenses; fewer than half actually did.
2. About 75% hoped for productivity improvements; only 22% achieved them.
3. More than half wanted to improve cash flow or increase shareholders' return on investment; fewer than 25% were able to do so.
4. More than half expected to reduce bureaucracy or speed up decision making; only 15% achieved these goals.
5. Many sought improvements in customer satisfaction and product quality. Others expected to become innovative or better able to utilize new technologies. But fewer than 10% felt that they had met their goals in these key areas.

These goals, to gain competitive advantage by reducing staff and reorganizing work, will clearly continue. The question yet to be answered is, how are they to be reached?

13.15 — Human Resources Information Management

The development of HRMSs is clearly tied to the current economic climate, current technology and contemporary trends in human resources management. But it also reflects the history of HR. The 1995 survey of HRMS users reveals some interesting facts and speculation.

There is a clear indication that HRMS users want to see a shift away from recordkeeping to what might be termed as "value-added management," but, as Table 13.1 illustrates, today's reality shows that few such systems are used for more than fundamental human resources functions and payroll recordkeeping.

13.15 Human Resources Management Systems

Table 13.1 Most Important HR Application for Internet

TODAY	NEXT 3-5 YEARS
• Staffing	• Staffing
• Employee records	• Competency profiling
• Attendance management	• Skills matching
• Career management	• Performance management
• Payroll	• Variable compensation
• Training management	• Career management

However, competency profiling was seen as the top priority over the next three to five years. (It is even among the top 10 today). This fact, together with the projected importance of succession, career and HR planning, demonstrates an awareness of the importance of creating an effective means of gathering, storing and analyzing human resources information for all types of organizations.

As the 1995 End User Survey revealed, a clear focus for HR and HRMSs in the future is the empowerment of line management to use human resources information effectively. In part this will be accomplished by giving line managers more direct access to HRMSs. Richards-Carpenter (1994) points out that delayering tiers of management, devolving the HRM function to business units and empowering management, all combine to make traditional computerized personnel information systems for the use of human resources alone completely inadequate.

The survey further indicates that cost justification is seen as the most significant barrier to acquiring new HRM systems, followed by a lack of top management commitment, a lack of a clear HRM strategy, outdated business processes and a lack of computer skills. Campbell and Mathews (1995) lay the blame on a failure to justify the need for the new system in language that is persuasive to other managers, including the organization's executive. Generally this means being able to demonstrate that the HRMS contributes to the organization's competitive advantage (see Table 13.2) to specify what value is added through better management information and to demonstrate potential savings in administrative costs (see also Chapter 3).

Table 13.2 Benefits of HRMS

• Integrated HR, Payroll, and Time processes	• Integrated HR, Payroll, and Time management activities
• Improved management of HR operations	• Improved management of Payroll operations
• Eliminate non-value add HR activities	• Improved HR productivity
• Empowers line management	• Empowers employees
• Brings information to supervisors when required	• Eliminate non-value add Payroll activities
• Complex metrics possible with minimal input	• Improved Payroll productivity

HRM practitioners must ask themselves how they can best help HR management to accomplish this in the years ahead.

Some other trends in HRM will include:

1. *User caution.* Some users will continue to be slow to invest in the latest technological trends, while insisting that their functional needs have top priority. The speed with which key technologies advance leave many wondering if there is ever a right time to buy a new computer or new software.

2. *Integration.* The integration of software has been a trend for several years. This is mirrored by the integration of human resources functions. As discussed in previous chapters, non-traditional HR management functions such as payroll, occupational health and safety and time and attendance need to be integrated with other human resources functions and to be considered strategically within the larger organizational context. This integration, in turn, must be reflected in the HRMS. Fortunately, open systems provide opportunities to integrate separate software packages if a "fully integrated" HRMS is not available.

3. *Privacy/Security.* Although often used as synonyms for one another, these are two distinct and equally important issues. The *Personnel Journal* (1994) emphasized the distinctions between database security and privacy. Security relates to proprietary, company-owned human resources data and systems, which are investments to be protected from theft or damage. Privacy is completely different; it concerns data contained in an HRMS that should not be made universally available. Security management policies and procedures can help resolve the privacy problems posed by the increased number of data elements and greater access, the latter being largely created by a new view of who the "users" of a system should be.

13.16 — Summary

A new business climate has evolved that, combined with trends in technology and human resources management, will have a significant effect on the future of human resources management systems.

Technology is expanding exponentially and in doing so, it is shrinking the world, making globalization easier and faster. For example, recent developments in electronic communications of all sorts, but particularly the Internet and related applications, are having a huge impact on the way that organizations do business. This chapter discusses how the human resources practitioner may access and use these new innovations in their every day work.

Throughout this book, but particularly in this chapter, the point is made that organizations built to prosper in old environments must restructure or perish.

Human resources, both employees and non-employees, must consequently be reinvented as a strategic and valued operational asset. New jobs, with titles like "New Metrics Analyst", "Virtual Organization Leader", "Content Engineer", "Chief Community Strategist", "Metamediary CEO", "Chief Knowledge Officer" and "Ethical Hacker" (drawn from New Jobs by Sean Donahue, pp. 102-109, *Business 2.0*, July 1999), are redefining and redrawing organization charts and parameters to challenge the status quo. Managing a virtual organization in a virtual office will prove to be an interesting challenge.

Although the tools to build new organizations are not entirely clear, effective HRMSs will be increasingly important in organizations as they strive to better manage their human resources to meet their business goals.

To meet new requirements, however, HRMSs, built on the two towers of human resources management and technology, must change as well. We hope that we have contributed to your understanding of the past, the opportunities of the present and the challenges of the future.

13.17 — References

Baig, E.C. 1995. "Welcome to the Officeless Office." *Business Week*, no. 3430 (June 26): 104-6.

Baig, E. C. 1995. "Taking Care of Business — Without Leaving Home." *Business Week*, no. 3420 (April): 106-7.

Bartholomew, D. 1995. "Better Systems, Brighter Numbers." *Informationweek*, no. 516 (February): 66-72.

Beck, N. 1992. *Shifting Gears*. Toronto: HarperCollins.

Belcourt, M., A.W. Sherman, G.W. Bohlander and S.A. Snell. 1996. *Managing Human Resources,* Canadian ed. Toronto: Nelson Canada.

Belcourt, M., A. and P. Wright. 1995. *Managing Performance through Training and Development.* Toronto: Nelson Canada.

Bryant, J. 1996. "Human Resources: Defining and Assessing Soft Skills." *The RESOURCE* (March): 16-18.

Burrus, D., with R. Gittines. 1993. *Technotrends.* New York: HarperBusiness.

Caldwell, B. 1995. "Making IT a Group Effort." *Information Week,* no. 545 (September 18): 170-74.

Campbell, I. and J. Matthews. 1995. *1995 End User Survey.* Softworld Report and Directory for Personnel and Human Resources Information Systems Infact Research and Interactive Information Services Ltd. London, England (September).

Copperman, H. 1995. Presentation to the International User Group Meeting of Ross Systems Inc. San Francisco (May 15).

Daniel, D. 1994. "A Whole New Way of Thinking Computing Canada." *Computing Canada* 20, no. 7 (March 30): 17.

Davis, S.M. 1987. *Future Perfect.* New York: Addison-Wesley Publishing.

Denton, D.K. 1992. "Multiskilled Teams replace Old Systems." *HR Magazine* 37, no. 9 (September): 40-50.

Dunivan, L. 1996. "Workflow Technology." *The RESOURCE* (March): 11.

Huva, W. 1995. "Globalization and the HRMS." *The RESOURCE* (September): 28-30.

Irwin, D. and V. Rocine. 1994. "Self-Directed Work Teams: Coming Soon to an Organization near You." *CMA Magazine* (September): 13-14.

Lasden, M. 1985. "Fad In, Fad Out." *Computer Decisions* (May): 74-88.

Miracle, M. 1993. "The Trend to Client/Server is Maturing into Acceptance." *National Underwriter Life/Health/Financial Services* 97, no. 45 (November): 2-8.

Mueller, B. 1994. "Changing Attitudes Help Shape HR Systems." *Systems Management (*March).

"New product news supplement." 1994. *Personnel Journal* (November): 16.

Parker, G. 1994. *Cross-Funcional Teams: Ways to Work with Allies, Enemies and Strangers.* Bristol, V.I.: Soundview Executive Book Summaries.

Prociuk, H. 1996. "The Electronic Highway May Be the Dominant Information Tool of the Future. How Do HR Departments Get Up to Speed?" *Human Resources Professional* (April): 7-8.

Richards-Carpenter, C. 1994. "Personnel Takes Pragmatic Approach to Technology." *Personnel Management* 26, no. 7 (July): 55-56.

Rivard, J. 1995. "Why is Outsourcing a Choice?" *RESOURCE* 4, no. 1 (March): 14.

Slofstra, M. 1994. "A Positive New Image in the Works." *Computing Canada* 20, no. 16 (August): 27.

Sookman, B. 1994. "The Legal Issues Abound."

Spencer, L.M., Jr. and S.M. Spencer. 1993. *Competence at Work: Models for Superior Performance.* Toronto: John Wiley and Sons, Inc.

Stewart, T. 1992. "Looking Ahead: the Search for the Organization of Tomorrow." *Fortune* (May 18): 93-98.

Tomasko, R.M. 1993. *Rethinking the Corporation: The Architecture of Change.* New York: The American Management Association.

Weizer, N., G. Gardner III, S. Lipoff, M.F. Roetter and F.G. Withington. 1991. *The Arthur D. Little Forecast on Information Technology and Productivity.* New York: John Wiley and Sons.

Wetherbe, J.C., N.P. Vitalari and A. Milner. 1994. "Key Trends in Systems Development in Europe and North America." *Journal of Global Informations Management* 2, no. 2 (Spring): 5-20.

INDEX

Benefits, see **Compensation: salary, benefits, pension, payroll and time and attendance**

Business/technological trends, see also **Trends in HRMS**
evolving trends, 16, 17
   coordinated strategic management, 16
   summary of trends, 17
summary, 22

Canadian Forces Personnel Applied Research Unit (CFPARU)
HRMS as data storage and reporting facility, 45
HRMS as important research tool, 45-47
   applied research areas, 46-47
   research studies, 45-46
   training cost savings, 46
needs analysis stage, 47-49
   longitudinal or long-term perspective, 47
   new applications enhancing cost benefit of system, 47-49
      example, 48-49
   personnel data being part of asset base, 47
period considered for ROI, 47
quality control of Canadian forces recruiting and selection, 48-49
   aptitude tests, upgrading, 48
   optical scanning equipment purchase justified, 48
   quality control exercise, 48
staffing, 163-165
   "applicant tracking files", 164
   Comprehensive Occupational Data Analysis Programs (CODAP), 164
   National Occupational Codes (NOCs), 164
   "onboarding", 165
   privacy laws, 165
   separate headquarter directorates, 164
   staffing functionality, 165
   training programs, 164
training and development, 191
   Canadian Forces Personnel Management Information System, 191
      employee module, 191
   Comprehensive Occupational Data Analysis Programs (CODAP), 191
   Directorate of Organizational Structures, 191

Compensation: salary, benefits, pension, payroll and time and attendance
HRMS requirements for total compensation, 207-223
   affiliation table, 208
   audit trails, 208
   data organization, 208
   deductions, 208
   effective date management, 208
   employee/position history, 209
   employment and pay equity, 209
   generally, 207-208
   heath tax, 209
   hourly employees, 209
   income tax statements, 209
   interfacing with other systems, 210
   job information, 210
   job/position definition, 210
   leaves of absence, 211
   mass changes, 211
   on-line communications and administration of benefits programs, 211
   organization, 212
      typical organization chart, 212-213
   pay equity, 213
   payroll variables, 213
   pension reports, 214
   performance evaluation, 214
   position management, 214-215, 216
      attributes of job, 215
      organization and people relationships, 214-215, 216
   record of employment, 215
   retroactive pay, 215
   salaried employees, 215
   salary market surveying, 216-217
      relation between salary policy line and actual salary line, 216-217
   salary policy lines, 217
   seniority, 217
   short-and-long term disability, 217
   time: actual, 218
   time and attendance, 221-223
      management of time and attendance, 221
      time and attendance management model, 221, 222
   time: available, 218
   time in lieu, 218
   time management reporting, 219

Index

time not at work, 219-220
time: overtime, 220
time: regular or standard, 220
time: scheduled, 220-221
trend toward coordination of information systems, 222
unsophisticated security as barrier to integrated systems, 222
work planning and review, 223
year-to-date information, 223
introduction, 195-204
benefits, 201-204
benefits and pension model, 201-203
benefits demand, 202
benefits programs per se, 203
benefits supply, 202
complexity of modules, 203
considerations in determining what programs to provide, 201
program evaluation, 203
benefits packages extended to both full-time and part-time employees, 201
capabilities of module to be considered, 203-204
integrated module vs. "stand-alone" module, 203
transfer of information, 204
HR model, 199-200
hands-on functions, 199-200
monitoring and auditing processes, 200
planning and development programs, 200
strategic context, 199, 200
cultural-based strategy, 200
Google, 200
influences, 200
salary distribution quartiles, 200
total compensation function, 199
payroll, 198
payroll increasingly reporting to HR, 198
payroll data and HR data largely same, 198
software security, sophistication of, 198
separation of duties, government focus on, 198
Sarbanes-Oxley (SOX) Act, 198
principles regarding internal controls, 198
total rewards/compensation functions of organization, 195-196
"compensation", meaning of, 195, 196
total compensation, 195, 196-197
additional considerations, 196
direct and indirect components, 196, 197
total compensation model, 197
total rewards, 195-196
modeling/analyses, 204
program evaluation/metrics, 223-224
automatic collection and calculation by HRMS software package, 224
measures for total compensation function, 223-224
Total Compensation Revenue Factor, calculation of, 224
references, 225-227
summary, 225
complexity greater in large organizations, 225
trends, 204-207
accessing benefits information "on-line", 207
changes updated quickly, 206
coordination of benefits, 205
"defined benefits" program, 206
usage and costs balanced, 206
flexible benefits, 205-206
design and development of program, 206
pension administration system, implementation of, 204-206
example of automating pension system, 206
pension plans, 207
plans becoming complicated, 204-205

Design and development of new HRMS
applications: breadth and depth, 74-77
breadth of system, 74
core or main module and secondary or optional modules, 74-75
comparison of core and secondary training module, 75
relationship between training module and counterpart on core module, 75, 76
data diagram and dictionary, 75
depth of system, 74
payroll function, 74
primary function, tracking movement of people in, 75
workforce participants, informing management about, 76-77
total workforce inclusion, 77
build or buy, 91-94

Index

best functional software vs. "enterprise-wide" software, 92-93
  integrated software modules, 92
"best-of-breed" (BoB) systems, 92, 93-94
  interfaces required for each system, 93
degree of variability not being minuscule, 92
  breadth of product from most vendors, 92
enterprise-wide systems, 92-94
  business process engineering (BPE), popularity of, 92-93
  integrated software modules, 92, 94
    addition of other modules more cost effective, 94
  strengths, 93, 94
    standardized foundation, 93, 94
  weaknesses, 93-94
    selection becoming more complex, 94
    software requirements not met in specialized industries, 94
    time-consuming and complexities, 93-94
external suppliers offering training and maintenance services, 92
matching needs and system off the shelf, 91-92
  amending system where close match, 91
  amount of fit desirable, 91
  more modifications causing maintenance difficulties, 91-92
  program developers regularly updating software, 92
  legislation, impact of, 92
selection of correct system, 91
strategic advantage of good information systems, 91
strategic applications not to be purchased "off the shelf", 91
  HRMS being strategic, 91
building or contracting out, 101-103
  contracting out example: payroll services, 101-102
    cost effectiveness, 102
    pay process, components of, 101-102
    payroll service, functions of, 102
    primary advantage, 102
    third party service providers, 102
  multiple software applications, 102-103
business processes, analysis of, 83-86
  business process re-engineering, 84-85
    core steps, 84-85
      analysis phase, 84
      problem-solving phase, 84-85
      degree of change to effect restructuring, 85
  re-engineering and re-structuring, 83-84
    "re-engineering", meaning of term, 84
    steps to follow in designing HRMS, 85-86
general design considerations, 74
HR metrics, 88-90
  best time to establish program, 89
  comparative surveys, participating in, 88
    Saratoga surveys in five subject areas, 88
    Saratoga's measures, 88
  output, measuring, 88
  performance measures, usefulness of, 89
  Saratoga metric, 88-90
    HR Expense Percent, 88-90
      industry, by, 89, 90
      number of employees, by, 89, 90
      size and industry making significant difference, 89
introduction, 73-74
  considerations addressed, 73
  questions addressed, 73
language and currency requirements, 77-78
  bilingual or unilingual systems, 77
  Charter of French Language, 77
  currencies, multiple, 77
  "Euro" and EU members, 77-78
  "home country currency", 77
references, 104-105
security and privacy, 78-83
  date effectivity, 80-81
  Internet, 83
  introduction, 78
    data security, 78
    user identification, 78
  flexible security structures, 78
    audit trails, 78
  privacy being legislated right, 78
  privacy generally, 78-79
    CSA Model Code, 79
    EU Data Protection Directive, 79
      transfer of personal information, 79
    factors driving protection of personal information, 78-79
  privacy in Canada, 79-80
    Personal Information and Electronic Documents Act (PIPEDA), 79-80
  privacy in United States, 80
    bi-lateral Safe Harbor Program, 80
    identity theft problems, 80
    international maze of data protection, 80
  reports, 81

Index

information generated from software application, 81
"standard" reports, 81
technical issues, 82-83
questions for project team, 82
screening and selecting software, 96-101
assessment of vendor responses, 98-100
account manager assigned, 99
acquisition path, 99
contact coordination, 99
misstatements and "lying", 99-100
warranty/disclaimer, 100
definition of requirements, 97
attributes of "user-friendly" systems, 97
three categories, 97
demonstrations, 100-101
generally, 96-97
reliability, supplier and product, 101
request for information (RFI), development of, 98
criteria for selection, 98
request for proposal (RFP), development of, 98
criteria for selection, 98
summary, 103
tools to assist in HRMS design and development, 86-88
benchmarking and best practices, 87-88
benchmarking, meaning of, 87
performance measurement, principles in, 87-88
flow charts, 86-87
automating paper flow, 86
data dictionary, 86
example of performance appraisal, 86-87
level of flow charting, appropriate, 86
limitations, 86
"work flow" concept, 86
software attributes for happy users, 87
typical HRMS components, 94-96
capability of systems, 96
cost of software packages, 95
full-suite HR packages, 95
key questions early planning process, 95-96
program modules, 94-95

Fit analysis, see also
Implementation of HRMS
deficiencies identified and reviewed, 118-119
recommendations submitted, 119
each task tested by team, 118
example of reviewing task, 118-119
simulated hiring of part time casual worker, 118-119
vendor, reliance on, 119-120
caveat emptor, 119
misstatements, 119
warranty/disclaimer, 119-120

Historical background
early 1980s and early 1990s, 12-16
associations formed to bridge the gap between HR and IS, 15-16
connectivity issue of microcomputers and mainframes, 13
Digital Revolution, 14
power of digital devices rapidly expanding, 14
Human Resources slower in utilizing networks, 14-15
HR practitioners generally not skilled in computer-related areas, 15
reasons related to specific considerations, 14
systems people developing complicated protocols, 15
process "owned" by management information specialists, 15
Local Area Networks (LANs) linking computers into networks, 13-14
MIS departments restricting access, 13
concerns expressed, 13
personal computer (PC) offering relief for many problems, 12-13
problems encountered by HR practitioners, 15
Internet, 10-11
ARPANET, 11
central mainframe method, 10
DARPA information processing office, 10
connecting separate physical networks, 10
electronic mail capabilities, 11
inter-networking, 10
International Packet Switched Service (IPSS), 11
mid-1950s and early 1960s, 6-7
computer technology, 6-7
cumbersome to program, 7
non-payroll personnel systems, 6-7
survey of employee skills, 7
Hollerith cards, use of, 7
television, cable and satellite, 6
mid-1960s, 7-9
American *Equal Pay Act* as impetus for automated personnel system, 8

Index

banks and insurance companies paring administrative costs, 8
Comprehensive Occupational Data Analysis Programs (CODAP), 9
    Ontario Hydro, 9
    U.S. Air Force, 9
costs, control of, 9
duplication of information, 7
Equal Opportunities Commission (EOC) and recordkeeping rules, 8
information accessed for variety of uses, 7-8
INSci developing first packaged personnel system, 8-9
mainframe-based HRMS system, 9
"longitudinal file" concept, 7-8
Management Information Systems (MIS) departments, 8
    payroll and personnel applications, 8
postwar period, 5-6
    payroll systems, 5-6
        "data dictionary", 6
        electrical accounting machinery (EAM), 5-6
        Employment Standards Act requirements, 6
        Fair Standards Act requirements, 6
pre-World War II, 5
    automation technology, late in applying, 5
    "Hollerith" punched cards, 5
    "IBM card", 5
    personnel department as reactive caretakers, 5
summary, 22
the 1800s, 4-5
    "informationalization" of devices, 4
    telegraph cables, 4
    telegraphy, 4
    telephone, 4
    ticker tape machines, 4
    wireless transmission, 4-5
the 1970s, 9-10
    Equal Employment Opportunity (EEO) programs, 9-10
        affirmative action, 10
        requirements for calculating "availability" and setting goals, 10
the 1980s, 11-12
    packaged HRMS products, 11-12
        early packages having limitations, 11-12
    personal computer (PC), 12
        Apple Computer and IBM, 12
        similar operating systems, use of, 12

HR metrics, see also
Design and development of new HRMS
best time to establish program, 89
comparative surveys, participating in, 88
    Saratoga surveys in five subject areas, 88
    Saratoga's measures, 88
output, measuring, 88
performance measures, usefulness of, 89
Saratoga metric, 88-90
    HR Expense Percent, 88-90
        industry, by, 89, 90
        number of employees, by, 89, 90
        size and industry making significant difference, 89
total compensation, 223-224
    automatic collection and calculation by HRMS software package, 224
    measures for total compensation function, 223-224

Implementation of HRMS
changes, 107-108
    business, 107-108
    technological change, 107, 108
        capabilities, increased, 108
        re-engineering, 108
conversion, 121-122
    algorithm written to convert data, 122
    conversion issues, 121-122
    data conversion, 122
    information, converting, 121
corporate/executive sponsor, 114-115
    steering committee, members of, 115-116
        individuals not generally included, 115
fit analysis, 118-120
    deficiencies identified and reviewed, 118-119
        recommendations submitted, 119
    each task tested by team, 118
    example of reviewing task, 118-119
        simulated hiring of part time casual worker, 118-119
    vendor, reliance on, 119-120
        caveat emptor, 119
        misstatements, 119
        warranty/disclaimer, 119-120
installation, 117-118
introduction, 107
manager, HRMS, 113
modification of system, 120
phases of implementation generally, 109
pitfalls in HRMS implementation, 108-109
planning, 109-111
    circulation of implementation plan, 111

Index

components of effective project plan, 110
priorities, 110
schedules, 111
policy and procedure issues, 113-114
   re-engineer business and revisit policies, 113
   review of policies and procedures, reasons for, 113-114
project implementation team, 111-112
   functional experts and project manager, 111
   other members of team, 112
   specialists added to team, 111-112
references, 123-125
steering committee, 114-115
   members, 114-115
   not generally members, 115
   role of, 114
summary, 123
testing, parallel, 122-123
   duplication of certain uses, 123
   payroll processing, test of, 122
   parallel trial period, 122-123
testing, unit, 120-121
   incorrect data used in testing, 121
   problems detected and discussed, 121
   review of every major process planned for system, 121
   "user-driven" activity, 121
training of project team, 115-117
   extended team training, 117
   generally, 115
   other users, training of, 117
   technical team training, 116-117
   training plan, 115-116
      components of effective plan, 115-116
      where adopting new area of technology, 116

Internet/Intranet, see also
Trends in HRMS
coordination with other clients/users, 131-132
e-Commerce, 255-258
networking, 258-263
staffing and Internet job sites, 166-170
   applying on-line, 166
      applicant's perspective, 166
      employer's perspective, 166
      negative aspects, 166-167
         focus on efficiency rather than effectiveness, 147
         no geographic boundaries, 166-167
      positive aspects, 166
   job seekers beware, 167-170

      disposable e-mail address, 169
      record keeping, 170
      résumés and privacy issues, 167-170
         deleting résumé from job site, 170
         résumé databases, 169
         Social Insurance Numbers, 168
         things to omit, 169
   job sites replacing newspapers, 166

Maintaining HRMS
business process maintenance, 133-134
   business process engineering (BPE), 134
   "excellence" defined, 133
   excellence, managing for, 133
   management improvement philosophies, 133-134
      continuous change reflecting need to maintain business processes, 134
      Total Quality Management (TQM), 133-134
         prominence receding, 133-134
      "value analysis", 134
coordination with other clients/users, 131-132
   Internet, 131-132
hardware and communications maintenance, 132
introduction, 127-128
   annual maintenance fees, 127
   continuous use affecting upgrades, 128
   mix of services, determining, 128
   monitoring effectiveness of system, 128
   usage patterns shifting, 128
new functional requirements, 137
references, 137-138
responsibilities, 135-137
   functional maintenance, 135-136
      example, 136
   functional/technical maintenance, 136-137
   technical maintenance, 136
roles, 134-135
shared services, 128-129
   centralization, 129
   "service centre", 128-129
      benefits of, 129
      meaning of, 128
   software maintenance, 132-133
      adaptive maintenance, 132
      corrective maintenance, 132
      perfective maintenance, 132-133
summary, 137
user support, 137
vendor relations, 129-131
   account manager, 130
   acquisition path, 129-130

Index

user groups, 130-131
  annual meeting, 130, 131
    survey of perceived requirements, 131
  electronic bulletin boards, 131
  future development priorities, setting, 130
  multi-product user conferences, 130-131
  networking and exchanging ideas, 130
  requirements, combining, 131

Models of human resources function
human resources model, 18-21
  addition of human resources/succession planning, 19
  administering and managing HR programs, 18
  four capabilities, 19
  new developments in HRMS software and hardware, 18
  strategic and contextual focus, 20-22
    HRMIS, 21
    model organized into rows and columns, 20-22
human resources programs, administering or managing, 17
organizations looking to obtain new HRMS, 18-19
tools to satisfy legislative requirements, 18

Need for effective HRMS
applicant tracking, 29
attrition reporting/monitoring, 26-27
  analyzed, and options considered, 27
employee lists, 25-26
  accessibility to identify groups of employees or to communicate, 26
  basic lists, 25
  identifying groups of employees with specific characteristics, 26
  purposes of lists, 26
employment equity tracking/monitoring, 8, 9-10, 27-28
  employment equity legislation, 27-28
    legislation requiring accurate and accessible information systems, 27
grievance tracking and analysis, 29
HRMS "reports", 30
Human resources/strategic planning, 30-32
  generally, 30
  internal population analysis, 31-32
  strategic planning, 31
    business plans, monitoring, 31
      strategic business and operating plans, 31
    succession planning, 31
introduction, 25
  accurate and timely information, need for, 25
  cost effective to implement and maintain HRMS, 25
  information requirements more complex, 25
references, 32-34
salary/benefits, 28
  budget management, 28
  "what-if" analyses, 28
seniority lists, 28-29
summary, 32
workers' compensation (WC) and long-term disability (LTD) tracking, 29-30
  benefits of effective management, 30
  financial inducements for reducing workplace accidents and minimizing costs, 30

Occupational health and safety (OH&S)
accident reporting, 235-237
  accident report information contained in HRMS module, 235
  accident/injury process flow, 235-236
    steps after accident at work, 235-236
    use of HRMS to capture, analyze and report data, 235-236
application, 232-233
  HRMS, use of, 232-233
  Pulp and Paper Research Institute of Canada (Paprican), 232
    organization's commitment to health and safety, 232
awareness of OH&S issues, 237-239
  differences and connections between OH&S and rest of HRM community, 238
  factors raising awareness, 237-238
    health care costs, 237
    technology and telecommuting, 237-238
    Workers' Compensation Board costs, 237
  OH&S modules not generally well handled by HRMS packages, 238-239
    organizational structure being fragmented, 238-239
health and employability, 240-241
  genetic information, use of, 241
  overweight employees, 240-241
    cost of obese employees, 241
inspections, 234-235
  checklist items, 234
  documenting and reporting, 235

Index

introduction, 229
   major aims of OH&S legislation, 229
legislation, 231-232
   "due diligence", organizations required to exercise, 231-232
      investigation of accident or unsafe working conditions, 231-232
    federal legislation, 231
    provincial responsibility, 231
occupational health and safety model, 229-231
   general activities covered, 230
   hazards associated with workplace, 229, 230-231
      pandemics, 230-231
   HR model applied to occupational health and safety, 229-230
references, 242-243
relationships between OH&S and HRM data, 233-234
   areas where share information, 233-234
   selected HRMS data requirements, 234
   security and privacy, 239-240
   confidentiality of health records, maintaining, 239-240
   health professionals pressured to provide health-related information, 239-240
   PIPEDA providing protection for personal health information, 240
summary, 241-242

Overview
ages spiral ever faster, 1, 2
automation and information technology revolutionizing business, 2
example of HRMS as essential business support tool, 2-3
   candidates' qualifications compared, 2
   candidates' test administered, 2
   career development information, 3
   employee feedback, 3
      tracking of changes in employee attitude, 3
   hiring of candidate and file opened, 2-3
      HRMS file continually updated, 2-3
      monthly reports, 3
   interactive voice response attachment, 3
   work planning process: goals and objectives, 3
human resources management systems (HRMS), meaning of, 3-4
   "Information Age", 1
   information as scarce resource, 1
Intangible Economy, 1

four key resources, 1
   collaboration assets, 1
   engagement assets, 1
   knowledge assets, 1
   time quality, 1
Knowledge Economy, 1

Pension administration, see **Compensation: salary, benefits, pension, payroll and time and attendance**

Planning new HRMS, see also **Strategic and tactical planning**
change, dealing with, 63-66
   capacity for change varying among organizations, 63
   employee responses, examples of, 65-66
   "empowering" employees to assume responsibility, 65
   degree of change, understating, 65
   example of overstating readiness of employees, 65
   example of employees implementing change to personal information, 64
   nature of system being implemented, 65
   whether substantially altering underlying business processes, 65
   process re-engineering, 64
      example: process engendering sense of trust, 64
communication process, 59-60
   line managers and project employees, dependence on, 60
   model for communication: five R's of reception, 59
   strategic and operational decisions, 59
   team members, guidelines in developing, 60
   telling and listening, 59
   time spent in ensuring that participants understanding project, 59-60
critical success factors, 60-63
   business process integration, 62-63
   organization's structure and culture, 60
   project manager's status and involvement, 61
      areas of expertise required, 61
      project managers vs. project champions, 61
   project team, 61, 62
   steering committee, 61-62
   systems support, 62
introduction, 53
planning generally, 53-54

Index

design and development planning, 53
goal-oriented, 54
implementation planning, 53-54
maintenance planning, 54
overplanning, avoiding, 54
training and documentation, user friendly, 54
planning implementation, 66
planning process, 54-55
major steps of planning process, 54-55
project management, 55-59
each unique task linked to specific objective, 55
performance appraisal, 67
planning and scheduling methodology, 57
software tools, 57-58
features offered in support of project activities, 57-58
CPM, 58
GANTT Chart, 57, 58
PERT charts, 57-58
project management software, 58
steps in HRMS planning, 56
references, 71-72
summary, 70-71
training and documentation, 66-70
documentation, timeliness of, 69-70
distinction between documentation and training reduced, 69
modifications necessary, 69
on-line aids and instructions, 69-70
written technical manuals, 70
generally, 66-67
in-house or off-the-shelf systems, 68-69
purpose, 67
systems documentation as record of technical underpinnings, 67
teaching methods, 67
training phases, 67-68
needs analysis, 67-68
methods of training, 68
skill maintenance, 68
training, timeliness of, 70

Privacy, see also **Design and development of new HRMS**
occupational health and safety, 239-240
confidentiality of health records, maintaining, 239-240
health professionals pressured to provide health-related information, 239-240
PIPEDA providing protection for personal health information, 240
privacy being legislated right, 78
privacy generally, 78-79, 147
CSA Model Code, 79
EU Data Protection Directive, 79
transfer of personal information, 79
factors driving protection of personal information, 78-79
privacy in Canada, 79-80
Personal Information and Electronic Documents Act (PIPEDA), 79-80
privacy in United States, 80
bi-lateral Safe Harbor Program, 80
identity theft problems, 80
international maze of data protection, 80
trends in HRM, 269

Return on investment (ROI)
cost/benefit analysis justifying first-time implementation or replacement, 39-49
employee lists, 40-41
address labels, example of producing, 40
cost saving in information officer producing labels, 40
legislative requirements, 41-42
Canadian university not activating position control module, 41-42
female dominated group, 41-42
tracking required to be done by hand retroactively, 41-42
employment equity legislation, 41
pay equity legislation, 41
penalty for failure to meet requirements, 41
planning, development, research and related issues, 45-49
Canadian Forces Personnel Applied Research Unit (CFPARU), 45-49
HRMS as data storage and reporting facility, 45
HRMS as important research tool, 45-47
applied research areas, 46-47
research studies, 45-46
training cost savings, 46
needs analysis stage, 47-49
longitudinal or long-term perspective, 47
new applications enhancing cost benefit of system, 47-49
example, 48-49
personnel data being part of asset base, 47
period considered for ROI, 47
Canadian forces recruiting and selection, quality control of, 48-49

Index

aptitude tests, upgrading, 48
optical scanning equipment purchase justified, 48
quality control exercise, 48
salary/benefits reporting and modeling, 42-45
  benefits options, analysis of, 43
  employers picking up more of overall cost, 42
  examples, 43-45
    labour negotiations, 43-44
      benefit costs, controlling, 44
        HRMS producing accurate picture of organization's financial situation, 43
        HRMS providing union with accurate and timely information, 43-44
        healthy labour relations climate achieved, 43-44
    organization projecting future costs trends by tracking past benefits costs, 44-45
      cost-control program, highlights of, 44-45
  social programs altered to shift costs to employers, 42
  "what if" models on demand, 42-43
introduction, 35-39
  contributions of human resources function undervalued, 36-37
  cost justification, 35
  cost/benefit analysis, 35, 37
  example of Organization XXX, 37-39
    licence fee or price ratio, 37, 38
    sample purchase model, 37-38
    total compensation model and costs continued over seven years, 38-39
    variables, 39
  HRMS, justifying purchase and implementation of, 35
  operating costs of organization, 35
    human resources as largest portion, 35
  questioning of long-term ROI of "new" HRMS, 37
  ROI models, 35-36
    Canadian Tire example, 36
    Silicon Graphics example, 36
    typical measures, 36
  techniques for assessing value of human resources programs, 37
    analysis largely based on HR Metrics, 37
references, 49-51

summary, 49

Staffing
applications, 163-175
  Internet job sites, 166-170
    applying on-line, 166
      applicant's perspective, 166
      employer's perspective, 166
      negative aspects, 166-167
        focus on efficiency rather than effectiveness, 147
        no geographic boundaries, 166-167
      positive aspects, 166
    job seekers beware, 167-170
      disposable e-mail address, 169
      record keeping, 170
      résumés and privacy issues, 167-170
        deleting résumé from job site, 170
        résumé databases, 169
        Social Insurance Numbers, 168
        things to omit, 169
    job sites replacing newspapers, 166
  large organizations: military, 163-165
    "applicant tracking files", 164
    Comprehensive Occupational Data Analysis Programs (CODAP), 164
    National Occupational Codes (NOCs), 164
    "onboarding", 165
    privacy laws, 165
    Pulp and Paper Research Institute of Canada (PAPRICAN), 165
    separate headquarter directorates, 164
    staffing functionality, 165
    training programs, 164
  managing staffing, 171-175
    "applicant tracking", 171
      access method, 171
    HR and staffing functions, 171-174
      accommodation, 173-174
        ergonomics, 173
        technological tools, 173-174
      exit interviews, 173
      recruitment on-line, 171-172
        job opportunities page/section, 171-172
      referral programs, 172
        employee referral programs (ERPs), 172
      whether staffing software, 174
    recruitment tools, 174-175
      screening tool, 174-175
  qualified workers, shortage of, 165-166
introduction, 161

Index

program monitoring for staffing, 175-176
   measures for staffing function, 175-176
references, 177-178
staffing model, 161-163
   human resources model applied to staffing, 161-162
staffing programs: overview, 162, 163
   job descriptions/job requirements, 163
      documented BFORs, 163
   recruiting and selection conducted objectively, 163
summary, 176-177

Strategic and tactical planning, see also **Planning new HRMS**
case study: application of HRMS in human resources planning, 150-151
   forecasting activities, 151
   foundation activities, 150-151
   Managerial Self-Service (MSS), 151
case study: safety statistics, 154-158
   comparative statistics, 155
   data concerning accidents and injuries entered, 154
   display alternatives, 156-158
      actionable management information gathered, 158
      "executive dashboard", 156-157
         comparative information displayed, 157-158
         example of lost day accident data, 156
      Intranet, use of, 156
   Managerial Self-Service (MSS) utilized, 154-155
      four screens/panels, 155
   safety record improvements, 155
   strategic goals achieved, 155
   up-to-date information, 155
demand and supply forecasting, 142-144
   demand forecasting, 142
   external recruitment, 143
   human resource planning vs. succession planning, 143
   internal selection, 143
      succession planning, 143
   modules for positions and employees, 143-144
      analyses using information in modules, 143-144
      organization module, 143
   reports created, 144
   specialty software applications, 144
   succession planning, 143, 144
   supply forecasting, 142-143

effective human resources planning, importance of, 142
   corporate strategic decision making, contribution to, 142
   means of facilitating goals, 142
HRMS' use in human resources/succession planning, 145-149
   committees formed from senior management team, 149
   example of documentation for succession planning, 148-149
   human resources/succession planning module, 148
   line (operational) management, questions asked by, 145-147
      credibility gained in providing analyses and reports, 147
      data required to answer questions, 146
   job descriptions related to modules, 147
   Managerial Self-Service model, 147-148
      "what if" modeling, 147-148
   model for large communication corporation, 145, 146
   organizational charting function, 148
   performance review and career development reports, 148
   potential successors identified, 148
   privacy, 147
   security, worthy of highest, 147
   statistical overviews, 147
   HRMS-vision of world, 147
internal and external trends, 141-142
   importance of strategic and tactical planning, 141-142
introduction, 139-141
   core human resource functions, 139
   "Human Resource Management" (HRM), meaning of, 139
   "Human Resources" (HR), meaning of, 139-140
      transactional administrative activities, 139
   strategic vs. transactional HR, 140-141
      existence of strategic HR, 140
      HR manager joining executive suite, 140
      transactional activities, challenges of, 140
measuring HRM practices and value, 151-153
   date management and data history, 152
   measurement by four key attributes, 151
   measures applied to any functional area, 152
   staffing replacement worker: flow chart, 153

Index

two HR timetables, 153
terminology used in measurement activities, 151-152
outsourcing, 153-154
   Service Level Agreement (SLA), 154
references, 159-160
summary, 158-159
   key learning points, 158-159

Succession planning, see **Strategic and tactical planning**

Training and development
application, 191-192
   Canadian forces, 191
      Canadian Forces Personnel Management Information System, 191
      employee module, 191
      Comprehensive Occupational Data Analysis Programs (CODAP), 191
      Directorate of Organizational Structures, 191
   large organizations, 191-192
   Western military forces, 191
      occupational and training courses, 191
attitude surveys, 192
   sociometric surveys, 192
introduction, 179
   "knowledge worker", meaning of, 179-180
references, 193-194
strategic context, 179-180
   recent development in Canada, 179-180
summary, 192-193
training and development: HR model, 182-184
   corporate goals and objectives, 182
   demand forecasting, 184
   internal and external labour supply, 184
   interrelationship between strategic planning and HR training and development, 182
   inventory of skills, providing, 184
   relationships among training and development processes, 182, 183
   training needs analysis, 184
      training and development programs, 184
   training specialists, knowledge and skills of, 182-184
      membership associations and networking, 183-184
training and development options, 180-182
   corporate content providers, 181-182
      eCornell courses, 181-182
   eLearning, aspects of, 181

life-long learning", 180
training delivery, 190-191
   computer-assisted training, 190
   eLearning, 190-191
      multimedia presentations, 190
training management information, 185-190
   training and development modules, 185-190
      data elements, 185
      data storage, 188
      health and safety training, 189-190
         serious medical accidents or injuries, 189
      reports, 189
      training management, 189
      typical data gathered for course management purposes, 185, 187
         sample course detail, 187
      typical information gathered on each individual, 185, 186
         employee training request, 186
      useful data on each individual relative to course, 185, 188
         sample course enrolment detail, 185, 188

Trends in HRMS
e-Commerce, 255-258
   e-Business, scope of, 255
   global marketing or self-service, implications for, 256-257
   HR information management, impact on, 257-258
      knowledge workers as dominant workforce, 258
   Internet usage, growth in, 256
   "metamarkets" emerging, 256
   value flowing from connectivity, 257
flexibility, 248
globalization, 246
human resources information management, 267-269
   barriers to acquiring new HRM systems, 268
   benefits of HRMS, 269
   fundamental recordkeeping, 267-268
   line managers to be given more direct access to HRMSs, 268
      delayering tiers of management, 268
   other trends, 269
   "value-added management", 267
information management, 263-265
   demands of post-industrialism, 264-265

Index

Groupware permitting groups of people to share data and applications, 263
"human resources" definition changing, 263
line management taking more direct role, 264
technological advances, impact of, 264
   human resources information specialists, 264
"telecommuting", 263
Internet and related innovations, 249-251
   computer supported technology, improvements in, 251
   electronic mail, 250
   fax machines, 251
   HRMS information via Internet, 251
   Internet users, growth in, 249-250
   World Wide Web, access to, 250-251
Internet/Intranet, 251-255
   applications of corporate Intranets, 252-254
      communicating, 252-253
      on-line feedback, providing direct, 253
      personal data, updating, 253
      recruiting and staffing, 253
      sharing information with employees, 252
      survey of applications, 254
   characteristics and advantages of Intranet applications, 254-255
   types of Intranets, 252
   Universal Resource Locator (URL), 252
introduction, 245
networking, 258-263
   e-mail discussion groups, 261
   electronic discussion groups, 259-261
      directory, 260
      HRIS-L being largest list, 260
      "lurking" approach suggested, 259
      packaged software used, 259
      posting question, 259-260
      business letter approach where question for everyone, 260
      replying to posts, 260
      subscription to groups or lists, 259, 260-261
         "digest" subscription, 260, 261
         "index" subscription, 260
   filters, 261
   forums, 261-262
      benefits, 262
      formats for HR forums, 262
      rules or netiquette, 262
   popular HR discussion groups, 261
   professional associations and meetings, 258
new economy, 245-246
   engines driving economy, 245
   features of new economy, 245-246
   phases of driving forces in organizational processes, 245
non-traditional HRM approaches, 265-267
   downsizing, 267
      rightsizing not necessarily answer, 267
   job-competency approach, 265
   teams, 266
      teamwork increasing organizational flexibility, 266
   workflow, 266
outsourcing/contracting out, 246
   advantages, 246
   technology resources, 246
references, 270-271
restructuring work, 247
summary, 270
technical issues, other, 248-249
   client-server (C/S), 248, 249
   imaging, 249
   interactive voice response (IVR), 249
technological advances, 247-248
   functional applications of information technology, 247